LEATHERHEAD
(01372)
373149

EPSOM
01372 721707

30. DEC 1997	29 JUL 2000	– 8 NOV 2005
14 FEB 1998	3/03	26. NOV 2005
19. JAN. 1999	16 AUG 2004	– 5 APR 2006
27. AUG 1999	3/09	23 MAY 2005
04 JAN 2000	EXTENDED LOAN DUE FOR RETURN BY 5 NOV 2004 SUBJECT TO RECALL	1 0 JUL 2008
14 APR 2000		
– 5 MAY 2000	– 1 DEC 2004	
1 4 JUL 2000		

COUNTY
LIBRARIES
AND LEISURE
SERVICE

Charges will be payable at
the Adult rate if this item
is not returned by the
latest date stamped above.

L21B

 SURREY
COUNTY COUNCIL

LONDON'S PARISH CHURCHES

LONDON'S PARISH CHURCHES

FOREWORD BY
THE RT. REVD. RICHARD CHARTRES,
BISHOP OF LONDON
AND
THE RT. REVD. ROY WILLIAMSON,
BISHOP OF SOUTHWARK

JOHN LEONARD

The Breedon Books
Publishing Company
Derby

First published in Great Britain by
The Breedon Books Publishing Company Limited
Breedon House, 44 Friar Gate, Derby, DE1 1DA.
1997

He by the vast metropolis immured,
Where pity shrinks from unremitting calls,
Where numbers overwhelm humanity
And neighbourhood serves rather to divide
Than to unite – what sighs more deep than his?
Wordsworth *The Recluse*

Whilst building began with the domestic need for shelter, architecture began with the
desire to give meaningful form to sacred space.
Lawrence Malcic

For Mark and Miriam

All royalties from the sale of this book will be devoted to the Church Urban Funds of the
Dioceses of London and Southwark.

By the same author: *Derbyshire Parish Churches*
                       Shropshire Parish Churches
                       Staffordshire Parish Churches

ISBN 1 85983 105 2

Printed and bound by Butler & Tanner Ltd., Selwood Printing Works, Caxton Road, Frome,
Somerset.

Colour separations by RPS, Leicester.

Jackets printed by Lawrence-Allen, Weston-super-Mare, Avon.

Contents

Acknowledgements

Mrs June Morgan of Photoworld Altrincham has once again performed miracles of developing and printing – I calculate that she handled over 1,800 photographs before the final selection was made. Mr Gordon Hamilton kindly read the text, saved me from numerous errors of fact and judgement, and generously enriched my knowledge of the subject; responsibility for any errors that remain is, of course, mine. I record with thanks permission from Faber & Faber Ltd to reproduce plans of the Wren churches from Eduard Sekler's book *Wren and his place in European Architecture* (1956); and from Philip Wilson Publishers permission to reproduce plans for Hawksmoor's churches from Kerry Downes' *Hawksmoor* (second edition 1979). Dr John Salmon has helped greatly in my search for excellence in modern churches, recommending especially the churches of E.C. Shearman. And I am greatly indebted to the many incumbents, churchwardens and other church officers who have guided me round their various buildings with never-failing patience and courtesy. Above all, I thank my wife Marjorie for allowing me to make numerous journeys to London from the heart of rural Shropshire, and for her constant encouragement and love.

Foreword

It is not known when the Christian faith was first brought to London. There may have been churches in the City in the later part of the Roman period but apart from finding a Christian symbol scratched on the base of a pewter bowl from Copthall Court, archaeology has produced few Christian traces.

What we do know is that when St Augustine of Canterbury arrived in Britain 1,400 years ago London was in pagan hands. According to Bede, Augustine soon 'consecrated Mellitus to preach in the province of the East Saxons, which is divided from Kent by the river Thames and borders on the sea to the east. Its chief City is London, which is on the banks of that river and is an emporium for many nations who come to it by land and sea.' London's Christian people soon began to robe their destiny in stone and build their places of worship.

John Leonard's timely book allows us to enter the history of a thousand years of Christianity in our capital City. He describes nearly 130 churches with insight and a lightness of touch. It is obvious that he holds a great love for his subject and strongly adheres to the truth that 'if we are to keep our inheritance, we must first learn about it.' The author is also very generously donating the royalties from his work to the Church Urban Fund in the dioceses of London and Southwark.

We warmly commend *London's Parish Churches* to you. It is a companionable guide which will make London's heritage more accessible to the visitor and to those who have the privilege of living in its midst.

Richard Londin and
Roy Southwark

Introduction: Visiting London's Churches

LONDON'S undervalued parish churches are treasures too much ignored by Londoners and visitors alike. What other capital city can boast 25 churches by one architect of world renown? Yet these buildings, the glory of London's architectural heritage, are sometimes difficult to find, and even more difficult to find open. Of course there is more to London's churches than the works of Sir Christopher Wren: yet who would dream of going to Stepney to see St George-in-the-East (Fig 1)?; or to Deptford, to see St Paul's (Fig 2)? For over two hundred years from the time of the Great Fire (1666) a very high propor-

(Fig 2) **St Paul, Deptford** *The semi-circular portico and the tower.*

name the architect? The truth is that three generations of Londoners have grown up in ignorance of their most precious architectural inheritance.

In this book, I trace the story of London's churches from Norman times to the present day, and describe over 120 of those which appear most rewarding

(Fig 1) **St George-in-the-East** *From the south-east.*

tion of the finest churches in the country were built in the capital, and with few exceptions they are virtually unknown to the general public. This would not have been so one hundred years ago. Even now, most people may have heard of St Martin-in-the-Fields (Fig 3); but how many can

(Fig 3) **St Martin-in-the-Fields** *The nave and ceiling.*

for visitors. All the medieval survivors in central London are here, with a few from further afield, and all the surviving Wren churches are described and illustrated, together with, I believe, the best churches of the eighteenth and nineteenth centuries. There may yet be no agreed consensus about the worthiest buildings of the present century, but a selection of these is included.

Post-Reformation church-building in London was concentrated in four distinct phases: the Wren churches built after the Great Fire of 1666; the twelve great churches built after the Fifty New Churches Act of 1711; the Commissioners' churches built after the Church Building Act of 1818, when Greek and Gothic styles struggled for supremacy; and the great Gothic revival which extended from 1840 to the outbreak of World War One.

Any writer on London's churches has to be selective: how to choose from perhaps two thousand churches those which are most worth visiting? How large an area should one cover? Should churches of all denominations be included? To keep the task (and the book!) within manageable limits, I have studied only Anglican churches, and, with one or two exceptions, all are, or have been, parish churches. I have largely restricted the study to inner London, broadly corresponding with the area covered by the old London County Council. Only in the search for good modern churches have I ventured further afield. That is not to deny that there are excellent churches of other denominations, and in outer London: of course, there are.

One of the most striking (and unexpected) lessons to emerge from a study of London's churches is their fragility. If a village church is solidly built and of good foundation, there is no reason why it should not last five hundred, perhaps a thousand, years. Not so in cities, especially in London, where the churches have been, and still are, liable to many misfortunes. The Great Fire of 1666 destroyed the vast majority of the

City's medieval buildings, so there are few churches in central London over 350 years old. Air raids in World War Two destroyed a number of Wren's and other churches, and damaged many more. And a combination of demographic change, commercial pressure, and clerical and artistic indifference was responsible for the frequent demolition of City churches in the nineteenth and early twentieth centuries.

It might be thought that these hazards were a thing of the past: but within the past ten years, fire has grievously damaged St Mary-at-Hill, one of Wren's finest churches, and there has been slight fire damage at another Wren church, St Magnus the Martyr. IRA terrorism has all but destroyed St Ethelburga's and seriously damaged St Helen's. And although we can now be reasonably sure that no seventeenth- or eighteenth-century church will be wilfully demolished because of indifference, the worry remains that the interior of some may be ravaged by unsympathetic attempts

(Fig 4) **St Stephen, Rosslyn Hill** *The nave and chancel.*

to find new uses for redundant buildings. Moreover, the threat to some outstanding Victorian churches persists: St Stephen, Rosslyn Hill (Fig 4) is in a shameful state, and there are others whose future is in doubt.

When the last steeple was added to Wren's churches in 1717 (Fig 5), the master was still alive, aged 85, and 51 years had passed since the Great Fire. London's skyline was dominated by the new St Paul's Cathedral, but Wren had also ensured

(Fig 5) **St James Garlickhythe** *The steeple.*

that a forest of spires should extend throughout the City, towering over the low and mean buildings. The scene is memorably recorded in a painting by Canaletto, *London and the Thames from Somerset House looking towards the City* (reproduced in Whinney [a]). Now, half of Wren's steeples have gone, and the remainder, and even St

Paul's, are hemmed in by giant blocks of glass and concrete. The skyline has been ruined: even so, one of the great delights in London is to walk through the City, and catch unexpected glimpses of towers and steeples in between the modern

(Fig 6) **St Helen Bishopsgate** *The twin naves separated by the Perpendicular arcade.*

office-blocks. It remains astonishing how close the City's churches are to each other – there are

(Fig 7) **St Stephen Walbrook** *Wren's reredos and Henry Moore's altar.*

(Fig 10) **St James the Less** *The nave and chancel.*

(Fig 9) **All Saints, Margaret Street** *The low marble wall and gate to the chancel; beyond fine metalwork in the grille, with Geometrical tracery above and blind arcading to the right.*

(Fig 8) **Christ Church Spitalfields** *The portico, tower and steeple.*

still 37 in the square mile – yet they are vulnerable, vulnerable to fire, vulnerable to bombs, vulnerable above all to neglect.

If we are to keep our inheritance, we must first learn about it, and I hope that this book will help to guide Londoners and visitors alike to the most rewarding churches. The book may be used in two ways: firstly, as a narrative account of the building of the capital's churches over a period of one thousand years; and secondly, as a reference book for descriptions and illustrations of the 122 churches mentioned in some detail.

Where should the visitor to London's churches start? If you can spare only one day for London's churches, then see the

(Fig 11) **St Augustine, Kilburn** *The vaulted nave, from the west gallery.*

(Fig 12) **St Pancras, Upper Woburn Place** *The finest church of the Greek revival.*

(Fig 14) **St Leonard, Shoreditch** *The steeple.*

following, all in the City of London or within walking distance of it: St Helen Bishopsgate (Fig 6), the best medieval church; St Mary Abchurch and St Stephen Walbrook (Fig 7), two of Wren's finest interiors; Christchurch Spitalfields (Fig 8) and St Mary Woolnoth, both outstanding churches by Hawksmoor. If you can spare a second day, then go a little further afield – perhaps to some of the following: All Saints, Margaret Street (Fig 9), St James the Less (Fig 10) and St Augustine, Kilburn (Fig 11), three of the best Victorian churches; St Martin-in-the-Fields; St George, Bloomsbury, Hawksmoor's subtlest church; St Paul, Deptford, the best church south of the river; St Pancras, Upper Woburn Place (Fig 12), the finest church of the Greek revival; or admire the elegant interior of Sir John Soane's at St Peter, Walworth (Fig 13). And if you have still more time, then return to the City and East End to St Mary Aldermary, St Magnus the Martyr, St James, Garlickhythe (all by Wren); St Leonard, Shoreditch (Fig 14); St Anne, Limehouse. And do not ignore the best churches of the twentieth

(Fig 13) **St Peter, Walworth** *The nave and chancel.*

(Fig 15) **St John, Peckham** *Diagonal view of the interior.*

century – e.g. St Saviour, Eltham, St John, Peckham (Fig 15) or St Paul, Harringay.

But there is more to churches than the build-ing: and a visitor to many of these churches cannot fail to be impressed by the ministry and witness exercised therein. In all, the gospel is proclaimed, and the worship of God ordered; and in many, the rejected from society are welcomed, the homeless, the alcoholics, the drug-abusers, the victims of domestic violence, the poor, the lonely, the desperate.

'In the streets of every City
'Where the bruised and lonely dwell
Let us show the Saviour's pity
Let us of his mercy tell' (Hugh Sherlock)

This is what London's churches are for: they deserve your love and support.

The Medieval Legacy

THE medieval churches surviving in London fall naturally into two groups, namely, those within and those outside the City. At the time of the Great Fire, there were 106 parish churches in the City, and all perished except a few whose survival depended on their peripheral situation, away from the centre of the blaze. These surviving churches are in a great arc around the City, beginning with Temple Church in the west, proceeding to St Sepulchre, St Bartholomew the Great and St Giles Cripplegate in the north, curving to the south along Bishopsgate (St Helen, St Ethelburga) and then to St Andrew Undershaft, St Olave Hart Street and All Hallows-by-the-Tower.

Outside the City walls, there is St Margaret, Westminster, two miles upstream; and across the river from the City the Priory Church of St Saviour, later known as St Mary Overie and now Southwark Cathedral. St Mary Magdalene, East Ham, St Dunstan, Stepney and Chelsea Old Church are included in this chapter as representative of the large number of medieval churches which were established in villages then quite separate from London, but now of course engulfed in its urban sprawl. Most of the other medieval churches in outer London have either been totally or partially destroyed, or have been 'restored' out of all recognition.

There are no surviving Anglo-Saxon churches in London, so the earliest Christian buildings date from the Norman period, which began after the Battle of Hastings, 1066. I have used the traditional classification of medieval churches into Norman, Early English, Decorated and Perpen-

(Fig 16) **St Bartholomew the Great** *Rahere's monument, a fifteenth-century structure with a Norman column on the left.*

dicular (as first described by Rickman (see p 140). These named periods are the result of retrospective analysis of building styles; they did not, of course, exist in the minds of the builders. One style merged imperceptibly into the next, usually as a result of new trends imported from the continent; so that, (except for Perpendicular) they appeared first in London and the south-east, and then spread very slowly through the rest of the country.

The **Norman** (or Romanesque) style persisted throughout the whole of the twelfth century, and the best Norman parish church in London is the Priory Church of St Bartholomew the Great (Fig 21, p 19). Norman churches are characterised by solidly-built arcades and towers, the arches are rounded, the cylindrical columns massive (Fig 16). The columns or piers are surmounted by square-edged capitals, which effect the transition from the round column to the square abacus above which supports the arch. The inferior surface of the capital is often carved into a cushion (a rounding-off of the lower angles into the cylindrical shaft below), scallop (a further modification in which the surface is elaborated into a series of truncated cones – see the column in Fig 16 – or volute (spiral scrolls). Semicircular arches are, of course, the hallmark of Norman or Romanesque building, and in addition to the arcades, are found above doorways and windows. They were often decorated by geometric designs, the commonest being the chevron or zigzag which was introduced *c*.1120. Norman windows are usually small and round-headed, and may be deeply splayed to maximise the provision of light, glass being expensive.

The introduction of the pointed arch, which ushered in Gothic architecture, and which was to revolutionise church building, was primarily for structural reasons, such an arch being able to transmit a larger proportion of the thrust directly to the ground (Foster). It appears to have been first used at Autun Cathedral, France, around 1120-1130, and in London was used later in the twelfth century at St Bartholomew the Great and at Temple Church (Fig 17). From about 1160 to 1200 it may be seen side by side with semicircular arches (the Transitional period), but after 1200 semicircular arches are seen no more and the Early English period is said to have begun. The **Early English** style lasted throughout the whole of the thirteenth century, and is characterised by pointed arches, supported by less substantial piers; at first they usually remained cylindrical, but later octagonal or multi-shafted piers may be seen. The capitals are now usually rounded rather than square, and may be decorated with 'stiff-leaf' foliage. The other major characteristic of the Early English style is the lancet window – a tall narrow window with an acutely pointed upper end. Often these may be paired, or grouped in a series of three or more, sometimes provided with a common hood-mould to throw the rainwater clear of the window. Later in the century, the area enclosed by a common hood-mould was often pierced, resulting in plate- or Y-tracery above the windows; from this germ, the development of complex tracery seen in the next century evolved. There is not much Early English work in London's parish churches, the best example being the chancel and retrochoir at St Mary Overie (now Southwark Cathedral; Fig 18, and Fig 37, p 25).

(Fig 17) **Temple Church** *The round nave, with pointed arches. Blind arcading below the windows and in the triforium.*

(Fig 18) **Southwark Cathedral** *Thirteenth-century Early English chancel. The statues in the reredos are Victorian.*

The **Decorated** style was introduced around 1300, and lasted for about 50 years. It was seen in the mid-nineteenth century as the perfect period of Gothic architecture. Decorated arches are not so acutely pointed, and the piers are more often octagonal or multi-shafted than circular in cross-section. Carvings on the moulded capitals are freer and more elaborate, and when foliage is seen it is more realistic than the stiff-leaf carving of the previous century. Y-tracery developed into intersecting tracery, in which each vertical mullion branched into two curved bars. But the most characteristic Decorated feature was the ogee arch–two shallow S-shaped curves meeting upwards in a sharp point, often embellished with crockets and other ornamental features. In windows, this led to complicated patterns of flowing tracery, some of which may be described as geometrical, curvilinear or reticulated. There is very little original building in the Decorated style in London parish churches; the best surviving work is in the Catholic church of St Etheldreda, Ely Place, Holborn. The tomb of Rahere (Fig 16, p 16) in St Bartholomew the Great, though said to date from the fifteenth century, certainly looks Decorated–note the elaborate canopy, with ogee curves sweeping up in an inverted V, adorned with crockets and cusps and finials. There are, of course, a number of nineteenth-century churches built in the Decorated style, e.g. St Stephen, Rochester Row (p 148).

The **Perpendicular** style evolved in the middle of the fourteenth century, and was first seen in Gloucester. It is the only medieval style which is confined to Great Britain and it held sway for two hundred years, until the Reformation. Most of the surviving medieval churches in London are built in this style, many of them being rather late Perpendicular; indeed St Giles Cripplegate is so late (1545-1550) that it is effectively post-Reformation. Their quality is variable; some are good, but it is idle to pretend that London's Perpendicular can compare with the glorious churches which may be seen in, e.g. the Cotswolds or East Anglia.

In Perpendicular building, the emphasis throughout is on verticality; straight lines replace the sinuous tracery of the Decorated style; the pointed arches become flatter. This 'alters the proportions of the arcade: a large part of its height is now taken up by the piers. The piers being both taller and thinner make the arcade appear loftier (Fig 19), and produce the impression of height and lightness of structure that is so characteristic of the Perpendicular style …the preference for straight lines shows particularly clearly in window tracery. There the vertical mullions that divide a window into its lights rise almost without interruption to the head of the window, ruling its tracery into tiers of rectangular compartments' (Foster). Steeply sloping roofs of earlier centuries were often replaced by low-pitched roofs; this enabled the side walls of the nave to be

(Fig 19) **St Andrew Undershaft** *Perpendicular arcades, east window and roof.*

heightened, thus allowing for the insertion of a clerestory.

The Priory Church of St Bartholomew the Great

The Priory Church of St Bartholomew the Great is the only Norman parish church remaining in the City of London, and yet what we see today is but a fragment – the crossing, choir and sanctuary – of the original, the nave of ten bays having been totally destroyed after the Dissolution of the Monasteries. Such a large church must indeed have been impressive, so close to the medieval St Paul's. After the dissolution, the choir and transepts were then left to form a parish church, but the transepts and Lady Chapel were put to various secular purposes for three hundred years

(Fig 21) **St Bartholomew the Great** *The south wall of the Norman choir; the eastern apse is a Victorian reconstruction.*

and fell into decay. Eventually, Sir Aston Webb carried out a brilliant reconstruction in the 1880s and 1890s.

The external appearance is deceptive. The priory is entered by a thirteenth-century porch, above which is an Elizabethan half-timbered gatehouse (Fig 20). The arch of this porch is almost the sole remnant of the original nave and marks the west end of the medieval building. The brick tower houses the oldest ring of bells in England and occupies the angle between the south transept and the truncated nave; it dates from the 1620s. The west front of the church dates from 1893.

Inside, the twelfth century takes over, for a priory of Augustinian canons (and St Bartholomew's Hospital) were founded by Rahere, a courtier of King Henry I, in 1123. What one now sees is the Norman crossing and choir, the massive columns being separated by plain semicircular arches (Fig 21). At the crossing, the eastern and western arches are semicircular, but the northern and southern are pointed, said to be the earliest Gothic arches in London, and dating from *c.*1150. There is scallop carving under the capitals of the arcades (Fig 16), and above a Norman triforium runs all round the church. Over the triforium is a clerestory which was built in the late fifteenth century.

Interrupting the triforium on the south side is an endearing oddity, a glazed Tudor oriel window

(Fig 20) **St Bartholomew the Great** *Thirteenth-century porch, with Elizabethan gatehouse above.*

(Fig 22) **St Bartholomew the Great** *The early sixteenth-century oriel window.*

(Fig 23) **Temple Church** *The Norman west portal.*

(Fig 22) of the early sixteenth century, through which the prior of the day (Prior Bolton) could keep an eye on the monks and pilgrims below. Under the window is a rebus, a pictorial pun, on the prior's name; it shows a bolt (from an arrow) and a barrel (a tun) – thus bolt-tun. The apsidal east end of the sanctuary (Fig 21) was reconstructed by Sir Aston Webb. Beyond the sanctuary is an ambulatory, and to the east of this a heavily-restored Lady Chapel. On the left of the high altar is Rahere's monument (Fig 16), consisting of an effigy on a tomb-chest under a canopy. There are a number of other monuments in the church, but none is memorable apart from the epitaph to John and Margaret Whiting:

> Shee first deceased. Hee for a little Tryd
> To live without her, likd it not and dyd.

Access: Nearest Underground station: Barbican.

Temple Church

The Knights Templar were founded in Jerusalem early in the twelfth century and their first establishment in London was in Holborn, around 1128. About 30 years later, they began to build the nave of the present church on a new site near the River Thames, and the most remarkable feature of this building is that the nave is round; scarcely less remarkable at such an early date are the pointed arches of the arcade. After the Gothic arches of the crossing at St Bartholomew the Great, these are the earliest pointed arches in London. So, as Pevsner points out, here we have not Transitional architecture (Norman columns supporting pointed arches) but Norman and Gothic features side by side, a very unusual combination. Round naves are rare: there are parish churches with such naves in Cambridge and Northampton, and at Little Maplestead, Essex, and there is a round nave in the chapel in Ludlow Castle; others, mostly connected with the Templars, are known from excavation. The form was designed to resemble that of the Holy Sepulchre in Jerusalem. The chancel of the Temple Church was added in the thirteenth century. Towards the end of the fourteenth century, apprentices of the Law acquired the tenancy of the church and have retained it ever since. Henry VIII confiscated the church from the Templars in 1540, and James I presented it to the Societies of the Inner and Middle Temple. The church escaped major damage in the Fire, but it was bombed in 1941 and has since been extensively restored. It has never been a parish church, but is a royal peculiar (i.e. it is exempt from control by the Bishop of London, and the Crown retains the right of appointment of the Master).

The west portal (Fig 23) is pure Norman, with three orders of columns and much Norman decoration of the arches above the door. The porch in front of the portal is, however, rib-vaulted, with Gothic detail, and has a pointed archway. The round nave (Figs 17, 24) has a group of six piers of Purbeck marble, very different from the usual massive stone columns of the twelfth century. Purbeck marble is a shelly limestone, much in vogue for wealthier churches in the twelfth and thirteenth centuries, and usually polished for interior use, where its dark colour provides a striking contrast (Clifton-Taylor). The piers support

(Fig 24) **Temple Church** *The round nave, with piers of Purbeck marble and effigies of knights.*

(Fig 25) **Temple Church** *Monument of Edward Plowden (1584).*

(Fig 26) **Temple Church** *Monument of Richard Martin (1618).*

headed windows. Further blind arcading is seen at ground level around the nave. In the nave is a series of knights from the thirteenth century (Fig 24). All are recumbent, with their legs crossed. They were badly damaged during the war, but have since been restored. The best preserved is that to Robert de Ros (1227). Between the nave and the chancel are much later monuments: Edmund Plowden (1584) Treasurer of the Middle Temple, recumbent on a tombchest (Fig 25); and Richard Martin (1618) Recorder of London, kneeling before a desk (Fig 26). Although basically a marble monument, it has

a circular arcade, above which is a triforium consisting of blind arcading with regularly spaced open windows above the apices of the arches below; above this again is a clerestory with round-been pointed out that a surprisingly high proportion is of plaster, painted to look like marble (Esdaile).

The fine chancel was built in the thirteenth

century, and is notable for the full height of the aisles. Slender multi-shafted columns of Purbeck marble support an Early English arcade. There is rib-vaulting above, and lancet windows in the aisles. The windows are in groups of three, with interior shafts. The reredos was added in 1682; it was carved by William Emmett, who was supervised by Wren.

Access: Nearest Underground station: Temple.

St Mary Magdalene, East Ham

This church is claimed to be the only Norman parish church in London still used as such. Almost as remarkable as the church is the churchyard, said, at 9.5 acres, to be the largest in the country and now managed as a nature reserve by the borough of Newham. The church is built of a variety of materials-the ubiquitous Kentish ragstone, but also flints and chalk from Surrey, Caen stone from Normandy, and tiles purloined from nearby Roman sites. The west tower of stone and brick was added in the sixteenth century. The church consists of an unaisled nave, chancel and apse; entrance to the nave is from under the tower, and the later construction of the tower has fortuitously preserved the fine mouldings of the doorway, three columns with scalloped capitals on each side. Deeply splayed Norman windows remain in the nave, together with some later additional windows. The bowl of the handsome font (Fig 27) is dated 1639.

The chancel (Fig 28)

(Fig 27) **St Mary Magdalene, East Ham** *The elegant seventeenth-century font.*

is noteworthy for the excellent Norman blind intersecting arcading which survives on the north wall; originally the south wall had similar arcading, but only vestiges remain after the insertion of a large window in the seventeenth century. Between the nave and chancel on the north side can be seen the remains of the stairway to the former rood-loft. Also in the north wall of the chancel is the entrance to a former anchorite's cell; above this is the monument to Giles Breame and his wife (1621).

The semicircular apse is a rare feature of a Norman church in England, though frequent enough on the continent. Uniquely, above the apse is a Norman timber roof, discovered only in 1931, and said to have survived unchanged since the twelfth century. There is a large Jacobean monument in the apse to Edmund Nevill and his wife

(Fig 28) **St Mary Magdalene, East Ham** *The chancel and apse, with blind intersecting arcading on the north wall.*

(Fig 29) **St Mary Magdalene, East Ham** *Monument to Edmund Nevill and his wife.*

(Fig 29), and on the opposite wall is a double piscina dating from the thirteenth century.

Access: Nearest Underground station: East Ham; then by bus.

The Cathedral Church of St Saviour and St Mary Overie

Southward Cathedral is included in a book of parish churches because it was indeed a parish church for nearly four hundred years. It was founded as the Priory Church of St Mary Overie (meaning 'over the river') in 1106, and served a community of Augustinian canons. This Norman church was almost totally burnt down in 1212, and was replaced by a Gothic structure during the thirteenth century. Severe damage was again done by fire in the 1390s, and extensive repairs were necessary. Then in 1469 the roof of the nave collapsed, and was replaced by a wooden structure. The priory was abolished by Henry VIII in 1539, and the church then became the parish church of St Saviour; the conventual buildings of the priory fell into ruin. St Saviour's continued as a parish church from 1539 until 1905, but early in the nineteenth century further repairs became necessary. The retrochoir and tower (Fig 30) were restored in 1822; then the wooden roof of the nave became unsafe and was taken down in 1831, the walls being dismantled later and replaced by a structure which received universal condemnation. Finally, the present nave was designed by Sir Arthur Blomfield in the 1890s, and St Saviour's became the Cathedral Church of St Saviour and St Mary Overie in 1905.

So what one sees now is a Victorian nave, with the transepts, tower, choir and retrochoir dating from the Middle Ages, though much restored. As a building, it cannot of course compare with St Paul's Cathedral or Westminster Abbey, but this is an unfair comparison; it is more rewarding to view Southwark Cathedral as one of the most

(Fig 30) **Southwark Cathedral (St Mary Overie)** *The medieval tower.*

interesting partly medieval parish churches in London, and then it can be appreciated on its own terms.

Blomfield's nave (Fig 31) is attractive and competent, without being particularly distinguished, and it certainly fits in well with the older fabric. The arcades are in the Early English style, with triforium and clerestory above, and over all a groin vault. In the north aisle is the medieval memorial to the poet John Gower (Fig 32), friend of Chaucer, who died in 1408. At the east end of the south aisle is the monument to Shakespeare; the Globe theatre where the playwright acted was quite close to St Saviour's, and Shakespeare's brother Edmund was buried in the church in

(Fig 31) **Southwark Cathedral** *The nave (nineteenth century).*

1608. The memorial to William Shakespeare was carved by Henry McCarthy in 1912.

The transepts are medieval, the north Norman and Early English, the south Perpendicular. In the north transept (Fig 33), the Norman west and north walls have been largely concealed by blind arcading of the thirteenth century, the shafts being of Purbeck marble. The finest monument here is that to Joyce Austin (1633), showing an allegorical harvest scene with wheatsheaves, farm girls

and above a standing figure of Agriculture (Fig 34); it is by Nicholas Stone (1586-1647), best known for the shrouded monument to John Donne at St Paul's Cathedral. Also in this transept are bewigged monuments to Lionel Lockyer (1672), a semi-recumbent physician under a broken segmental pediment; and to Richard Blisse, gentleman (1703). Off the east wall is the Harvard Chapel; John Harvard, founder of the university, was baptised in St Saviour's in 1607. The chapel contains a Tabernacle for the reserved sacrament designed by Pugin in 1851. It was previously in Pugin's church in Ramsgate and was transferred to Southwark in 1971.

The chancel (Fig 18, p 18) is Early English, with arcades of five bays, the piers being alternately octagonal and circular, and above a triforium and clerestory. Behind the High Altar is Bishop Fox's early sixteenth-century screen, separating the sanctuary from

(Fig 32) **Southwark Cathedral** *Tomb-chest of John Gower.*

(Fig 34) **Southwark Cathedral** *Monument of Joyce Austin (1633).*

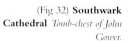

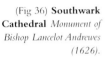

(Fig 35) **Southwark Cathedral** *Monument of Alderman Richard Humble (1616) and his wives.*

(Fig 36) **Southwark Cathedral** *Monument of Bishop Lancelot Andrewes (1626).*

the retrochoir; the statues were added four hundred years later. On either side of the choir are the north and south choir aisles, each containing some excellent monuments. On the north side is the oldest memorial in the cathedral, the wooden effigy of an unknown knight dating from *c.*1275. Nearby is the gaudily-painted monument to John Trehearne and his wife (1618), and between the choir and the north choir aisle the kneeling figures of Richard

(Fig 37) **Southwark Cathedral** *Early English retrochoir.*

Humble and his two wives (1616; Fig 35); this is thought to be by Nicholas Cure II (Esdaile). In the south choir aisle is the monument to Lancelot Andrewes, Bishop of Winchester (1626; Fig 36); he was a noted Anglican divine, one of the most learned theologians of his time, who took part in the translation of the Authorised Version of the Bible. The canopy above by Sir Ninian Comper has been described as 'a clever twentieth-century sham' (Harwood and Saint).

I have left until the end the most impressive part of the cathedral, the unusual Early English retrochoir which extends transversely behind the reredos. It is graced by slender piers supporting the vault (Fig 37); at the east end are a row of four chapels, with screens and furnishings by Comper. *Access:* Nearest Underground station: London Bridge.

St Helen Bishopsgate

St Helen's survival, restoration and re-ordering after damage by two IRA bombs in 1992-93 is a vivid illustration of the peculiar dangers which still dog urban churches today. Before the bombing, the church was renowned for the finest assembly of monuments in any parish church in London, and these have fortunately survived unscathed. Less fortunate were four people who died; but the devastation gave the opportunity for a fundamental re-organisation of the interior which has greatly enhanced its potential for modern worship, though the result has not been without controversy: where, for instance, is the altar? There is no disputing, however, that St Helen's is a stunning church–a compelling amalgam of medieval architecture with artefacts mostly of the sixteenth and seventeenth centuries.

The parish church, dedicated to the mother of Constantine, the first Christian Emperor of Rome, dates back at least to the twelfth century. Later, around 1210, a Benedictine nunnery was

(Fig 38) **St Helen Bishopsgate.**

founded, and as a result, St Helen's presents the unusual spectacle of a two-naved church separated by a single arcade (Fig 6, p 12); the north nave was the nuns' church, while the south nave was parochial. Such an arrangement is not unique: similar structures may be seen, for example, at Highham Ferrers in Northamptonshire, and at Leominster Priory, Herefordshire. Most of the fabric of St Helen's is thirteenth-century, but the Perpendicular arcade dates from about 1475. In addition, there is a large south transept. The attractive west front (Fig 38) has twin gables, with a central seventeenth-century bell-turret between. In the wall of the south transept is a stone doorway dated 1633 (Fig 39), of classical style, and contemporary with St Paul's, Covent Garden and St Katherine Cree; compare this rather fumbling assembly of Renaissance

(Fig 39) **St Helen Bishopsgate** *The stone south doorway of 1633.*

motifs with the sophisticated doorway at St Mary-le-Bow designed by Wren about 45 years later (Fig 169, p 80).

There are numerous monuments and artefacts in St Helen's, and only a few can be mentioned. In the north wall is the canopied tomb-chest of Hugh Pemberton (1500); at the east end of the same wall is an Easter Sepulchre, which houses the consecrated Host from Maundy Thursday to

Easter Day-below the recess is a blank stone arcade. There are two sword-rests, one of which is very early and made of wood, the other of wrought-iron. There are also two spectacular door-cases, the finer one in the south wall (Fig 40), west of the pulpit, adorned with columns; the other, simpler one is in the west wall of the south transept. The wonderful Jacobean pulpit Fig 41) is in the middle of the south nave, and since the bombing, the seating has been re-arranged so that the congregation is gathered on each side to face the pulpit, symbolising the importance of the preaching of the word. Nearby is the black and red marble font, dated 1632 (Fig 42). In the south transept, note the late fifteenth-century alabaster monuments to John de Oteswich and his wife (formerly in the church of St Martin Outwich) and to Sir John and Lady Crosby (1476; Fig 43); also here are the table tombs of Sir Julius Caesar Adelmare (1636; designed by Nicholas Stone) and Sir Thomas Gresham (1579), financier and

(Fig 40) **St Helen Bishopsgate** *The south nave with screen, pulpit, door-case and font.*

(Fig 41) **St Helen Bishopsgate** *Jacobean pulpit.*

(Fig 42) **St Helen Bishopsgate** *The font.*

(Fig 45) **St Helen Bishopsgate** *The rood screen, now sited between the south nave and the transept.*

(Fig 43) **St Helen Bishopsgate** *Effigies of Sir John and Lady Crosby (1476).*

(Fig 44) **St Helen Bishopsgate** *Effigy of Sir William Pickering (1574).*

founder of the Royal Exchange and of Gresham's College. Nearby is the fine Elizabethan monument to Sir William Pickering (1574; Fig 44) surrounded by railings, possibly the work of William Cure I (Whinney [b]). The rood-screen (Fig 45) has now been moved so that it functions as a parclose screen between the south nave and the south transept.

Access: Nearest Underground station: Liverpool Street.

St Dunstan and All Saints, Stepney

Stepney Parish Church is a pleasant surprise in an area of London not noted for great things: for here is a genuine medieval church with one outstanding treasure and many other points of interest.

The church dates back a thousand years, and was originally dedicated to 'All the Saints'; when Dunstan, Bishop of London, who had built a stone church here in 962, was canonised in 1029, his name was added to the dedication, and so it has remained. Dunstan's church has been replaced; the chancel of the present building dates from the thirteenth century, the remainder some two hundred years later. The building is of Kentish ragstone. In the early Middle Ages, Stepney was quite distinct from London, and was the centre of a large parish extending to the Middlesex/Essex border at the River Lea. In the fourteenth century, new churches were built in the parish at Whitechapel (the white chapel) and at Bow.

It must have been quite a large settlement for those times, and this is reflected in the size of the present church. In the Domesday survey–which did not cover London– it was described as Stibenhed, the manor belonging to the bishop of London; seven mills are mentioned, but no

(Fig 46) **St Dunstan, Stepney** *The nave, looking east.*

(Fig 47) **St Dunstan, Stepney** *The Anglo-Saxon rood.*

(Fig 48) **St Dunstan, Stepney** *Thirteenth-century sedilia.*

church. The nave of St Dunstan's is long (Fig 46), and is separated from the aisles by an arcade of seven bays built in the Perpendicular style. Originally, the easternmost two bays were for the choir, for the staircase leading to the former rood-loft can be seen about two-thirds along the south aisle.

But the greatest treasures of St Dunstan's are in the chancel–and above all, the Anglo-Saxon rood–arguably the most remarkable artefact in any London church. The sculpture displays the Crucifixion, with the figures of St John and the Virgin Mary on either side, and is dated to the tenth or eleventh centuries (Fig 47). Apparently it was placed outside the church until 1899, so it is not surprising that the figures are somewhat indistinct; it remains, however, a fine work from an era which has left relatively few artefacts in London.

ormation had come, sweeping away medieval fashions: and Robert Clarke (died 1610) and his wife are portrayed in the Jacobean mode as kneeling figures facing each other. The modern stained glass in the east window is by Hugh Easton, and shows Christ above the ruins of Stepney after the blitz (Fig 50).

Access: Nearest Underground station: Stepney Green.

(Fig 49) **St Dunstan, Stepney** *The canopy above the tomb-chest of Sir Henry Colet (1510), twice Lord Mayor of London.*

(Fig 50) **St Dunstan, Stepney** *The east window by High Easton.*

St Olave Hart Street

King Olave was a Norwegian who, early in the eleventh century came to the aid of the Saxon king Ethelred (the Unready) by destroying London bridge and with it the Danish intruders. Because of this feat, at least five churches in London were dedicated to him after his canonisation in 1031, but this church in Hart Street is the sole survivor. Its origin is lost in antiquity; maybe there was a wooden church here before the end of the eleventh century, but the earliest written reference to St Olave's is from the end of the thirteenth century. This fits in with the crypt of the present church, which dates from this time and consists of two bays with ribbed vaults.

The present building is basically of the fifteenth century; it escaped the Great Fire thanks to the

On the south side of the chancel is an excellent set of sedilia (Fig 48), carved in the Early English (thirteenth-century) manner; and on the north side an impressive tomb-chest with canopy above, enriched with pendant arches (Fig 49). This commemorates Sir Henry Colet (died 1510), twice Lord Mayor of London. The other fine memorial is from exactly a century later, and is in an entirely different style-for in between the Ref-

(Fig 51) **St Olave Hart Street** *The north arcade.*

actions of Samuel Pepys and Sir William Penn, who organised the tearing down of surrounding dwellings, but it was severely damaged by bombing in World War Two. It was rebuilt after the war and fortunately retains many of the original furnishings and monuments. The church consists of nave and aisles, separated by arcades of Purbeck limestone columns (Fig 51). The windows are Perpendicular, and the vestry doorway is also fifteenth-century (Fig 52). The upper part of the tower was rebuilt in brick in 1731-32.

The greatest interest in St Olave's, however, attaches to the furnishings and monuments. The pulpit (Fig 53), from the Wren church of St Benet, Gracechurch Street, has lovely carving, reputedly by Grinling Gibbons. A series of four wrought-iron sword-rests may be seen; two of them came from All Hallows Staining, a medieval church whose tower still stands in Mark Lane. Sword-rests were set up whenever a parishioner was elected Lord Mayor of London. There are brasses to Sir Richard Haddon (died 1524) and to Thomas Morley (died 1566) and several monuments, notably the kneeling figures of Sir James Deane and his wife (1608), the kneeling figures of the Bayning brothers (died 1610 and 1616; Fig 54), and the standing figure of Sir Andrew Riccard (1672). But the best known monument is the Pepys memorial: Samuel Pepys had a long association with St Olave's, and is buried in a vault by the

(Fig 54) **St Olave Hart Street** *Monuments to Paul and Andrew Bayning (1610 and 1616).*

(Fig 53) **St Olave Hart Street** *Seventeenth-century pulpit.*

communion table. He erected a monument in memory of his wife Elizabeth in the east end of the sanctuary, a lively bust probably the work of John Bushnell (1630-1701); he was described by Margaret Whinney [b] as 'the first English artist to show any knowledge of baroque sculpture'.

Access: Nearest Underground station: Tower Hill.

St Sepulchre without Newgate

The largest parish church in the City was originally dedicated to St Edmund, but from the time of the Crusades took its name from the church of the Holy Sepulchre. In the twelfth century, the church belonged to the Priory of St Bartholomew, who exercised the right of appointment to the benefice.

The tower, porch and walls of the fifteenth century survive today, though the body of the church was destroyed in the Fire; so that what one now sees is a much-altered late medieval shell enclosing the rebuilding of 1670. The porch is noteworthy: a three-storeyed structure, with fan-vaulting, dating from 1458. The ragstone tower (Fig 55) carries four heavy pinnacles added in 1878; it houses a ring of twelve bells, famous as 'the bells of Old Bailey'.

(Fig 52) **St Olave Hart Street** *The fifteenth-century vestry doorway.*

(Fig 55) **St Sepulchre** *Medieval tower and three-storeyed porch.*

The interior has majestic north and south arcades dating from 1670, with Tuscan columns; these were erected by impatient parishioners who would not wait for Christopher Wren's services. The contrast between the classical columns and the Perpendicular tower arch at the west end is striking (Fig 56), but not displeasing. Above are vaulted plaster ceilings installed in 1834. The reredos (Fig 57) and the marble font date from 1670; the wrought-iron communion rails are a little later. St Sepulchre's has had a special relationship with music, and the north chapel contains memorials to John Ireland, Sir Henry Wood and other musicians. The organ (Fig 58) is a distinguished instrument built by Renatus Harris (1640-1715); he was of French origin, and built

(Fig 56) **St Sepulchre** *Arcades of Tuscan columns (1670) and coffered ceiling of 1834.*

(Fig 57) **St Sepulchre** *The chancel, showing the reredos of c.1670, and early eighteenth-century wrought-iron communion rail.*

many organs for parish churches and cathedrals. Sir Henry Wood, founder of the Promenade Concerts, played on this instrument in his early days.

Previously, the church has been described as

(Fig 58) **St Sepulchre** *The organ by Renatus Harris.*

'cluttered', but now that the pews have been cleared away, the seventeenth-century interior can be appreciated-although some may feel that the classical arcades do not accord with the Perpendicular tower arch and the nineteenth-century ceiling (Young), I feel that it has a dignified simplicity of its own. The church, alas, is now closed, and its future is quite uncertain.

Access: Nearest Underground station: St Paul's.

All Hallows-by-the-Tower (All Hallows Barking)

All Hallows (Fig 59) is of awesome antiquity, for it was founded by Erkenwald, Bishop of London in 675. From the beginning it was attached to Barking Abbey in Essex, which the bishop had founded eleven years earlier, his sister being the first abbess. The relationship with Barking Abbey persisted, with interruptions, until the Dissolution of the Monasteries in 1536. But the oldest artefact in All Hallows is still older: parts of Roman tessellated pavements in the undercroft were originally in a floor of a second-century domestic house.

Excavations after the bombing in 1940 have revealed that the Saxon church was originally 70 feet by 24 feet, and an arch from this building may now be seen in the south-west corner of the church, next to the baptistry. Roman tiles may be

(Fig 59) **All Hallows-by-the-Tower.**

seen in the arch. Fragments of Saxon crosses are also displayed in the undercroft.

The church was enlarged in the twelfth century, and in the fifteenth century was substantially rebuilt. The brick tower, which survives, was added in 1658-59. Seven years later, the church, like St Olave Hart Street, escaped destruction in the Fire by the demolition of buildings surrounding it: Samuel Pepys watched the melancholy scene from the new tower. But Hitler's bombs did what the Fire failed to do, and the nave was almost totally destroyed in 1940. The church was reconstructed after the war, and re-dedicated in 1957. The aisles still retain their Perpendicular fifteenth-century windows.

In spite of the destruction, some fine furnishings remain. Easily the best is the 1682 font-cover by Grinling Gibbons (Fig 60), a riot of

(Fig 60) **All Hallows-by-the-Tower** *The font cover by Grinling Gibbons.*

cherubs, fruit and flowers, surmounted by a dove. The contract reveals that he was paid £12 for this work. The Tate altar-panel comprises four panels from a Flemish winged triptych by an unknown artist, dating from *c.*1500; the outer panels portray the donor, Sir Robert Tate, with St John the Baptist, and opposite St Joseph; the inner panels show St Ambrose of Milan and St Jerome with his lion. The seventeenth-century pulpit comes from the bombed Wren church of St Swithin London Stone; it has segmental pediments around the top, 'suggesting undulating gesticulation in the preacher' (Young [a]). There are three gilded wrought-iron sword-rests which would have been used when the Lord Mayor visited the church in state.

Of the monuments, the best is the tomb-chest of Alderman John Croke (1477), which has been reassembled after being blown into 150 fragments during the bombing; at the back of the tomb are brasses showing the effigies of the alderman and his wife and their thirteen children. On the tomb is the casket given by the Prince of Wales in 1922 to commemorate the founding of Toc H by the vicar, the Reverend Philip Clayton. There are a number of excellent brasses, mainly in the floors of the sanctuary and Lady Chapel.

Access: Nearest Underground station: Tower Hill.

St Margaret, Westminster

St Margaret's, Westminster, usually thought of as the parish church of the House of Commons, is

(Fig 61) **St Margaret, Westminster.**

in fact not now a parish church at all, but is part of Westminster Abbey, under the care of the Dean and Chapter of Westminster, and as such is part of a 'royal peculiar' i.e. it is outside the responsibility of the diocese in which it is geographically situated, and under the direct patronage of the crown. Except for the period from 1840-1972, when it *was* a parish church and part of the diocese of London, it has enjoyed the status of a royal peculiar since 1189.

Westminster Abbey was founded by Edward the Confessor in 1065 as a Benedictine monastery, and St Margaret's was probably founded not long after to minister to the ordinary population of Westminster. The present church is the third to be built upon the site, and was begun in the late fifteenth century and completed in 1523, on the eve of the

(Fig 62) **St Margaret, Westminster** *South arcade and aisle.*

(Fig 63) **St Margaret, Westminster** *The chancel.*

Reformation. It is therefore in late Perpendicular style, but has been much affected by subsequent restorations. In 1734 the walls were encased in Portland stone, and the north-west tower was rebuilt by John James in 1735-37 (Fig 61).

The nave (Fig 62) is divided from the aisles by an arcade of eight bays, with no division between nave and chancel. The piers are typically Perpendicular-slender columns with four shafts-and there are Perpendicular windows at both east and west ends. The east window (Fig 63) is the glory of the church, and contains pre-Reformation Flemish glass with a crucifixion scene and kneeling figures of Catherine of Aragon and her first husband Prince Arthur. (As he died young and Catherine subsequently married his brother who became Henry VIII, it is not surprising that that self-willed king banished the glass, and after being rusticated in various places it was not installed at St Margaret's until 1758.) Below the east window, in the centre of the reredos, is a limewood carving

in bas relief based on Titian's *Supper at Emmaus.* There are a considerable number of monuments: note the kneeling life-like representation of Blanche Parry (1590), maid of honour to Elizabeth I. Some excellent modern glass by John Piper may be seen in the windows of the south aisle. *Access:* Nearest Underground station: Westminster.

Chelsea Old Church (All Saints)

The medieval church in Chelsea was very severely damaged during an air-raid in 1941; fortunately the More chapel and the monuments were less damaged than the rest of the building. It is these which now draw visitors, for the church contains one of the best assemblies in London.

Originally this was the parish church of the village of Chelsea, which was quite separate from London. Before 1941, the church consisted of a thirteenth-century chancel, with chapels to the north and south, and a nave and tower which dated from *c.*1670. The north chapel belonged to the Lord of the Manor of Chelsea; the south chapel was rebuilt as his private chapel in 1528 by Sir Thomas More, who lived at Beaufort House nearby and who was then Chancellor of the Duchy of Lancaster. The next year he became Henry VIII's Lord Chancellor, against his own wishes but he resigned in 1532 in protest against Henry's ecclesiastical policies. More refused to accept the king as head of the English Church, and this led to his conviction for high treason, for

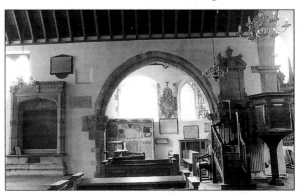

(Fig 64) **Chelsea Old Church** *View into the south chapel.*

(Fig 65) **Chelsea Old Church** *Capital in Italian Renaissance style (1528).*

(Fig 67) **Chelsea Old Church** *Memorial arch to Richard Jervoise (1563).*

which he was beheaded in 1535.

In the 1950s, the church was restored on its old foundations, the square nave being re-built in seventeenth-century style, with the medieval chancel and chapels seen through three arches (Fig 64). The capitals of the pillars leading to the south chapel were carved in 1528; one bears a plaque carved with this date. They are said to be very similar to a capital in the chateau at Chambord in the Loire valley dated 1532 and are probably the work of French carvers. The attribution to Holbein is said to be a guess dating only from 1898 (Summerson [b]). They are exquisitely carved in Renaissance style (Fig 65); 1528 is a very early date for Renaissance art in England.

In the chancel, the More monument (1532) is on the south wall and consists of a recess, with arch above, and an inscription composed by Sir Thomas himself. On the opposite wall is the plain tomb-chest commemorating Sir Edmund Bray (1539). In the south chapel is the monument to

(Fig 66) **Chelsea Old Church** *Monument to Lady Jane Cheyne (1672) designed by Pietro Bernini.*

Jane Guildford, Duchess of North-umberland, (1555), mother-in-law of Lady Jane Grey and mother of Robert Dudley, earl of Leicester and future favour-ite of Elizabeth I.

(Fig 68) **Chelsea Old Church** *Monument to Sir Robert Stanley (1632).*

Along the south wall of the nave is the imposing monument to Lord Dacre and his wife Ann Sackville (1595) – two recumbent figures on a tomb-chest, and above a superstructure and coat-of-arms. On the opposite (north) wall of the nave is a memorial to Lady Jane Cheyne (1669; Fig

66); Lady Jane lies semi-recumbent flanked by tall columns, with a segmental pediment above. Proceeding from here to the north chapel, one passes through the triumphal arch which com-memorates Richard Jervoise (1563; Fig 67). In the north chapel are the monuments to Sir Robert Stanley (a large standing wall-monument; 1632; Fig 68), Sir Thomas Lawrence and his wife (kneeling figures; 1593) and their daughter Sara Colville (1632) portrayed rising in her shroud from her tomb.

Access: Nearest Underground station: South Kensington; then by bus.

St Andrew Undershaft

The name 'Undershaft' derives from a long shaft or maypole which used to be set up there on May Day. John Stow, the London historian who is buried here, tells the story of the erection of the maypole every May Day in front of the south door of the church. As the shaft overtopped the steeple, the church received the name of St Andrew Undershaft. The maypole was finally destroyed when the parish-

(Fig 69) **St Andrew Undershaft.**

(Fig 70) **St Andrew Undershaft** *Pulpit from the school of Grinling Gibbons.*

(Fig 72) **St Andrew Undershaft** *Monument of Sir Thomas Offley (1582) and family.*

(Fig 71) **St Andrew Undershaft** *Monument of John Stow (1605).*

ioners were accused by the curate of St Katherine Cree of setting up an idol, as they had named their church 'under the shaft' (Bumpus).

The original church was built in 1362, but this was replaced by the present building between 1520 and 1532. St Andrew's stands at the corner of Leadenhall Street and St Mary Axe, and its rather unprepossessing exterior does not prepare one for the splendours within. The lower stages of the tower are from the previous church, and a prominent newel staircase terminates above in a turret (Fig 69). The upper stage of the tower is Victorian.

The interior has a continuous nave and chancel, separated from the aisles by tall Perpendicular arcades, with slender columns; above is a clerestory. The roofs are original from the sixteenth century, of low pitch, divided by ribs into squares, with gilded bosses at the intersections (Fig 19, p 18). There are large east and west Perpendicular windows; the fine stained glass in the west window, much of it dating from the seventeenth century, was destroyed by an IRA bomb, and the window has not yet been restored. There is a seventeenth-century font by Nicholas Stone, who was master mason to James I and Charles I; the bowl is hewn from a block of white marble set on a octagonal stem of black marble. The excellent pulpit (Fig 70) comes from the school of Grinling Gibbons, and the organ was built by Renatus Harris in 1696. At this time, there was intense competition between Harris and the famous Father Smith (or Schmidt) who built the organ in St Paul's Cathedral. Of the monuments, the best known is that of John Stow (died 1605), author of the *Survey of London*; he is depicted seated at his desk, quill in hand (Fig 71). An annual service is held in which his pen is replaced. Next to him is the brass to Nicholas Leveson (1539), with his wife and family. The monument to Sir Thomas Offley (1582) shows two kneeling figures facing each other across a prayer-desk, with kneeling children between (Fig 72).

Access: Nearest Underground station: Liverpool Street or Aldgate.

St Giles Cripplegate

The visitor may be forgiven for thinking that St Giles Cripplegate was a stronghold of seventeenth-century Puritanism, for here John Milton was buried, Oliver Cromwell was married, and John Bunyan preached – and all three are suitably commemorated in the church. And at the end of the previous century, the vicar of St Giles was Lancelot Andrewes, later Bishop of Chichester, Ely and Winchester, one of the early Anglican divines who is buried in Southwark Cathedral (p 26). But in fact St Giles goes back to 1090, when it was founded by Alfune who was

(Fig 73) **St Giles Cripplegate** *Perpendicular arcades.*

(Fig 74) **St Giles Cripplegate.**

later associated with Rahere in the foundation of St Bartholomew's Hospital. The name Cripplegate may relate to a hospital for the lame said to have been situated nearby, or alternatively may indicate the great number of cripples who begged in the area. St Giles was the patron saint of cripples and blacksmiths. The early medieval church was rebuilt in the fourteenth century, but this building was virtually destroyed by fire in 1545. The present church was built in 1545-50 when the Reformation was well under way during the reigns of Henry VIII and Edward VI. It is the last medieval parish church in London.

So the new St Giles was built in a very late Perpendicular style. But that was not the end of the church's troubles: although it escaped the Fire of 1666, it was severely damaged in the Second World War, and only the shell remained; it was later restored by Godfrey Allen and re-opened in 1960. The church is now adjacent to the Barbican, which gives it once more a resident congregation, and it is attractively situated opposite the lake and the Arts Centre.

The exterior (Fig 74) appears a rather Victorianised Perpendicular, with a battlemented nave and aisles; but a watercolour of 1815 by George Shepherd shows the clerestory built of brick, and no battlements. In fact, the north and south fronts were faced with Kentish ragstone and the walls crenellated in the 1850s. The tower had been heightened in 1682-84, when the top storey was encased in brick and the turrets and cupola added.

Inside, the long nave is flanked by Perpendicular arcades of seven bays (Fig 73); the east and west windows, roofs and panelling are new. The burial place of Milton is marked by a stone at the threshold of the chancel, and there is a bust of the great poet by the elder John Bacon (1793). Other famous men buried in St Giles include John Foxe, author of *Foxe's Book of Martyrs* (1587), Sir Martin Frobisher, Elizabethan sailor and explorer (1594) and John Speed, map-maker (1629). The eighteenth-century organ came from the church of St Luke, Old Street.

Access: Nearest Underground station: Barbican.

The Age of Inigo Jones (1573-1652)

THE Reformation brought an abrupt end to church building in London, as elsewhere in England. The last medieval parish church to be built in the capital was, as we have seen, St Giles Cripplegate, completed in 1550. Then for eighty years there was nothing, until St Katherine Cree and St Paul's, Covent Garden were built around 1630.

The intervening years, covering the reigns of Elizabeth and James I were, of course, momentous in the course of English history. They witnessed the emergence of England as the leading Protestant power in Europe, the union of the crown with the crown of Scotland, and the final establishment of the reformed religion through-out the whole of Great Britain. They also saw the gradual spread of Renaissance ideas throughout Europe, but Protestant England was remarkably slow in adopting classical designs in parish churches. Churches were still occasionally being built in the provinces in a so-called debased form of Perpendicular style until well on in the seventeenth century– e.g. Broughton, Stafford-shire, 1634; Foremark, Derbyshire, 1662.

But before we look at post-Reformation churches in London, it is necessary to learn a little about the classical style of architecture which was employed: and for that, we must go in imagination to Italy. In that country at the end of the sixteenth century, the Renaissance was a *fait accompli*, the baroque had yet to begin. Vitruvius, a Roman author, had, before AD27, written the only Roman treatise on architecture to have survived, and accordingly his writings were treated with enormous reverence. In *De Architectura* he had described the classical 'orders' of architecture, Tuscan, Doric, Ionic, Corinthian, to which a fifth order, the Composite (a synthesis of Ionic and Corinthian), was added in the fifteenth century

(Fig 75) **St Michael Cornhill** *Tuscan columns.*

by a Renaissance architect, Alberti. In 1537, Serlio, an Italian architect, published the first of a series of fully illustrated books, from which all later treatises have been derived.

Each Roman order consists of a column or shaft, plain or fluted, standing on a base and ped-

(Fig 76) **St Leonard, Shoreditch** *Doric columns: two simple mouldings at the top of the shaft, then a square capital (abacus), a frieze with vertical patterning (triglyph) and then the cornice from which the arches rise.*

estal; Tuscan columns are always plain, but all the other orders may be plain or fluted. Above the column, the capital supports an entablature consisting of an architrave, a frieze and a cornice.

Tuscan – the simplest and most primitive. The columns are massive, the capital simple, with only one or two plain mouldings; the entablature also is plain (Fig 75, and also Fig 255, p 125).

Doric – the columns are slightly less massive, the capital still simple, but tending to have smaller

(Fig 77) **St Giles-in-the-Fields** *Ionic columns.*

(Fig 78) **St Paul, Deptford** *Corinthian columns.*

(Fig 79) **Christ Church Spitalfields** *Composite columns.*

mouldings than the Tuscan; the frieze is decorated with vertical mouldings known as triglyphs (Fig 76).

Ionic – distinguished by the presence in the capital of volutes (coiled scrolls) (Fig 77, and also Figs 163, 166 and 283 on pp 77, 79 and 139 respectively).

Corinthian – the capital is luxuriantly decorated with two or three ranks of carved acanthus leaves (Fig 78, and also Figs 193, 219 and 241 on pp 90, 103 and 116 respectively).

Composite – the capital combines features of the Ionic and the Corinthian, i.e. volutes above acanthus leaves (Fig 79).

Sometimes the orders are said to have characters – thus Tuscan and Doric are thought to be plain, masculine, tough; Ionic scholarly or matronly; Corinthian virginal, suitable above all for the Virgin Mary; Composite luxuriant. Not too much significance should be read into these interpretations. The reader desiring a fuller description is referred to Sir John Summerson's *The Classical Language of Architecture.*

Although, as we have seen, England was tardy in adopting classical ideas in the field of church architecture (perhaps because no churches were built in the Elizabethan age!), in domestic architecture it was a different story. In the second half of the sixteenth century, such buildings as the former Somerset House (1547-54), Longleat (from 1554 onwards), and other great Elizabethan houses such as Wollaton Hall, Nottinghamshire and Hardwick Hall, Derbyshire, were steeped in Renaissance ideas, and it was clear that the Channel could not forever exclude the wind of artistic change sweeping through the continent.

Into this climate of English nationalism and relative insularity was born, in 1573, Inigo Jones, a Londoner just nine years younger than Shakespeare. Crucially, as a young man he went to Italy, and afterwards he was employed at Copenhagen by King Christian IV of Denmark, brother-in-law of James I. By 1605, he was back in England and then began his career as a producer of court masques and designer of theatrical scenery. In 1609, he was appointed surveyor to Henry, Prince of Wales, but after the Prince's death at the age of 16 in 1612, Inigo Jones departed again to Italy.

There he made extensive direct studies of Roman remains and the work of Palladio.

The latter, who modelled his architectural style on Vitruvius, had died in 1580. Scamozzi, a pupil of Palladio, had, like his master, expounded the classical orders, and Inigo Jones met Scamozzi in Venice in 1614 (Summerson [b]), but was not greatly impressed (Hamilton). After seeing Scamozzi, Inigo Jones returned to London, and was appointed Surveyor-General to the King. He was now 39, and had never practised as an architect: but the time was ripe, in fact overdue, for the full-scale introduction of classical architecture into England.

There ensued a series of buildings which transformed for ever the face of English architecture. First Jones designed the Queen's house at Greenwich, begun for Anne of Denmark in 1616, but not completed until 1629-35, when Henrietta Maria was Queen. The Banqueting House for the royal palace at Whitehall followed in 1619-22. In 1623, Jones designed the Queen's chapel as a Catholic chapel in St James' Palace, at first for the Infanta of Spain who was intended to marry Prince Charles; and when this match failed, for Henrietta Maria, daughter of the King of France, whom Charles married in 1625. The chapel was complete by 1627. It has a large Venetian window at the east end; the west front has a door and two windows at ground level, and above, three windows, the central one round-headed, the lateral ones flat-headed. There are substantial pediments at both east and west ends. Unfortunately, the Queen's chapel is not open to the public except during services (Anglican) on Sundays.

Then, in 1630, came St Paul's, Covent Garden.

St Paul, Covent Garden

Covent Garden (originally Convent Garden) was in medieval times literally a market garden for Westminster Abbey. By the reign of Charles I, it was on the fringe of an expanding London and ripe for development by the owner, the Earl of Bedford. It appears that the King and his advisers persuaded the earl that the area should be developed as a whole, and that the buildings should have architectural merit. Inigo Jones was entrusted with the design, and in 1630-31 he created London's first open space, a piazza in the Italian fashion, with arcaded buildings on the north and east sides, St Paul's church on the west, and an open area on the south adjoining the private garden of Bedford House. Unfortunately none of these buildings, apart from St Paul's, survives. The earl did not intend his new church to be grand, little more than a barn; 'My Lord', replied Jones, 'You shall have the handsomest barn in England.' And so it proved.

The most rewarding aspect of the building is the east front, facing the square. There is the giant portico (Fig 80), with four Tuscan columns scrupulously founded on Vitruvian designs, and above an enormous pediment with far over-reaching eaves. The choice of the Tuscan order for the columns is surely significant: this is the plainest of the orders, and thus

(Fig 80) **St Paul, Covent Garden** *Tuscan columns in the portico.*

(Fig 81) **St Paul, Covent Garden** *The interior of 'the handsomest barn in England'.*

suitable for Protestant worship. The two out-ermost columns are square in cross-section, the inner ones circular. The side-arches are wider than those originally designed by Jones. The west front, which is the main entrance to the church, has two round-headed windows on either side of the door, and again is surmounted by a huge pediment. The north and south sides have simple round-headed windows.

The interior (Fig 81) is a plain 'barn': no division between nave and sanctuary, no arcades nor aisles. It is light and friendly, with a west gallery on Doric columns. The ceiling is beautifully proportioned; the original was painted by Matthew Goodrich. The altar is flanked by short colonnades, the columns of which previously supported the original galleries.

The later history of St Paul's follows an all-too-familiar pattern in London churches: severe damage by fire in 1795, faithful reconstruction by Thomas Hardwick, removal of the side-galleries in 1872, with redecoration of the ceiling and renewal of the brick facing. Perhaps most harmful of all has been the demolition in the eighteenth and nineteenth centuries of all Jones' other buildings in the piazza, which now make it impossible for us to visualise the grandeur of the original conception.

Nevertheless, St Paul's remains as the earliest classical parish church in England, and as such has an assured place in the affections of all who love parish churches.

Access: Nearest Underground station: Covent Garden.

St Katherine Cree

This church, unique in style in London, was a medieval foundation, being in the twelfth century part of the Augustinian Priory of Holy Trinity, or Christchurch, Aldgate; Cree stands for Christ-church. Later there was a fourteenth-century church, and the tower was built in 1504. By the

seventeenth century, the church was dilapidated, and it was rebuilt in 1628-30 under the influence of William Laud, the 'high-church' Bishop of London. The architect is unknown: but, like many churches built in the first half of the seventeenth century, St Katherine Cree is ambiguous: Janus-like, it looks backward to the Perpendicular past, and forward to the classical future.

The tower of 1504 survives (Fig 82) and is surmounted by a cupola constructed in 1776. The windows are unusual: to the east is a straight-headed 'Tudor' window of five lights, and above this a rose window set in a square. The south windows consist of three lights, again straight-headed, and the large west window is pedimented.

The interior (Fig 83) is a feast of colour, predominantly pale blue and gold. There is a nave

(Fig 82) **St Katherine Cree** *The tower (1504).*

(Fig 84) **St Katherine Cree** *The font (c. 1630-40).*

of six bays, and florid Corinthian columns supporting semicircular arches. The contrast between the Corinthian of St Katherine Cree and the austere Tuscan of the portico of St Paul's, Covent Garden is very striking, reflecting, perhaps, differences in churchmanship in the Church of England which were widening in the first half of the seventeenth century. Above the arcade is a Perpendicular clerestory and then a plastered ceiling with ridge-ribs and tiercerons, adorned with bosses displaying the arms of City companies.

The reredos comes from a demolished church, St James, Duke's Place. There is an elegant seventeenth-century font (Fig 84) and an eighteenth-century pulpit (Fig 85) and communion table. The best monument is that to the Elizabethan Sir Nicholas Throckmorton (1570; Fig 86). He lies recumbent, in the medieval manner, but flanked by Tuscan columns-another example of the stylistic ambiguity of St Katherine Cree?

Access: Nearest Underground station: Aldgate.

(Fig 83) **St Katherine Cree** *The interior (1628-31); Corinthian columns, rose window, clerestory and plaster vault.*

(Fig 85) **St Katherine Cree** *Eighteenth-century pulpit.*

(Fig 86) **St Katherine Cree** *Monument to Sir Nicholas Throckmorton (1570).*

(Fig 87) **St Luke, Charlton.**

(Fig 88) **St Luke, Charlton** *The nave and chancel of c.1630 and the arcade (1693).*

St Luke, Charlton

Sir Adam Newton, Tutor to Prince Henry, built his Jacobean mansion Charlton House around 1610. Twenty years later, he rebuilt the village church of Charlton, and thus St Luke's is

(Fig 90) **St Luke, Charlton**
Bust of Spencer Perceval, by Sir Francis Chantrey (1812).

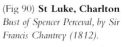

(Fig 89) **St Luke, Charlton**
Seventeenth-century font.

contemporary with the preceding two churches. It is, however, utterly different from both: whereas St Paul's is Renaissance, and St Katherine Cree looks both backwards and forwards with a sophisticated air, St Luke's is unashamedly a simple village church of uncertain style and totally without pretension. Built of red brick, the church stands prominently at the top of the hill leading up from Charlton station.

The church consists of a plain west tower (Fig 87), and inside there is a nave and chancel, with a north aisle added later in the seventeenth century (Fig 88). The porch has a Dutch gable. Both nave and chancel have a wagon roof, that of the chancel being original. The arcade is low, the arches being rounded and the columns square with attached shafts. There is a seventeenth-century reredos, with Creed, Commandments and Lord's Prayer. The font (Fig 89) is late seventeenth-century, with a baluster stem and shallow bowl. There is a good array of monuments: perhaps the most striking being that to Lady Newton by Nicholas Stone (1630), and the bust of Britain's only assassinated prime minister, Spencer Percival, by Sir Francis Chantrey (1812; Fig 90).

Access: By train from London Bridge to Charlton Station.

Sir Christopher Wren (1632-1723)

TWO or three years after the construction of St Paul's, Covent Garden, a more important St Paul's occupied Inigo Jones' attention. London's medieval cathedral was by the 1630s showing signs of severe dilapidation, and Inigo Jones recased the exterior of the nave and added a giant Corinthian western portico, which must have appeared somewhat incongruous against its Gothic background.

In the same year that Jones was at work on the cathedral, the man was born who was ultimately to build the new St Paul's. Christopher was born in a Wiltshire rectory to a staunchly royalist and Laudian family. The Wrens, in contrast to the Joneses, moved in relatively high circles: Christopher's father held livings in Wiltshire and Oxfordshire, and was also Dean of Windsor and as such was responsible for the treasures of the Order of the Garter. His more famous uncle, Matthew Wren, became Bishop of Hereford in 1635 and of Ely three years later. By 1641 the bishop's high-church leanings had earned the displeasure of the Puritans, and he was arrested and confined to the Tower for nearly 20 years. At the same time, Laud, inspirer of the church of St Katherine Cree, Bishop of London from 1628 and Archbishop of Canterbury from 1633, was also arrested and thrown into the Tower; he was less fortunate than Matthew Wren, and in 1645 he was found guilty of 'endeavouring to subvert the laws, to overthrow the Protestant religion, and to act as an enemy of Parliament'. He was beheaded on Tower Hill.

During these troubled years, young Christopher Wren was at Westminster School under the remarkable headmastership of Richard Busby, who, though a Laudian Royalist, managed to survive the Civil War and Commonwealth undisturbed in Parliamentary London. From Westminster, Wren went to Wadham College, Oxford in 1650, and soon showed his brilliance at mathematics and physics. He became a Fellow of All Souls', and then in 1657 professor of astronomy at Gresham College, London. After the Restoration, he returned to Oxford as professor of astronomy in 1661.

In the seventeenth century, professional specialisation barely existed, and it would not have been thought strange for a man to encompass mathematics, physics, engineering and astronomy, and then turn his attention to architecture. And so it happened that Wren's introduction to building came in 1662, when he designed the Sheldonian theatre in Oxford; this was followed in the next year by the chapel for Pembroke College, Cambridge. Both these buildings are in the classical style, following the example of Inigo Jones 30 years earlier. The front of the chapel has four Corinthian pilasters, with a pediment above. Just as in the time of Inigo Jones, the condition of St Paul's Cathedral was again causing grave concern, the tower above the crossing showing some signs of impending collapse. A Commission was established in April 1663 to undertake restoration, and opinions were sought from various authorities, including Wren.

The last major outbreak of bubonic plague ravaged England, and especially London, in 1665, and coincidentally that year Wren made his only journey to the continent, visiting France for nine months, returning early in 1666. This tour was crucially important for Wren's development as an architect, though detailed information about his journey is lacking. He was certainly introduced to the leading Italian architect, Bernini, who was in Paris to design a rebuilding of part of the Louvre, and Wren returned to England laden with engravings of contemporary French buildings. On his return, he was once more immersed in the problems of St Paul's, and in May 1666 he proposed a radical reconstruction, replacing the tower with a dome, surmounted by a cupola, lantern and spire. On August 27th, 1666, these plans were discussed at a meeting attended by John Evelyn, the diarist, the Bishop of London, the Dean of St Paul's, Wren and others, and Wren's proposals received a cautious acceptance. Six days later came the Great Fire, and old St Paul's perished.

The fire devastated the narrow crowded streets of the city of London: 13,200 dwellings were destroyed, most of them built of wood. In addition to the cathedral, 86 parish churches were destroyed; 20 survived, but only eight remain today (p 16). One positive by-product of the fire was that plague came to an end, never to return to the capital. Within a week of the end of the fire, Wren had submitted to the king proposals for the rebuilding of the city; Evelyn followed with his plans two days later.

The fate of these plans, and the whole subject of the rebuilding of the cathedral are outside the scope of this work. But the rebuilding of the parish churches very much concerns us. Many parishes were amalgamated, and the 86 churches were eventually replaced by 51, designed by Wren with or without the assistance of others (see below). In addition, Wren built a new church outside the city, St James Piccadilly, making 52 in all. These churches are listed in Tables I and II.

These, especially Table II, make melancholy reading. Of the 52 churches, only 25 survive today (Table I), and of these, 14 have been restored following damage in World War Two. Sadder still are the 27 lost churches of Table II. Eight were destroyed in the war, but 19 were pulled down for

Table I – Wren's Churches (Surviving)	Tower Completed By:
1670-72 St Michael Cornhill	
1670-72 St Vedast Foster Lane★; later 1695-99	1712
1670-75 St Mary-le-Bow	1680
1670-76 St Mary-at-Hill	
1670-79 St Edmund the King	1707
1670-84 St Bride Fleet Street★	1703
1671-76 St Magnus the Martyr	1705
1671-78 St Nicholas Cole Abbey★	
1671-80 St Lawrence Jewry★	
1672-79 St Stephen Walbrook★	1717
1676-83 St James Garlickhythe★	1717
1677-80 St Anne & St Agnes★	
1677-81 St Peter Cornhill	
1677-83 St Benet Paul's Wharf	
1677-84 St Martin Ludgate	1705
1679-82 St Mary Aldermary	1703
1680-82 St Clement Danes★	
1681-86 St Mary Abchurch★	
1682-84 St James Piccadilly★	
1683-87 St Clement Eastcheap	
1683-88 St Margaret Lothbury	1713
1684-87 St Margaret Pattens	1702
1684-90 St Andrew Holborn★	
1685-93 St Andrew-by-the-Wardrobe★	
1686-94 St Michael Paternoster Royal★	1717

★ = Damaged 1940-44 and restored

a variety of reasons between 1786 and 1939. The architecture of Wren was out of favour during Victorian times: by 1846, four churches had been lost, but between 1872 and 1904, no fewer than 14 were demolished – a rate of almost one every two years. It is incredible to us to learn that the last Wren church to be wilfully destroyed was as late as 1939 (All Hallows, Lombard Street). The reasons for the loss of churches were many: they included commercial pressures, road-widening schemes, the departure of the resident population from the City, and artistic and clerical indifference.

Table II – Wren's Churches (Demolished)			
1668-71 St Dunstan-in-the-East	Bombed 1940	1677-82 All Hallows-the-Great	Demolished 1894
1670-71 St Christopher-le-Stocks	Demolished 1786	1677-84 All Hallows Bread Street	Demolished 1877
1670-73 St Michael Wood Street	Demolished 1897	1677-87 Christchurch Newgate★	Bombed 1940
1670-74 St Mary Albermanbury	Bombed 1940	1678-83 St Antholin Budge Row	Demolished 1876
1670-77 St Dionis Backchurch	Demolished 1878	1680-86 St Augustine Old Change★	Bombed 1941
1670-77 St Mildred Poultry	Demolished 1872	1681-86 St Matthew Friday Street	Demolished 1885
1670-79 St Olave Jewry★	Demolished 1887	1681-86 St Benet Gracechurch Street	Demolished 1876
1670-81 St Benet Fink	Demolished 1846	1681-87 St Mildred Bread Street	Bombed 1941
1671-79 St George Botolph Lane	Demolished 1904	1682-87 St Alban Wood Street★	Bombed 1940
1674-77 St Stephen Coleman Street	Bombed 1940	1683-87 St Mary Magdalene Fish Street	Demolished 1890
1674-81 St Bartholomew Exchange	Demolished 1841	1684-87 St Michael Crooked Lane	Demolished 1831
1676-79 St Michael Bassishaw	Demolished 1900	1686-94 All Hallows Lombard Street	Demolished 1939
1676-80 St Michael Queenhythe	Demolished 1876	1686-94 St Mary Somerset★	Demolished 1871
1677-81 St Swithin London Stone	Bombed 1941	★ = Tower survives	

Summary:

Demolished 1786-1939	19
Bombed 1940-41 and destroyed	8
Bombed 1940-41 and restored	14
Survive relatively unscathed	11
Total	52

The New Churches

Four years after the Great Fire, in 1670, an Act was passed to provide for the rebuilding of London's churches. The fabric would be provided from the proceeds of a tax on coal, but the fittings would remain the responsibility of the parishes. Wren had been appointed Surveyor-General in 1669, and after the passage of the Act he was assisted by three surveyors, Robert Hooke, Edward Woodroffe and John Oliver. Three Commissioners were appointed to approve the designs: the Archbishop of Canterbury and the Bishop and Lord Mayor of London; Wren became

their executive officer. Rebuilding proceeded quickly: about fourteen were begun in 1670, immediately after the passage of the Act, and by 1677 nearly 30 were under construction (Summerson [b]); by 1686 rebuilding was virtually over, though nearly all the greatest steeples followed in the 20 years between 1697 and 1717.

The initiative for the rebuilding lay with the parish vestries, who approached Sir Christopher Wren. In at least one instance (St Sepulchre, p 32) the vestry was too impatient to wait for his services and proceeded without his advice: as it turned out, an unwise move. But most of the vestries were only too anxious to work through the official channels, because they would then have access to public funds and hence minimise the cost to the parishioners.

Wren faced an unprecedented task: not only had he to design over 50 parish churches and the new St Paul's, but also over the years he had many other commissions. There has been much debate about the division of responsibility between Wren and his assistants in the design for the new churches: the traditional view, first put forward by

Wren's son, is that Sir Christopher designed all the 51 new churches in the City: this is not now generally accepted. Paul Jeffery [b], in a recent scholarly review (1996) concludes that there is *documentary* evidence supporting Wren's claim in only about six churches (St James Piccadilly, St Stephen Walbrook, St Mary-le-Bow, St Andrew Holborn, St Bride Fleet Street, St Clement Danes); but on the other hand there is no documentary evidence in favour of other designers. In addition, no stylistic features have been found which clearly differentiate Wren's work from that of his main assistant Robert Hooke. It seems that we must conclude that some churches are wholly by Wren; others are by Wren, with help from Hooke; others mainly by Hooke, with help from Wren; and some *may* be entirely the work of Hooke, with only nominal supervision by Wren.

Wren's (or Wren/Hooke's) fecundity of imagination is astonishing: every one of the new churches is different, and the sites they were wrestling with were often cramped, and hemmed in by streets and new buildings. 'It was a stroke of extraordinary good fortune that gave him the City churches to design just when he had finally devoted himself to architecture, and an even greater that the carrying out of the St Paul's design was delayed until the experience on the City churches had been digested. For it was his work on the City churches that helped to develop that superb gift for space composition that distinguishes the completed St Paul's' (Webb).

Some of the churches had not been wholly destroyed by the Fire, and required repair rather than total rebuilding. Thus the repair of St Dunstan-in-the-East started as early as 1668, but even here Tuscan pillars and arches replaced medieval arcades; the steeple followed 30 years later. St Mary Woolnoth was another building repaired by Wren: but the church was totally rebuilt by Hawksmoor in 1716-27. In some cases (e.g. St Mary-at-Hill, St Michael Cornhill, St Peter Cornhill and St Christopher-le-Stocks) part

of the medieval fabric was incorporated in the new building. But in virtually all other instances, the new church was a total rebuild, although often utilising the foundations of the earlier church. Just outside the City, St Andrew Holborn and St Clement Danes were medieval churches which escaped destruction by fire but whose fabric was decaying and required replacement. Finally, St James Piccadilly was a totally new church for a developing part of London.

Most of the money for the rebuilt churches

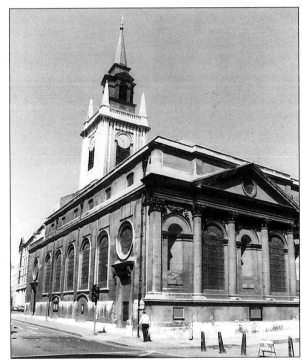

(Fig 91) **St Lawrence Jewry.**

came from the new coal-tax, but some funds came from private benefactors. The majority of the churches were built of Wren's favourite material, Portland stone, but brick was used for a few (e.g. St Benet Paul's Wharf, and St Anne and St Agnes) sometimes with dressings of stone.

Although it is in general true that the exteriors of Wren's churches are less arresting than the interiors, there is in most of the churches at least one façade that is worth studying. Undoubtedly the finest is the east façade of St Lawrence Jewry

(Fig 92) **St Nicholas Cole Abbey.**

(Fig 91): here four giant Corinthian columns support a pediment, with Corinthian pilasters at each corner. The demolished church of St Michael Wood Street also had a distinguished east façade; there was a giant pediment with protruding clock, and three round-headed windows separated by Ionic pilasters and rustication at the corners. St Nicholas Cole Abbey has a good south front (Fig 92), with arched windows under straight hoods. Both St Mary-at-Hill (Fig 93) and St Peter Cornhill have striking east façades, with pediments above; at St Peter's the upper floor is connected with the wider lower floor by Italianate curved pieces; a similar motif can be seen in the south front of St Edmund the King on either side of the tower (Fig 110, p 58). At St Martin Ludgate the tower is connected to the lower part of the façade by volutes. At St Benet Paul's Wharf, the combination of brick walls with quoins of Portland stone and stone-carved garlands above the windows produces a stunning

(Fig 93) **St Mary-at-Hill** *The east façade.*

effect (Fig 105, p 56). Similar garlands were present above the windows in St Swithin London Stone (now demolished).

Towers and Steeples of Wren's Churches

If the exteriors of Wren's churches are sometimes dull, in contrast the towers and steeples are fascinating; here Wren's fertile imagination endowed them with infinite variety and appeal-though as with the bodies of the churches the authorship of the steeples has engendered much discussion. The hand of Hooke has often been detected in the earlier steeples (most of those in Groups I and II below); and in the last group (Group III, except for St Mary-le-Bow) the influence of Hawksmoor has been suggested (Jeffery [b]). For ease of comparison of the towers and steeples, I thought it most helpful to collect together illustrations of all the surviving towers, rather than to include them with the description of each individual church.

Gerald Cobb, in his 'The Old Churches of London', attempted a complicated classification of Wren's towers into no less than twelve separate groups. For the sake of simplicity, I have regrouped the 28 surviving towers into three major categories (Table III). Three towers of Wren's churches are referred to elsewhere because they are definitely not the work of Wren: that of St Michael Cornhill is by Hawksmoor, St Clement Danes by Gibbs, and St Mary-at-Hill by Gwilt. Six towers survive when the rest of the church has been destroyed or demolished (St Olave Jewry, St Mary Somerset, St Alban Wood Street, St Augustine Old Change, Christchurch Newgate and St Dunstan-in-the-East). When the steeple was completed long after the church, the date of completion is given in parenthesis.

Wren rebuilt three towers in the Gothic style-St Mary Aldermary, St Alban Wood Street and St Dunstan-in-the-East; in addition, the Hawks-moor tower of St Michael Cornhill is Gothic. Two other churches (St Christopher-le-Stocks and St Sepulchre) were also repaired in the Gothic style with new windows and pinnacles, either by Wren, or more likely, by Dickenson, a Gothic expert (Downes).

**Table III
Towers and Steeples of Wren's Churches**

1) Towers without spires
St Clement Eastcheap
St Andrew-by-the-Wardrobe
St Andrew Holborn
St Mary Aldermary
St Anne & St Agnes
St Olave Jewry
St Alban Wood Street
St Mary Somerset

2) Towers with lead spires
St James Piccadilly
St Margaret Lothbury
St Mary Abchurch
St Benet Paul's Wharf
St Peter Cornhill
St Lawrence Jewry
St Margaret Pattens
St Augustine Old Change
St Edmund the King
St Nicholas Cole Abbey
St Magnus the Martyr
St Martin Ludgate

3) Towers with stone spires
St Mary-le-Bow
St Dunstan-in-the-East
St Bride Fleet Street
Christchurch Newgate
St Vedast Foster Lane
St Michael Paternoster Royal
St James Garlickhythe
St Stephen Walbrook

Group 1 – towers without spires

Even this, the plainest group, exhibits considerable variety. Three (**St Clement Eastcheap** (Fig 94), **St Andrew-by-the-Wardrobe** 1703,

(Fig 94) **St Clement Eastcheap** *South-west tower with brick exposed in upper parts, stone quoins and balustrade.*

(Fig 95) **St Andrew-by-the-Wardrobe** *A brick south-west tower with stone quoins and at the belfry stage, stone pilaster strips at the angles.*

(Fig 95), and **St Andrew Holborn** (Fig 96) are surmounted by a parapet, with or without urns. **St Mary Aldermary** (1702; Fig 97) is a rebuilt Gothic tower, while **St Anne and St Agnes** (1714, Fig 98) has a small cupola. Most notable are three towers which now stand alone: **St Olave Jewry** (Fig 99) has a big doorway with segmental pediment; above, the tower has four obelisk pinnacles

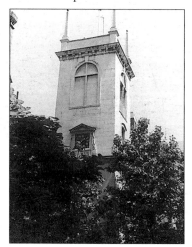

(Fig 99) **St Olave Jewry** *Tower with obelisk pinnacles at the corners.*

(Fig 96) **St Andrew Holborn** *A fifteenth-century tower refaced in 1703; segment-headed windows under round-headed frames; scrolled pedestals at corners of parapet, with urns carrying vases above.*

at the corners. **St Alban Wood Street** is a Gothic tower, with buttresses at the angles and sides, and Perpendicular windows at the upper stage; above is a parapet with eight crocketed pinnacles (Fig 100). Finest of this group is **St**

(Fig 97) **St Mary Aldermary** *The lowest stage is dated to 1511 and the second stage to 1625-29 (Pevsner). Wren rebuilt the upper stages.*

(Fig 98) **St Anne and St Agnes** *The western tower is rendered and above is a new cupola.*

(Fig 101) **St Mary Somerset** *On each face a vertical series of windows, alternately circular and round-headed; above, a crown of eight pinnacles: four obelisks set on pedestals and four fluted vases at the corners.*

(Fig 100) **St Alban Wood Street** *A Gothic tower with buttresses at the angles and sides and Perpendicular windows; above, a parapet and eight crocketed pinnacles.*

Mary Somerset: (Fig 101) on each face is a vertical series of windows, alternately circular and round-headed; above are tall obelisks set on pedestals, and at the corners four fluted vases, giving a noble crown of eight pinnacles.

(Fig 102) **St James Piccadilly** *A brick tower with stone quoins and a plain parapet. The spire was replaced according to Wren's design in 1968; it has a clock on each face and above, a lantern and a short spirelet.*

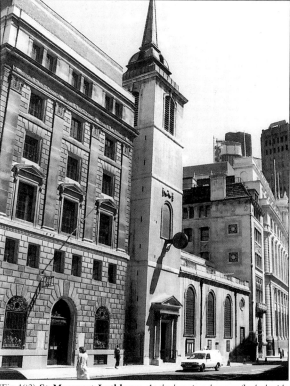

(Fig 103) **St Margaret Lothbury** *At the base is a doorway flanked with columns and a pediment above. The tower is crowned with a bell-shaped cupola and a lead spire.*

Group II – with lead spires

Twelve churches have lead spires of varying complexity. Simplest is **St James Piccadilly** (1700; Fig 102), which has a lantern and a short spirelet. **St Margaret Lothbury** has a lead dome with spire (Fig 103), while three (**St Mary Abchurch** Fig 104, **St Benet Paul's Wharf** Fig 105, and **St Peter Cornhill** Fig

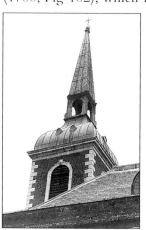

(Fig 104) **St Mary Abchurch** *A brick tower with stone quoins. An ogee-shaped dome carries a lantern and a short spire.*

(Fig 105) **St Benet Paul's Wharf** *The brick tower with stone quoins, and above a lead dome and spire.*

(Fig 106) **St Peter Cornhill** *The brick tower contrasts happily with the stuccoed nave; at the belfry level are three arched windows on each face. The dome sustains an octagonal lantern and spire. The finial bears a large key (symbol of St Peter) as the vane.*

(Fig 107) **St Lawrence Jewry** *A plain tower with a parapet and obelisks at each corner. The recessed lead spire has arched openings and a pediment on each face; above a spirelet carries a vane in the form of a grid-iron (symbol of St Lawrence).*

106) have a dome, lantern and spire. **St Law-rence Jewry** (Fig 107) has a parapet with stone obelisks at each corner, and then a recessed spire with arched

(Fig 108) **St Margaret Pattens** *The tower is capped by a balustrade; at the corners pointed stone pinnacles rise from a scrolled base. The spire is composed of transverse bands of lead, punctuated at intervals by small windows, and soars nearly 200 feet above the street.*

(Fig 109) **St Augustine Old Change** *The graceful lead spire at the east end of St Paul's.*

openings and a pediment on each face. **St Marg-aret Pattens'** tower (1703; Fig 108) is capped by a balustrade with tall pinnacles at each corner, and then a very tall lead spire, transversely banded and punctuated at intervals by small windows, soars up to two hundred feet above ground level.

Five lead spires are even more complex. That of

(Fig 110) **St Edmund the King** *The tower rises above a pediment, and is linked to the outer bays of the nave by Italianate concave masonry. Above the belfry, pineapples and vases on the parapet, then a recessed lead spire terminating in a cornice which bears the finial.*

(Fig 111) **St Nicholas Cole Abbey** *(Rebuilt to Wren's design in 1961-62.) The round-headed belfry windows are crowned with a pediment; four plain vases at the corners, and above a recessed curved lead spire sustains a balcony with a pedestal bearing a bulbous ornament beneath the ball and ship's weathervane (from St Michael Queenhythe).*

(Fig 112) **St Magnus the Martyr** *A massive tower, with clock projecting from the west wall. The parapet has two urns placed diagonally at each corner. Recessed within the parapet is a tall octagonal stone lantern, then an ogee-shaped dome, a small lantern and graceful spire.*

St Augustine Old Change was destroyed in the war, but has been restored according to Wren's original design (Fig 109). The handsome tower, now embodied into the choir school, terminates in a parapet with obelisks at the corners; the recessed spire has a lantern stage, with smaller obelisks, and then a bulbous swelling narrows to a fine point. The tower of **St Edmund the King** (1707; Fig 110) has a parapet with pineapples and vases, and then a recessed lead spire terminates in a cornice which bears the finial. **St Nicholas Cole Abbey** (Fig 111) has a tower with a pediment above the belfry windows and four vases at the corners; above, the recessed curved spire sustains a pedestal with a bulbous ornament beneath a ball and ship's weathervane. The tower of **St Magnus the Martyr** (1705; Fig 112) is massive, and the parapet has two urns placed diagonally at each corner; an octagonal stone lantern is recessed within the parapet, and this bears an ogee-shaped dome, a small lantern and a graceful spire. Finest of all in this group is **St Martin Ludgate** (Fig 113): above the tower is a short octagonal stage, then an ogee dome carrying a balcony, lantern and spire. Wren is said consciously to have designed this steeple to act as a foil to the dome and towers of St Paul's.

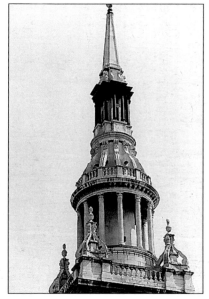

(Fig 114) **St Mary-le-Bow** *At the corners of the balustrade, urns are enclosed by open volutes leading to a short pinnacle. Above, a central core of stone is encompassed by Corinthian columns. Then a further balustrade, an ogee dome, and a lantern with colonnettes supporting an obelisk.*

(Fig 113) **St Martin Ludgate** *The finest of the lead spires, with the dome, portico and south-west tower of St Pauls. Above St Martin's tower is a short octagonal stage, then an ogee dome carrying balcony, lantern and spire.*

Group III – with stone spires

This group comprises Wren's most ingenious designs, whose complexity never fails to delight and intrigue. Apart from the steeple of St Mary-le-Bow, which was completed in 1680, all of them are late, and they are arranged here in chronological order of the date of completion. If the influence of Hawksmoor is to be sought, it is perhaps most convincing in the towers of St Vedast and Christchurch Newgate.

St Mary-le-Bow (1680; Fig 114): The tower is tall and at the bell-stage are paired pilasters. At the corners of the balustrade are urns encompassed by open volutes which lead to a short pinnacle. Within the balustrade a cylindrical core of stone rises, around which is a series of free-standing columns. Above this is a further balustrade, then an ogee dome and then a lantern again encircled with twelve slender colonnettes, and supporting an obelisk.

St Dunstan-in-the-East (1697; Fig 115): In the Gothic style, the tower is said to be modelled on the pre-Fire tower of St Mary-le-Bow. It

terminates in four corner pinnacles which are embellished with decoration. The main spire, again embellished, is supported by four flying buttresses which arise from the corners of the tower to lift the spire high above the pinnacles.

(Fig 115) **St Dunstan-in-the-East** *The Gothic tower ends in four decorated pinnacles at the corners. The main spire, again embellished, is carried by four flying buttresses far above the pinnacles.*

(Fig 118) **St Vedast Foster Lane** *The most baroque of Wren's steeples (Pevsner). Above the belfry, a lantern with concave walls and pilasters grouped at the angles. The upper lantern has convex walls between pilasters and carries the spire.*

St Bride Fleet Street (1703; Fig 116): This spire, the tallest and most famous of Wren's spires, is said to be the inspiration behind the multi-tiered wedding cake! It has five diminishing stages; an odd feature is that although the total height of each successive stage is less, the base below the lights becomes higher, noticeable especially in the third stage, giving an effect of 'lift-off'.

Christchurch Newgate (1704; Fig 117): In contrast to St Bride's, the tower of Christchurch is solid and sober. (In view of the suggestion that this tower may be the work of Hawksmoor, the reader might like to compare Fig 117 with the illustrations of Hawksmoor's towers – Figs 210, 213, 217, 221, 225.) The belfry stage has three

(Fig 116) **St Bride Fleet Street** *The spire is said to have inspired the multi-tiered wedding cake! An odd feature of the five stages is that the height of each successive lantern diminishes but the stone base beneath the lights increases, giving an effect of 'lift-off'.*

(Fig 117)
Christchurch Newgate *The belfry stage has three lights on each face, with a cornice and segmental pediment above. Then recessed within a parapet, a square stage with a free-standing colonnade, and a vase above each column. Above, a slender lantern bears the short spire.*

lights on each face, with cornice and segmental pediment above. Then recessed within a parapet is a square stage with a free-standing colonnade, each column bearing aloft a vase. Above this, a slender lantern carries a short spire.

St Vedast Foster Lane (1712; Fig 118): Said by Pevsner to be the most baroque of all Wren's steeples, the tower itself is relatively plain; but then above the belfry rises a lantern with concave walls between pilasters grouped at the four corners. Above this is a smaller lantern with convex walls between pilasters, and then finally a short spire.

The remaining three are, so far as we know, Sir Christopher's last designs in the course of his long life. They share certain resemblances, yet all are still amazingly different. In each, the tower ends in a parapet with vases at the corners; within the parapet rises the complex recessed spire.

(Fig 119) **St Michael Paternoster Royal** *Within the parapet with corner vases rises a recessed octagon with columns at the angles bearing a protruding section of architrave. Two smaller octagonal stages above (Pevsner).*

St Michael Paternoster Royal (1717; Fig 119): In contrast to the four-square solidity of Christchurch, the steeple of St Michael's is all delicacy and light. The southwest tower ends in a parapet with corner vases, and then rises 'a recessed transparent octagon with eight columns set in front of the angles, each with its own projecting piece of architrave. Two yet smaller octagonal stages above' (Pevsner).

St James Garlickhythe (1717; Fig 120): The steeple resembles the preceding one, but is a little more solid. Again the tower ends in a parapet with corner vases, and within is a square stage, with paired columns placed diagonally at the corners, each carrying the entablature which

(Fig 120) **St James Garlickhythe** *Above the parapet with corner vases is a square stage with paired columns placed diagonally at the angles, each carrying the entablature which projects outwards. Above, two similar but smaller stages terminate in a minute dome.*

(Fig 121) **St Stephen Walbrook** *Recessed within the parapet is a hollow square, with three columns at each angle, the entablature projecting outwards. The second stage is similar without the columns, and above a small lantern bears a stepped spire.*

projects outwards. Two further smaller, but similar, stages above terminate in a minute dome.

St Stephen Walbrook (1717; Fig 121): Again recessed within a parapet, the first stage is a hollow square, with three columns placed at each angle, and again the entablature projects outwards. The pattern is repeated in the second stage, but without the columns, and then above is a small lantern carrying a stepped spire.

The Interiors of Wren's Churches

The interiors of Wren's churches reflect the revolution in worship which had occurred in England since the Reformation. Chancels were prominent in medieval churches, since there the Mass was enacted before a largely passive congregation. In the seventeenth century the situation changed: in Protestant churches there was much greater emphasis on preaching, but the Jesuits also were keen that their congregations should see and hear properly (Sekler). Pulpits in Wren's churches are therefore prominent, usually

with a sounding-board, or tester, above to provide the necessary resonance. The altar (or communion table) is no longer placed in a remote chancel, but is brought forward, still usually at the east end of the church, and enclosed within communion rails. Behind is a reredos, simple or elaborate, often painted with the Commandments, Lord's Prayer and Creed, and flanked by paintings of Moses and Aaron.

As with the steeples, there is great variety in the interiors of Wren's churches, often in response to the cramped and irregular boundaries of the sites. They range from the plain square or oblong plans of St Edmund the King or St Margaret Pattens to the highly sophisticated St Stephen Walbrook. The designs of the interiors of the surviving churches are classified in Table IV, and further details are given in the descriptions of each church which follow.

The designs of some of Wren's lost churches deserve some comment, for some of them were of considerable interest and beauty. Four churches had tunnel-vaulted naves with flat ceilings above the galleries: Christchurch Newgate, St Dionis Backchurch, St Mary Aldermanbury and St Michael Bassishaw. These were buildings on a considerable scale, comparable with groups 3c and 3d in Table IV. Four churches had domes: St Mildred Bread Street and St Swithin London Stone were undivided, like St Mary Abchurch; the other two were especially remarkable, and

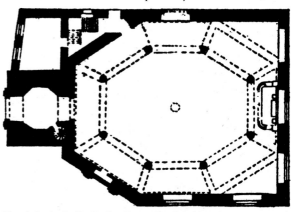

(Plan I) **St Antholin Budge Row** *(demolished 1874).*

their loss is grievous: St Antholin (Plan I) had a dome on an elongated octagon, and St Benet Fink (Plan II) was ten-sided, with an elliptical dome on six columns.

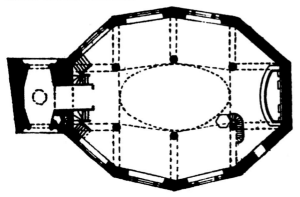

(Plan II) **St Benet Fink** *(demolished 1843)*

St Edmund the King

St Edmund, King of East Anglia, was killed by the Danes in 870, and this church in Lombard Street was first mentioned *c.*1100. The earlier church perished in the Fire, and work on the new building began in August 1670; the church was

(Fig 122) **St Edmund the King.**

Table IV – The Interiors of Wren's Churches

1) Undivided
St Edmund the King
St Nicholas Cole Abbey
St Michael Paternoster Royal
St Mary Abchurch (domed)

2) Nave with north or south aisle
St Clement Eastcheap
St Lawrence Jewry
St Margaret Lothbury
St Margaret Pattens
St Vedast Foster Lane
St Benet Paul's Wharf (west aisle also)

3) Nave with north and south aisles
  a) Gothic
  St Mary Aldermary
  b) Flat Ceiling
  St James Garlickhythe

c) Tunnel-vaulted nave, transverse tunnel-vaulted aisles
  St Magnus the Martyr
  St Mary-le-Bow
  St Peter Cornhill
  St James Piccadilly

d) Tunnel-vaulted nave, groin vaulted aisles
  St Andrew-by-the-Wardrobe
  St Andrew Holborn
  St Bride Fleet Street
  St Clement Danes

e) Groin-vaulted nave and aisles
  St Michael Cornhill

4) Greek Cross design
  St Mary-at-Hill
  St Martin Ludgate
  St Anne and St Agnes
  St Stephen Walbrook (complex)

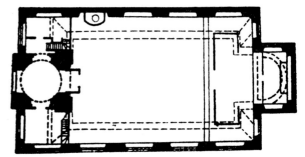

(Plan III) **St Edmund the King, Lombard Street** (north is to the right).

(Fig 124) **St Edmund the King** *The font and rail.*

(Fig 123) **St Edmund the King** *The interior.*

reredos has door-cases on each side, with paintings of Moses and Aaron by Etty, dated 1833. The church contains some excellent original wood-work, even though the box-pews were removed in Victorian times. The pulpit has lost its tester, but the twisted balusters around the font survive (Fig 124), the marble font still in the position decided for it in 1687. There is an iron sword-rest.

Access: Nearest Underground station: Bank.

opened for worship in 1676, but the tower was not completed until 1706. The alignment is unusual: the main façade and entrance faces south (Fig 122). A drawing survives of the handsome south front, and this is confidently ascribed to Robert Hooke, leading some authorities to ascribe at least the south façade, and maybe the whole church, to him and not to Wren (Summerson [b]). A clock projects above the entrance, and above this is a pediment. The tower rises above this, and is linked to the outer bays of the nave by Italianate concave masonry. Above the belfry, pineapples and vases bedeck the parapet, and then a recessed lead spire ends in a cornice bearing a finial.

The interior (Fig 123 and plan) is simple, without subdivisions, and the altar is placed north in a small recessed sanctuary. The ceiling is flat. The

St Nicholas Cole Abbey

St Nicholas dates from at least 1144, but the origin of the name 'Cole Abbey' is uncertain. It has been suggested that the name comes from 'Cold harbour'-a shelter for travellers in the Middle Ages. The medieval church was destroyed in the Fire, and rebuilt by Wren from 1671-77. Wren's church was severely damaged in the blitz in 1941 and 20 years later it was restored. It is now the home of the London congregation of the Free Church of Scotland.

The body of the church is rectangular, with a north-western tower, the upper part of which was rebuilt after the war. The tower has pediments above the belfry windows and plain vases at the corners (Fig 111, p 58). A short lead spire carries

(Fig 125) **St Nicholas Cole Abbey** *The east and north windows with Corinthian pilasters between.*

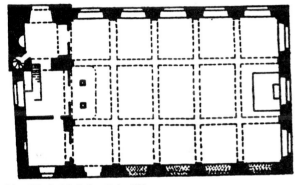

(Plan IV) **St Nicholas Cole Abbey**.

a weathervane of a ship from St Michael Queenhythe. The church is built of Portland stone, with a parapet all round the nave. The nave windows are arched under straight hoods (Fig 92, p 52). In the west wall can be seen some brickwork from the medieval church.

The interior (Fig 125 and plan) is a plain rectangle with Corinthian pilasters and a flat ceiling. It fortunately retains some furnishings from Wren's church which survived the bombing; these include the pulpit, font-cover, communion rail, royal arms, sword-rest and brass chandelier. The east windows contain modern stained glass by Keith New.

Access: Nearest Underground station: Mansion House.

St Michael Paternoster Royal

St Michael's was first mentioned in the thirteenth century, and the old church was rebuilt by Dick Whittington two hundred years later. He founded a college of priests (hence College Hill) and was buried in the church in 1423. The word 'royal' has nothing to do with kingly connections, but relates to the importation of wine from La Reole near Bordeaux by merchants who lived in College Hill.

Whittington's church was lost in the Great Fire, and was one of the last rebuilt by Wren, between 1686 and 1694. The tower is much later (1713; Fig 119, p 61). Wren's church, now the headquarters of the Mission to Seamen, was damaged by bombing in the Second World War and lost most of its furnishings. The blitz did, however, open up the prospect from the south, where it now presents an attractive face (Fig 126). Built of Portland stone and brick, there are five arched windows in the south façade, and in the southwest corner a square tower with parapet. Above this rises a recessed colonnaded octagon, with two smaller stages above supporting a vane.

The interior (Fig 127 and plan) is a simple rectangle, with excellent seventeenth-century furnishings, mainly imported from other

churches. The reredos (Fig 128), complete with Lord's Prayer, Creed and Ten Commandments, is lovely, as are the pulpit (Fig 129) and the lectern with a carved figure of Charity (Fig 130).

(Fig 126) **St Michael Paternoster Royal.**

(Fig 127) **St Michael Paternoster Royal** *The interior: stained glass in the east windows by John Hayward.*

(Fig 128) **St Michael Paternoster Royal** *The reredos.*

(Fig 133) **St Michael Paternoster Royal** *The font and font-cover.*

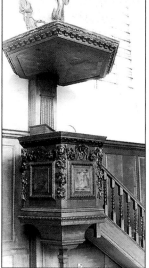

(Fig 129) **St Michael Paternoster Royal** *The pulpit.*

(Fig 130) **St Michael Paternoster Royal** *The lectern, with carved figure of Charity.*

(Fig 132) **St Michael Paternoster Royal** *Brass chandelier.*

(Fig 131) **St Michael Paternoster Royal** *The organ and Royal Arms.*

Note also the organ-case (Fig 131), the sword-rest, the original brass chandelier (Fig 132) and the font (Fig 133). Many of the furnishings came

from the demolished church of All Hallows-the-Great. The modern stained glass in the east windows was designed by John Hayward. *Access:* Nearest Underground station: Cannon Street.

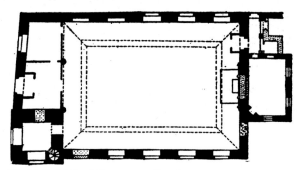

(Plan V) **St Michael Paternoster Royal.**

St Mary Abchurch

St Mary Abchurch is a pearl of great price, one of the finest of the surviving Wren churches. The subtlety of its architectural design is of course exceeded by St Stephen Walbrook, but for the quality of its furnishings it has no rival. The church was first mentioned in 1198; the derivation of the name is uncertain. The medieval church was destroyed in the Fire, and it was not until 1681 that the decision to rebuild was made. The building (Fig 134) is of red brick with stone

(Fig 135) **St Mary Abchurch** *The dome painted by William Snow.*

(Fig 134) **St Mary Abchurch.**

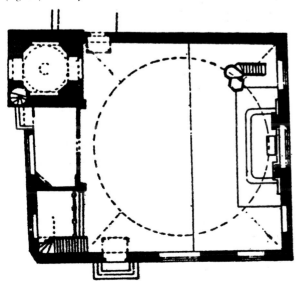

(Plan VI) **St Mary Abchurch.**

dressings, and is raised on the old foundations. The north-west tower is also brick, and above a small lantern carries a lead spire (Fig 104, p 56). The church suffered severely in the blitz: on 8 September 1940, blast destroyed the windows, south door and inner porch, and damaged the roof. More damage was incurred in four further air-raids between December, 1940 and 1945. Work on the roof began in 1948, and the shattered woodwork was restored during the next five years.

Internally the church is a plain rectangle (see plan), transformed by the tremendous dome resting, as in St Stephen Walbrook, on eight equal cantilever arches; the arches spring from Corinthian-like corbels. The dome (Fig 135) is pierced by four porthole windows, and is painted by William Snow. The painting, depicting eight female figures representing Christian virtues, and a choir of angels, was lovingly restored after damage in the war. Beneath the dome is a cornice elaborated with swags and shells. At the west end is a gallery, with a single Corinthian column.

The other chief glory of St Mary Abchurch is the great reredos by Grinling Gibbons himself (Fig 136). At the centre are two panels bearing the Creed, and above is a gilded pelican, and higher still swags of fruit and flowers carved in lime-

(Fig 136) **St Mary Abchurch** *Reredos by Grinling Gibbons (1686).*

(Fig 137) **St Mary Abchurch** *Pulpit with tester and communion rail.*

(Fig 138) **St Mary Abchurch** *Marble font (1686) and cover with statues of the four evangelists.*

(Fig 139) **St Mary Abchurch** *Monument to Sir Patience Ward (1696).*

wood. One either side are Corinthian columns, and flanking these are further panels with the Lord's Prayer and Ten Commandments. Almost as remarkable is the pulpit with large tester (Fig 137), dating from 1685, the work of William Grey. The marble font, crowned by a carved cover with statues of the four evangelists (Fig 138), is by William Kempster (1686). There are also notable door-cases and an organ-case of 1717 from All Hallows Bread Street. To the south of the reredos is the monument to Sir Patience Ward (Fig 139), who exhorted Wren to build the church.

Access: Nearest Underground station: Cannon Street.

St Clement Eastcheap

This church, which dates back to the thirteenth century, was rebuilt after the Fire between 1683 and 1687. It was built of brick with stone quoins, but has since been stuccoed except for the plain tower (Fig 94, p 54). The west front bears a pediment, but in spite of this St Clement's is not one of Wren's more impressive exteriors–perhaps because of the smallness and irregularity of the site.

Internally (see plan), there is a nave and south aisle, wider at the west end than at the east. Corinthian pilasters surround the interior (Fig 140), and an arcade of cast-iron columns separates the nave and aisle. Semicircular windows form a north and south clerestory. The flat plastered

(Fig 140) **St Clement Eastcheap** *The interior.*

(Fig 141) **St Clement Eastcheap** *The tester or sounding-board above the pulpit.*

(Fig 142) **St Clement Eastcheap** *The reredos, redecorated by Sir Ninian Comper in 1933; original communion rail and door-case.*

(Fig 143) **St Clement Eastcheap** *The marble font.*

ceiling above the nave has a huge wreath of fruit and flowers set in an oblong panel. The outstanding furnishing is the original pulpit with a large sounding-board above (Fig 141), exquisitely carved in the Grinling Gibbons manner. The reredos (Fig 142) was

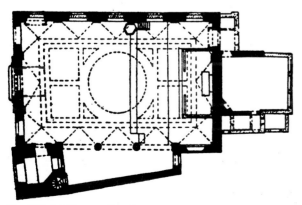

(Plan VII) **St Clement Eastcheap.**

redecorated by Sir Ninian Comper in 1933, and is now gold and blue, which does not fit well with the other furnishings. To the north of this is an impressive door-case. There is a seventeenth-century marble font (Fig 143) with a wooden cover, and other woodwork of this period includes the communion rail, panelling, doors and organ-case. There is also a gilded sword-rest.
Access: Nearest Underground station: Monument.

St Lawrence Jewry

From the time of the Norman Conquest until 1290, when Edward I expelled the community, this area had a substantial Jewish population. The church belonged in the twelfth century to the convent of St Sauve and St Guingalaens of Montreuil in the diocese of Amiens, and in the next century to Balliol College, Oxford. The church destroyed in the Fire had been thoroughly repaired in 1618 (Young [a]), and Wren's church was built between 1671 and 1687. This building was bombed in December, 1940, and lost virtually all its furnishings. It was restored in 1954-57 by Cecil Brown.

The quality of the east façade ensures that this is perhaps the only Wren church in which the exterior is possibly more interesting than the interior. It is the Corporation church of the City of London, and stands at the junction of Gresham Street and Guildhall Square. The east front (Fig 91, p 51) has a series of arched windows and niches separated by Corinthian columns, and with Corinthian pilasters at the corners. At the level of the capitals are swags of fruit and flowers. Along Gresham Street to the south is a further series of arched windows; the west end is plainer, and from it arises the stone tower, with pinnacles at the corner, and a lead spire (Fig 107, p 57).

The interior (Fig 144 and plan) is a simple rectangle (a double cube), with an aisle jutting out to the north. The walls of the nave are pilastered,

(Fig 144) **St Lawrence Jewry** *The interior.*

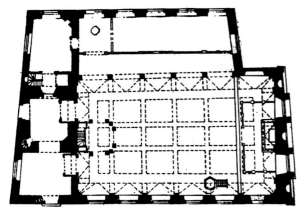

(Plan VIII) **St Lawrence Jewry**.

and on the north side the pilasters are replaced by Corinthian columns which separate the nave from the aisle (Fig 144). Between the columns are wrought-iron gates and a wooden screen. Above, groins spring to support a flat fretted ceiling of exceptional span (47 feet), now restored to its pre-war state. The nave is, perhaps, rather oppressively formal, which is not surprising in view of its municipal functions. There is an early seventeenth-century font from the church of Holy Trinity Minories.

Access: Nearest Underground station: St Paul's.

St Margaret Lothbury

This church, dedicated to St Margaret of Antioch, dates from Norman times and was rebuilt in 1440. That edifice was lost in the Fire, and its suc-

cessor was one of the last to be constructed afterwards, work not commencing until 1686 and being completed by 1690. Among the undamaged Wren churches, it ranks very high for the quality of its furnishings, many of them acquired from other (demolished) buildings. As so often with Wren, the exterior is unremarkable, the building of Portland stone plain and square, with three arched windows now facing and challenging the Bank of England, the very emblem, one might think, of the relation of God to Mammon. The plain tower is surmounted by a lead spire (Fig 103, p 56).

The interior is a seventeenth-century gem. Nave and south aisle are separated by Corinthian columns (Fig 145 and plan), and above the nave are a clerestory and a flat ceiling. In the aisle is an outstanding marble font (Fig 146); on the side of the bowl are a series of carved biblical subjects – Adam and Eve, Noah's Ark, the Baptism of Christ and the Baptism of the Eunuch; the font cover came from St Olave Jewry. From the same church came the altar-piece of the south aisle.

(Fig 145) **St Margaret Lothbury** *The Corinthian columns separating the nave and south aisle.*

The nave is dominated by a huge screen (Fig 147) which extends right across the church, one of only two screens in Wren's churches (cf St Peter Cornhill). It was carved *c.*1689, and was the

(Fig 146) **St Margaret Lothbury** *The font.*

(Fig 147) **St Margaret Lothbury** *The screen, originally from All Hallows the Great, extends across the nave.*

(Fig 148) **St Margaret Lothbury** *The reredos.*

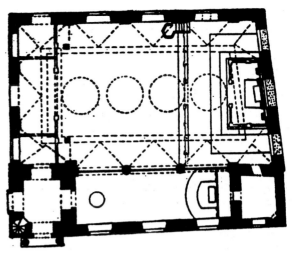

(Plan IX) **St Margaret Lothbury.**

gift of two German merchants, Theodore and Jacob Jacobsen to the church of All Hallows-the-Great. 'On either side of the middle entrance there are four open, round-headed sections separated by balusters. Each baluster takes the form of a cleverly carved double helix, two intertwined spirals …The entrance is bridged by an open segmental pediment in which the sloping upper sides of the triangle are replaced by a segment of a circle with a gap in the middle. Beneath is a large carved eagle with outspread wings, and above the compulsory Royal Coat of Arms' (Foster). To the north of the nave is the impressive pulpit, of equal quality to the screen; the fine tester above also came from All Hallows. Beyond the screen, the floor of the sanctuary is paved with black and white marble. Behind the communion table, the reredos (Fig 148) is richly carved, with Corinthian columns flanking panels inscribed with the Ten Commandments, Lord's Prayer and the Creed. On either side of the reredos are paintings of Moses and Aaron from St Christopher-le-Stocks. At the west end is the eighteenth-century gallery and organ-case. There are several monuments of which the best is the bust of Alderman Boydell (1791) designed by

Thomas Banks (1735-1805); perhaps his best-known work is the engaging figure of six-year-old Penelope Boothby in Ashbourne, Derbyshire. *Access:* Nearest Underground station: Bank.

St Margaret Pattens

St Margaret's was first mentioned in the eleventh century, and a medieval church was pulled down and rebuilt in 1538. This building perished in the Fire, and the present church dates from 1684-87; the tower is later (1699-1703). The unusual dedication refers firstly to St Margaret of Antioch, and secondly to the manufacture of pattens (wooden soles) which used to occur beside the church; the Pattenmakers' Company has been associated with St Margaret's since the fifteenth century. The exterior (Fig 149) is dominated by the tower (Fig 108, p 57) and spire, which rises to a height of 200 feet.

The interior is a plain rectangle (see plan), with originally a north aisle; unfortunately the north gallery is now converted into offices. The large east windows and clerestory provide plenty of light; the ceiling is flat. Corinthian pilasters on the south and east walls (Fig 150) are complemented by Corinthian columns on the north side. At the west end are a remarkable pair of churchwardens'

(Fig 149) **St Margaret Pattens.**

(Fig 150) **St Margaret Pattens** *The interior.*

canopied pews (Fig 151). At the east end is a fine reredos containing a painting of Christ in the Garden of Gethsemane, by the Italian painter Maratti; note also the communion

(Fig 151) **St Margaret Pattens** *Seventeenth-century canopied churchwarden's pew.*

rails, pulpit and lectern, all good examples of seventeenth-century woodwork. In the north chapel are two Della Robbia plaques given in 1984 in memory of Prebendary George Bosworth. The Royal Arms at the west end is very striking, and is the only set in the City erected during the reign of James II (1685-88).

Access: Nearest Underground station: Bank.

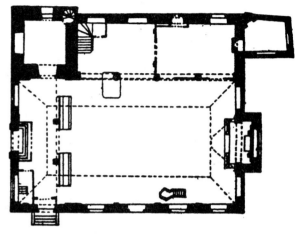

(Plan X) **St Margaret Pattens.**

St Vedast Foster Lane

Nestling beside the east end of St Paul's Cathedral is this church with the unusual dedication. Who was St Vedast? Apparently he was a sixth-century Bishop of Arras in Flanders who converted King Clovis to Christianity, and it has been conjectured that the church was founded in the twelfth or thirteenth centuries by a Flemish community (Jeffery [a]). There is one other English dedication to St Vedast at Tathwell in Lincolnshire (Cobban). The medieval building was damaged in the Fire, but at first only modest repairs and re-roofing were carried out in 1670-71 at the cost of the parish. This soon proved inadequate, and the parish later applied for public funds; the present structure was designed by Wren, the rebuilding starting again in 1695. The steeple came later (1709-12). On 29 December 1940, disaster struck again when the church was badly damaged by incendiary bombs. The roof and all the fittings were lost, but the tower and steeple survived. In the rebuilding that followed in the 1950s, the major internal change was the rearrangement of the pews in collegiate fashion, facing each other along the whole length of the nave.

(Fig 152) **St Vedast Foster Lane** *The interior, reconstructed after bombing, with pews arranged as in a college chapel.*

(Fig 153) **St Vedast Foster Lane** *The restored ceiling and east windows.*

(Fig 154) **St Vedast Foster Lane** *The reredos and communion rail from St Christopher-le-Stocks.*

The church is built of Portland stone, and from the east end of St Paul's, the tower and steeple of St Vedast's rise elegantly (Fig 118, p 60); some believe that Hawksmoor rather than Wren may have been responsible for the design (Jeffery [b]).

The interior (Fig 152 and plan) is chaste and cool, an academic atmosphere being inculcated by the arrangement of the pews. There is a south

(Fig 155) **St Vedast Foster Lane** *The pulpit came originally from All Hallows Bread Street.*

aisle, separated from the nave by an arcade of Tuscan columns. The ceiling (Fig 153) is flat, with an oblong plaster wreath enclosing further wreaths of flowers and leaves. The new east windows were designed by Brian Thomas. Some fine fittings have been imported from other churches to replace those lost. Thus the font and font-cover come from St Anne and St Agnes, the elaborately-carved pulpit (Fig 155) from All Hallows Bread Street, the organ from St Bartholomew-by-the-Exchange (originally), the altar-table from St Matthew Friday Street and the reredos and communion rail (Fig 154) from St Christopher-le-Stocks (via St Mary Magdalene, Great Burstead, Essex). The font is a seventeenth-century stone baluster, surmounted by an intricate

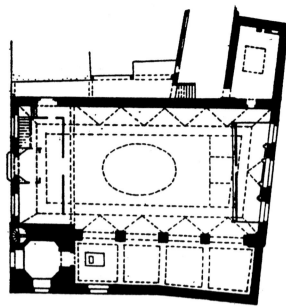

(Plan XI) **St Vedast Foster Lane**.

St Benet Paul's Wharf

There were three Wren churches with the dedication to St Bene't (or St Benedict), but this is the sole survivor. The church dates back to the twelfth century, but the medieval building was destroyed in the Fire. The present church was built between 1677 and 1683, and its design is unusual in that it has both a north and a west aisle (see plan).

The exterior is of brick, with prominent quoins of Portland stone at all corners, both of the main building and of the tower below the parapet. Above is a lead dome surmounted by a short lead spire (Fig 105, p 56). In addition to the stone quoins, there are stone garlands of fruit and flowers above the windows giving the church a domestic dimension, which many writers have described as Dutch. But Sacheverell Sitwell dissents: he likens St Benet's to a Quaker or Moravian meeting-house, and comments, 'Wren's

wooden cover. There are a sword-rest and a Royal Arms.

Access: Nearest Underground station: St Paul's.

(Fig 156) **St Benet Paul's Wharf** *The interior looking north-west.*

(Fig 157) **St Benet Paul's Wharf** *The reredos.*

Access: Nearest Underground station: Blackfriars. The church is usually closed except for Sunday services, which are in Welsh. St Benet's has been the London church of Welsh Episcopalians since 1877.

brick buildings may be Dutch by suggestion, but are not at all Dutch in spirit. Wren is only under Dutch influence till we have been to Holland. Then nevermore.'

The interior confirms Sitwell's opinion (compare the interior of St Benet with that of the Nieuwe Kerk, Haarlem, Figs 187-89, p 88). The plan is square, with a north aisle of three bays and a west aisle of two (Fig 156). The bases of the Corinthian columns support the galleries, the columns themselves springing from the level of the galleries. The south and east walls have Corinthian pilasters, and the fronts of the galleries are carved with fruit. The pews and pulpit are plain, but the communion table is elaborate, being inlaid on top and supported by carved angels. The

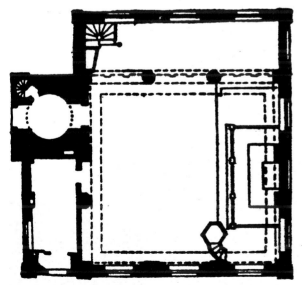

(Plan XII) **St Benet Paul's Wharf.**

reredos (Fig 157) has broken pediments and urns above. There is a striking west door-case, above which is the Royal Arms.

St Mary Aldermary

The medieval church dates back at least to the twelfth century, and the name probably denoted that it was the older church of St Mary, the younger being St Mary-le-Bow round the corner. The medieval church was lost in the Fire, only the lower part of the tower and portions of the east wall surviving. Wren completed the upper stages of the tower, and, most unusually, rebuilt the church in the Gothic style. This is said to derive

(Fig 158) **St Mary Aldermary** *The nave and plaster ceiling.*

(Fig 159) **St Mary Aldermary**
The door-case originally from St Antholin.

(Fig 160) **St Mary Aldermary**
The pulpit.

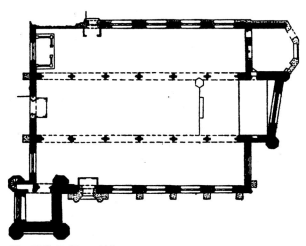

(Plan XIII) **St Mary Aldermary.**

from the terms of the bequest of Henry Rogers, who left £5,000 for the rebuilding, provided that it was done in Gothic. Dislike of modern architecture is evidently no new thing! In his defence, it may well be that the pre-Fire church, built in 1510, was one of the finest in the City.

The tower (Fig 97, p 55), at the west end of the south aisle, is flanked with polygonal corner buttresses which ascend to the top and are surmounted by rather heavy pinnacles; originally these ended in slender foliaged finials of stone. These were removed as unsafe in 1927 (Cobb), and have now been replaced by golden fibreglass finials.

The exterior leaves one quite unprepared for the glories within. For here one is immediately overwhelmed by the fan-vaulting which covers the nave and aisles above the Perpendicular arcades (Fig 158, and see plan), the epitome, one might think, of early sixteenth-century Gothic. But did any Gothic church really look like that? Of course, the answer is No; what has happened here is that Wren is deliberately building in an obsolete, antique style, much as Prokofiev did when he composed his Classical Symphony. No eighteenth-century symphony sounds like Prokofiev's, and no late-Perpendicular church looks like St Mary Aldermary. In any case, the fan-

vaulting is in plaster and not in stone, and a closer inspection reveals un-Gothic details such as the saucer-shaped domes between the fans. Elizabeth and Wayland Young, as so often, hit the nail on the head when they describe the vaults as beautiful, but with the sweetness of confectionery. Perhaps Wren's designs here should be regarded not as looking back to late Perpendicular, but as looking forward to the Gothick extravaganzas of Strawberry Hill (p 139) and Shobdon.

Most of the seventeenth-century furnishings were wantonly cleared out by a restoration in 1876. But there is still some good woodwork to see: best is the door-case at the west end (Fig 159), brought here from St Antholin Budge Row. Also noteworthy are the original pulpit (Fig 160), the font and font-cover (Fig 161) and the wooden sword-rest placed against a pillar on the south side of the nave.

Access: Nearest Underground station: Mansion House.

(Fig 161) **St Mary Aldermary**
The font (1682).

(Fig 162) **St James Garlickhythe.**

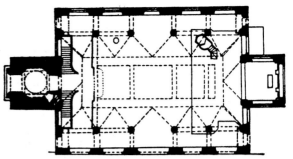

(Plan XIV) **St James Garlickhithe.**

(Fig 164) **St James Garlickhythe** *The reredos and above 'The Ascension' by Andrew Geddes.*

(Fig 163) **St James Garlickhythe** *The interior from the west gallery.*

St James Garlickhythe

The church was first mentioned in the twelfth century; the name indicates that garlic was sold nearby. The medieval church perished in the Fire, and Wren's replacement is one of his most elegant creations. It was damaged in the blitz, but was very well restored after the war. A falling crane in 1991 damaged the roof yet again.

The tower and steeple (Figs 5, p 12 and 120, p 62) are late creations of Wren. The church (Fig 162) was originally built in brick, with the west end and tower faced with Kentish ragstone (Harwood and Saint). Later the east end was rendered, and the upper stages of the tower have, since the war, been refaced in Portland stone. Arched windows are present on all four sides of the building, and above is a clerestory.

The impressive interior (Fig 163, and plan) is the tallest in the City, and since the stained glass has been removed the church is beautifully light. The nave is separated from the aisles by a series of Ionic columns; the columns are panelled with painted deal to gallery level, the bases now towering above the pews (previously they would have been much less conspicuous above the box-pews). The ceiling above both nave and aisles is flat; over the nave, there is coving pierced by clerestory windows. The entablature above the columns returns to the sides in the centre of the church, giving an impression of false transepts (Fig 163).

The chancel projects slightly and boasts a painting of the Ascension by Andrew Geddes, given to the church in 1815 (Fig 164); the top of the reredos was cut down to accommodate the picture. The communion table and communion rails and the door-cases now forming screens behind the choir-stalls came from St Michael Queen-hythe. Also from this church is the fine pulpit, complete with sounding-board, stair-case and wig-stand. The west gallery contains an organ of 1697 by the celebrated Father Smith (p 39). The font and font-cover are original. The excellent glass chandelier is modern (made by Arnold Montrose in 1967).

Access: Nearest Underground station: Mansion House.

St Magnus the Martyr

'Inexplicable splendour of Ionian white and gold' was T.S. Eliot's description (in *The Waste Land*, line 265) of the interior of this church, which was first recorded in the reign of William the Conqueror (1066-87); but when the church was dedicated to St Magnus the Martyr is uncertain. It is believed that the martyr referred to is the Earl of Orkney who was killed in 1116 and canonised in 1135.

The church stands at the north end of London Bridge. The relation to the bridge was so close that when the houses on the bridge were dem-olished in 1760, the aisles on either side of the west tower were shortened to allow a footway to pass through the tower, whose lowest storey thus became a porch (Pevsner). The square tower (Fig 165) with lantern, lead dome and spire (Fig 112, p 58) is one of Wren's most attractive construct-ions. One of the few surviving Wren clocks pro-jects from the west wall.

(Fig 165) **St Magnus the Martyr.**

Inside, one sees exactly what Eliot meant: the interior (Fig 166) is dominated by the sumptuous reredos, with its Protestant emphasis on the Lord's Prayer, the Commandments and Creed now balanced by the Catholic dimension of the rood above, and by six candlesticks-an addition of 1924-25 by Martin Travers. There are paintings of Moses and Aaron on either side of the communion table, a pelican above the commandments and a glory in the upper part. The delicate wrought-iron com-munion rails date from 1683. On either side of the reredos are side-altars behind which are reredoses formed from seventeenth-century door-cases.

(Fig 166) **St Magnus the Martyr** *Reredos and pulpit.*

The nave is divided from the aisles by a series of Ionic columns (see plan), with a continuous horizontal entablature from which the arcades spring; above, the nave is tunnel-vaulted, with circular clerestory windows on each side. At first

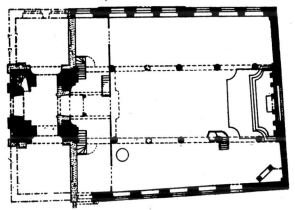

(Plan XV) **St Magnus the Martyr.**

the fourth bay from the east was wider, forming a groin-vaulted cross-axis, perhaps like the false transepts of the previous church (Fig 163; Pevsner). The crossing was filled with an extra pair of columns in the restoration of 1924.

The pulpit with tester is very fine, as is the font and font-cover given in 1683 (Fig 167). The oldest

(Fig 167) **St Magnus the Martyr**
Font and font-cover.

wrought-iron sword-rest in the City is here, dated 1708. The west gallery is splendid and has two staircases with twisted balusters. It houses an organ of 1712, said to be the earliest swell-organ. *Access:* Nearest Underground station: Monument.

St Mary-le-Bow

This most famous of Wren's churches–home of Bow Bells, the very definition of a Cockney, the bells that persuaded Dick Whittington to turn again, that tolled the curfew in medieval times–was severely damaged during the war; only the

(Fig 168) **St Mary-le-Bow** *The tower and steeple.*

(Fig 169) **St Mary-le-Bow** *The doorway at the base of the tower.*

tower, steeple and outer walls survived, the interior being reconstructed according to Wren's design by Laurence King from 1956-64. It was the most expensive of Wren's churches, costing £15,421 9s 0d – half of this being due to the tower and steeple.

St Mary's has a very ancient history, for beneath the present church is a crypt which dates back to *c.*1090. The crypt is said to be the oldest parochial building in London; it was opened up again by George Gwilt the younger in 1822. The columns have scalloped capitals, and the bays are groin-vaulted.

The entrance to the base of the tower (Fig 168) is through an impressive doorway between Doric columns (Fig 169); above the doorway is a classical triglyph frieze surmounted by two cherubs on either side of an oval window. The design is generally recognised to be derived from the Hotel de Conti in Paris by Francois Mansart, but Wren has given greater dignity to the design by the addition of the columns and frieze. The steeple (Fig 114, p 58) is generally considered to be Wren's finest.

There is documentary evidence that Wren's design of the church was based on the basilica of Maxentius in Rome. The nave is separated from the aisles by piers with Corinthian half-columns in front, from which spring the arches supporting the tunnel-vaulted ceiling. Originally there were galleries on three sides, but these were dismantled in 1867. The old church had a magnificent

(Fig 170) **St Mary-le-Bow.**

reredos, but this and other furnishings were lost in the blitz. The reconstructed church (Fig 170, and plan) is large and rather formal, without the intimacy of the best of Wren's churches. The altar has been brought forward, and there are wrought-iron

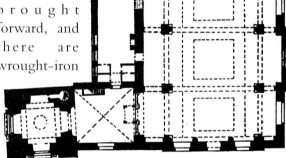

(Plan XVI) **St Mary-le-Bow.**

screens on each side. There is some excellent modern stained glass in the east windows by John Hayward, and a rather garish rood by the same artist is suspended from the ceiling.

Access: Nearest Underground station: St Paul's or Mansion House.

St Peter Cornhill

Claims, probably fanciful, have been made that this church was founded in 179 by Lucius, the first Christian king of Britain (Young [a]). But if this is myth, St Peter's certainly dates back to the eleventh century, and later the Fishmongers' Company and a grammar school were connected

(Fig 171) **St Peter Cornhill** *The screen and pulpit.*

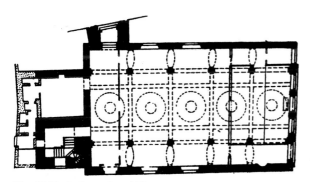

(Plan XVII) **St Peter Cornhill.**

with it. The old church was destroyed in the Fire, and was rebuilt by Wren between 1677 and 1681.

From the churchyard to the south, the brick tower contrasts well with the stuccoed nave; the tower is plain (Fig 106, p 57) and above it is a green copper dome and short spire with St Peter's keys at the top.

The nave is separated from the aisles by square columns (Fig 171, and plan); it is tunnel-vaulted, the aisles tunnel-vaulted transversely. There is much original woodwork: notable is the screen which runs right across the nave and aisles and is divided into sections by slender columns. The pulpit with its sounding-board is very fine, as is the western gallery and organ-case. The door-cases are also good, the doors being flanked by Corinthian pilasters.

Access: Nearest Underground station: Bank.

St James Piccadilly

A new church was required in the fashionable residential area being developed in the 1670s by Henry Jermyn, Lord St Albans and here at last Wren could develop a site with ample room, away from the constrictions and constraints of the City of London. The result was St James Piccadilly, whose design became a standard model for the town church of the eighteenth century. It was built between 1676 and 1684, and has always been a fashionable church-four rectors, including

(Fig 172) **St James Piccadilly** *Longitudiunal barrel-vault over nave, and transverse barrel-vaults over galleries.*

(Fig 173) **St James Piccadilly** *Reredos by Grinling Gibbons (1684).*

(Fig 174) **St James Piccadilly** *Detail of the reredos.*

spire built in 1968. The interior (see plan) is large and is said to hold a congregation of 2,000, though not all seated. Galleries on three sides are supported by square Doric columns, with Corinthian columns above supporting the longitudinal barrel-vault of the nave (Fig 172). A notable feature is that the entablature of each Corinthian column runs laterally to the side-walls, supporting transverse barrel-vaults, emphasising a north-south axis (cf St Clement Danes, p 86). The theme of transverse barrel-vaults across the bays of the aisles was also used by Hawksmoor at Christchurch Spitalfields (p 105; Summerson [b]).

The supreme attractions of St James are the works of Grinling Gibbons, the reredos and the font. The lime-wood reredos is spectacular (Figs 173, 174), with garlands of flowers, fruit and sea-shells and a pelican with her young at her breast. John Evelyn, the diarist, wrote in 1684 that 'There

the great William Temple, later became Archbishops of Canterbury. The church was severely damaged by bombing in 1940, in an air-raid in which the verger and his wife were killed. The exquisite reredos and font had been protected and were saved. After the war, St James' was restored by Sir Albert Richardson.

From the outside, the church is plain, built of brick with dressings and quoins of Portland stone (Fig 102, p 56). The tower again is simple, and carries a new

(Fig 175) **St James Piccadilly** *The font by Grinling Gibbons.*

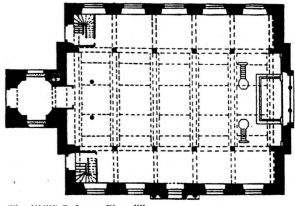

(Plan XVIII) **St James Piccadilly.**

was no altar anywhere in England, nor has there been any abroad, more handsomely adorned.' The font (Fig 175), carved by Gibbons in white marble, has a shaft representing the Tree of life encircled by a serpent, with Adam and Eve standing on either side; the bowl has bas-reliefs of Noah's Ark, the baptism of Christ, and the baptism of the Ethiopian by St Philip (Acts viii. 26-40). More work by Gibbons can be seen in the top of the organ-case, the organ by Renatus Harris having come from James II's Catholic chapel in Whitehall Palace; it was given to St James' church by Mary II in 1691.

Access: Nearest Underground station: Piccadilly Circus.

St Andrew-by-the-Wardrobe

St Andrew's dates originally from the thirteenth century, and was called 'by the wardrobe' after 1361 when the Great Wardrobe (the royal stores of arms and clothing), previously housed in the

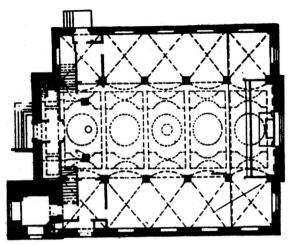

(Plan XIX) **St Andrew-by-the-Wardrobe.**

Tower, was given new quarters close by (Church guide). Both Wardrobe and church perished in the Fire, and the new church was built by Wren between 1685 and 1695. This building was gutted in December, 1940, and lost nearly all its furnishings but the tower and walls survived. It was restored in 1959-61.

From Queen Victoria Street, the church is stately, built of red brick with dressings of Portland stone. The south-western tower (Fig 95, p 54) is plain, surmounted by a parapet. The nave has an upper series of five round-headed windows, with four smaller windows and main entrance below.

The interior (see plan) followed the basilican plan of St James Piccadilly, with a barrel-vaulted nave, but

(Fig 177) **St Andrew-by-the-Wardrobe**
The font from St Matthews Friday Street and the cover from All Hallow Bread Street.

(Fig 178) **St Andrew-by-the-Wardrobe**
Statue of St Andrew.

(Fig 176) **St Andrew-by-the-Wardrobe**
The pulpit from St Matthew Friday Street.

(Fig 179) **St Andrew Holborn** *Barrel-vaulted nave and groin-vaulted aisles.*

here Wren designed groin-vaulting for the ceilings above the galleries, which diminishes the transverse axis noticeable at St James'. At the reconstruction, the aisles were closed off and are now used for offices. The only fittings which survived the bombing were two beadle's staves and a sword-rest. The pulpit (Fig 176) and font (Fig 177) came from St Matthew Friday Street, and the font-cover from All Hallows Bread street. The Royal Arms came from St Olave Jewry. On the north side of the sanctuary is a wooden figure of St Andrew, dated *c.*1600 (Fig 178).

Access: Nearest Underground station: Blackfriars.

St Andrew Holborn

St Andrew's dates from the thirteenth century; the medieval church escaped the Fire, but the building was by then in such a state of disrepair that at the request and expense of the parishioners it was rebuilt by Wren between 1684 and 1690.

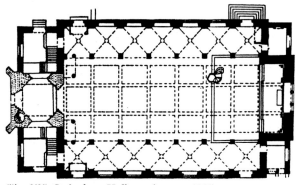

(Plan XX) **St Andrew Holborn** *(burnt out 1941).*

The parish was extensive, containing 3,000 dwellings (the average City parish of this time contained only 120–150 – Young [a]); so it is not surprising that this is the largest of Wren's churches. In 1703 the medieval tower was refaced with Portland stone and the top storey was added to complement the new building. Unfortunately the interior of the church was gutted during the blitz and all the furnishings and the fine eighteenth-century stained glass in the east windows were lost. The church was restored in 1960.

The western tower is simple, terminating in a balustrade with pinnacles at the corners (Fig 96, p 54). At the east end, there are further pinnacles at the apex and corners of the pediment above the two-storeyed Venetian window. Along the north and south sides is a row of seven round-headed windows.

The restored interior is light, and has galleries on three sides (Fig 179, and plan). Square panelled wooden columns support the gallery fronts, from which rise round stone Corinthian columns supporting the tunnel-vaulting over the nave and the groin-vaulting over the galleries. The design may have been used by Gibbs for St Martin-in-the-Fields (Summerson [b]). At the restoration, a Lady Chapel was formed at the west end, and the eighteenth-century reredos here came from St Luke, Old Street. Other good furnishings (font, organ, pulpit) came from the chapel of the Foundlings Hospital; this was established in the eighteenth century for the care of abandoned children by Thomas Coram, whose recently refurbished monument may be seen at the west end of the church. Handel is said to have given the original organ to the hospital, and to have given recitals in support of its work. The present organ is modern, but the upper part of the case is from the old hospital chapel. Appropriately, the church is now the headquarters of the Royal College of Organists.

Some famous people have been associated with St Andrew's: the church guide records *inter alia* the ordination of Samuel Wesley (father of John and Charles), the burial of Thomas Chatterton, the poet who committed suicide at the age of 17, the marriages of Brunel the engineer and Hazlitt the essayist, and the christening of Benjamin Disraeli. *Access:* Nearest Underground station: Chancery Lane.

St Bride Fleet Street

The 'parish church of Fleet Street' is said to be the eighth church on this site in the past 1500 years; the dedication to the Irish St Bridget is unique in England away from the north-west, where Irish influence was clearly stronger.

The present building was erected by Wren in 1671-78, and before the blitz it was magnificent. It is famous mainly for the marvellous stone spire (Fig 116, p 61) which rises to a height of 226 feet – Wren's tallest.

The church (see plan) was badly damaged by incendiary bombs in 1940; the interior was destroyed and all the furnishings were lost, including a superb reredos. The walls survived, and in the post-war restoration the galleries were not renewed; the seating was rearranged as in a college chapel (Fig 180). The nave is divided from the aisles by an unusual arcade of paired Doric columns, each pier consisting of two three-quarter columns fused together (Downes), now

(Fig 180) **St Bride Fleet Street** *The reconstructed interior.*

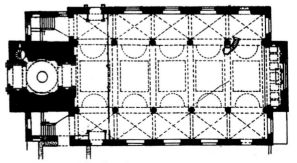
(Plan XXI) **St Bride Fleet Street.**

largely masked by the new woodwork. The arches spring from independent entablatures to support the barrel-vaulted ceiling and the groin-vaulted aisles. The altar was originally set in a slight chancel-like recess, but has now been brought forward; behind it is a Wren-style reredos, inserted into which is a vesica of stained glass. Above and around the east window, a painting by Glyn Jones gives the impression of an apsidal east end.

Excavations after the blitz revealed a Roman pavement, a Saxon church with an apse, and the foundations of the Norman tower. The crypt now houses an interesting exhibition of the history of St Bride's.

Access: Nearest Underground station: Blackfriars.

St Clement Danes

As the name indicates, this church probably goes back to Danish times in the eleventh century; later in the Middle Ages the church was held by the Templars, and later by the Prior of Warwick, and it was rebuilt in 1640. By the 1670s, it was again ruinous, and in 1680-82 it was rebuilt by Wren, who waived his professional fees. Wren's church was burnt out in 1941, and restored after the war. The interior is new, though reconstructed along Wren's designs, and St Clement's is now the official church of the Royal Air Force.

Set off well in its island site in the Strand, the church is best viewed from the south (Fig 181), where the double series of arched windows make a striking aspect. Wren encased the medieval tower in Portland stone, but the steeple was not built until 1719 when James Gibbs designed the present structure (Fig 238, p 113). Above the belfry, whence the bells ring out the old nursery rhyme 'Oranges and lemons say the bells of St Clement's', are three diminishing octagonal lanterns surmounted by a small obelisk.

The interior is all new, and has galleries on three sides. This is the only Wren church which has an apse at the east end (Fig 182 and plan). The former

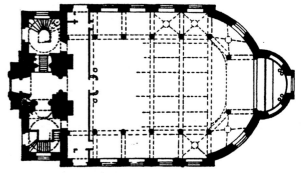

(Plan XXII) **St Clement Danes.**

(Fig 181) **St Clement Danes.**

building apparently had a rectangular chancel, with a south aisle cut short at the east end. Wren shortened both aisles symmetrically and curved their ends to provide a semicircular apse with a decorated semi-dome above (Downes). This gives, for a seventeenth-century Protestant church, unusual emphasis to the sanctuary. The galleries are supported by square masonry piers clad in wainscot, and above the Corinthian columns rise to support the barrel-vaulted ceiling of the nave and the groin-vaulted ceiling above the galleries (Fig 182).

(Fig 182) **St Clement Danes** *The reconstructed interior.*

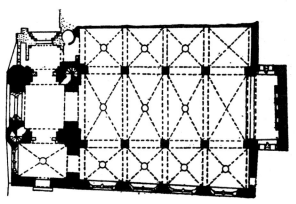

(Plan XXIII) **St Michael Cornhill.**

The plaster ceiling is decorated with flowers, fruit and cherub-heads, and a large Royal Coat of Arms. *Access:* Nearest Underground station: Temple or Aldwych.

St Michael Cornhill

The medieval church was destroyed in the Fire, but the lower part of the tower survived. Wren's rebuilding (1670-72) has suffered more than most of his churches by successive attempts at 'improvement' and modernisation. The earliest is, in fact, successful – being the Gothic tower added in 1715-22 by Hawksmoor, complete with corner turrets and multiple pinnacles (Fig 206, p 96). The north porch and south cloister were added by Sir George Gilbert Scott in the 1860s, and he also removed most of the furnishings. The altarpiece, for instance, is now in the vicarage of Great Waldingfield, Suffolk, and the communion rails are in the village church (Clarke [a]). Since the war, the interior of St Michael's has been again remodelled, and is now lighter both in atmosphere and in colour.

The nave is separated from the aisles by an arcade of four Tuscan columns (Fig 75, p 41 and see plan), with a groined ceiling which is now blue and gold. The ceilings of the aisles are lit by small lunettes. Angels in the spandrels are a Victorian legacy. The marble reredos (Fig 183) is by Scott, but contains seventeenth-century paintings of Moses and Aaron by R Streater. The pulpit (Fig 184), lectern (Fig 185) and bench-ends (Fig 186) are of excellent quality by the Victorian craftsman W.G.Rogers. The sum of all these changes is that there is not a great deal left of the seventeenth-century; perhaps it is best to admire St Michael's for the quality of its Victorian furnishings.
Access: Nearest Underground station: Bank.

(Fig 183) **St Michael Cornhill** *Reredos by Sir George Gilbert Scott.*

(Fig 184) **St Michael Cornhill** *Pulpit by W.G.Rogers, 1850.*

(Fig 186) **St Michael Cornhill** *Bench-end.*

(Fig 185) **St Michael Cornhill** *The lectern.*

The 'Greek Cross' design:

The remaining Wren churches are radically different from the preceding ones. Three of them are based on a 'Greek Cross' design, while the last, St Stephen Walbrook, is an elaboration of that design. All authorities are agreed that the inspiration behind this design came from Holland, where it was first seen at the Nieuwe Kerk in Haarlem. Wren never visited the Netherlands, but possibly Hooke did. 'The existence, in a portfolio of drawings by Hooke in the British Library, of a drawing of the Nieuwe Kerk of Haarlem, designed by Jacob van Campen (1645-49), with a roof support structure similar to that used at St Martin Ludgate, has been taken as evidence of a visit, but no confirmation of any such visit has been found.' (Jeffery [b]).

(Fig 187) **The Nieuwe Kerk, Haarlem** *Diagonal view of the interior.*

(Fig 188) **The Nieuwe Kerk, Haarlem** *Each corner with a flat, coffered ceiling, supported by a square and a cylindrical column.*

The Nieuwe Kerk, Haarlem

This church replaced an older building which was originally the St Anna Convent. A tower in Renaissance style was added to St Anna's in 1613, when the church became the first Protestant church of Haarlem. By 1645, the body of the church was becoming dilapidated, and it was replaced by the Nieuwe Kerk, built by van Campen to an original design.

The church is roughly square, and in the centre an area is delineated by four columns, square in cross-section, with Ionic capitals (Fig 187); this arrangement produces a Greek cross design (a square within a square), with arms of the cross of equal length (see plan). The columns rise to the ceiling and support arches from which barrel-vaults extend to the sides (Fig 188); above the central space, there is a cross-vault (Fig 189). The ceilings in the corners outside the central square are flat and coffered. In each corner area (Fig 187) are Ionic columns and pilasters. The pulpit is prominently sited between two of the columns

(Fig 189) **The Nieuwe Kerk, Haarlem** *The groin-vaulted central space.*

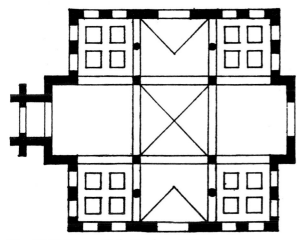

(Plan XXIV) **Nieuwe Kerk, Haarlem,** *1649.*

(Fig 190) **St Mary-at-Hill** *The tower, 1787-88, by George Gwilt.*

on the south side, and is square, with a staircase at each side. Above is a square sounding-board supported by four copper pillars. The pulpit abuts on to the central space; thus the design is eminently adapted for Protestant worship, with its emphasis on preaching the word of God; it is also strangely modern, with the communion table in the centre of the worshippers. A similar design was used at the Ooster Kerk in Amsterdam, around 1669-71.

Wren used this model for the following three churches, while St Stephen Walbrook is a sophisticated development of the design. Hawksmoor developed the theme further at several of his churches, notably at St Mary Woolnoth.

St Mary-at-Hill

St Mary's dates from at least the twelfth century, and the medieval church was damaged, but not destroyed, in the Fire. The tower and some of the walls survived, and the new church was built by Wren between 1670 and 1676. Its later history exemplifies just how prone urban churches are to disaster. Severely damaged by fire in the 1840s, it escaped major damage in the blitz only to succumb to a further severe fire in May 1988, which devastated the reredos and pulpit. As a result the interior is now plain, although it is hoped that much of the damage may be restored.

At the east end (Fig 93, p 52), there are two windows, with a central blind Venetian window surmounted by an arched pediment, and a clock projecting over the street-one of the few remaining in Wren's churches; the west end has a plain brick tower (Fig 190), which was rebuilt by George Gwilt in 1787-88.

Wren based the interior design on the Greek cross-arms of equal length resting on four Corinthian columns (Fig 191, and see plan). Pevsner traces the Greek cross design (the square within a square) back to early Christian and Byzantine times, but agrees that the immediate prototypes are the Dutch churches previously mentioned.

In the centre is a low dome (Fig 192) on pendentives (cf the following two churches). The plasterwork of the ceiling is later than Wren, and is in an Adam style, probably the work of Savage in 1826; this architect, who designed St Luke's, Chelsea, restored St Mary's in that year, and again after the fire in 1848-49.

Before the fire of 1988, the interior was thought by many to be the finest in the City. It was especially notable for its woodwork, some of it original, but much of it by the Victorian craftsman W.G.Rogers (cf St Michael Cornhill); his work was so good that experts found it impossible to distinguish from the work of Wren's original craftsmen. The best series of box-pews in the City, a fine reredos and pulpit and six magnificent

(Fig 192) **St Mary-at-Hill** *The dome.*

sword-rests-the best array in London-were on display in the church. It is hoped eventually to restore at least some of these treasures; in the meantime curtains replace the reredos.
Access: Nearest Underground station: Monument.

St Anne and St Agnes

This medieval church was destroyed in the Fire and rebuilt by Wren in 1677-80. It was burnt again in the blitz, and was restored according to Wren's design in the 1960s, when the opportunity was taken to simplify the interior and to use clear rather than stained glass, which is more suitable for Wren churches.

(Fig 191) **St Mary-at-Hill** *Corinthian columns supporting an entablature which runs continuously round the church.*

(Fig 193) **St Anne and St Agnes** *Corinthian columns on tall pedestals support entablatures which outline the form of a Greek cross.*

(Fig 194) **St Anne and St Agnes** *The groin-vaulted central dome.*

The church is built of red brick and set in an attractive garden; being of a plain and homely disposition, it is fitting that it should now be used for Lutheran worship. There is a western

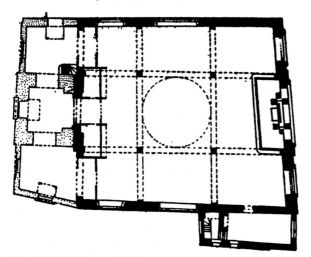
(Plan XXV) **St Mary-at-Hill.**

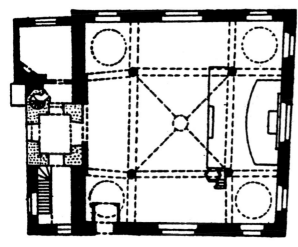

(Plan XXVI) **St Anne and St Agnes.**

(Fig 195) **St Anne and St Agnes** *The reredos.*

tower with cupola (Fig 98, p 55) and the other elevations show arched windows under a central pediment.

The interior is lovely (Fig 193, and see plan): as in other churches in this group, the plan is based on a Greek cross, with four Corinthian columns supporting barrel-vaults in each arm of the cross; the central area is groin-vaulted (Fig 194). The entablatures above the columns form the arms of the cross, being continued towards the sides of the church, and the ceilings over the squares in the corners are flat. The large windows admit plenty of light, which shows the plaster-

(Fig 196) **St Anne and St Agnes** *Font and font-cover.*

vaulted ceilings well. The reredos (Fig195), pulpit and font-cover (Fig 196) are all excellent.

Access: Nearest Underground station: St Paul's

St Martin Ludgate

Ludgate, at the foot of Ludgate Hill, led out from the City of London across the Fleet River towards

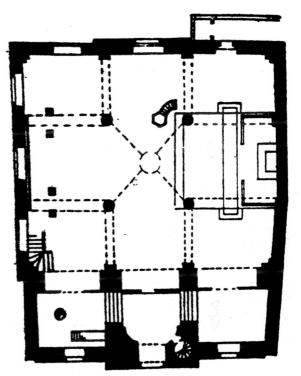

(Plan XXVII) **St Martin Ludgate.**

Westminster. The church of St Martin-within-Ludgate goes back at least to the twelfth century, and was apparently rebuilt in 1437; this building was destroyed in the Fire, and Wren's replacement followed in 1677-84.

The church fronts on to Ludgate Hill, the south façade showing three bays, with windows and doorways segment-headed. The tower rises from the middle, and is connected with scrolls at the angles with the rest of the façade. Above is an octagonal lantern and then an ogee dome, a balcony and a spire (Fig 113, p 59).

(Fig 197) **St Martin Ludgate** *Composite columns support entablatures which outline a Greek cross; here the entablature ends in a pilaster, to the left of the reredos (cf Fig 200).*

(Fig 198) **St Martin Ludgate** *The font (1673).*

(Fig 198), pulpit, communion rails, altar and reredos. This is one of the finest and least spoilt of Wren's interiors.

Access: Nearest Underground station: St Paul's.

St Stephen Walbrook

This survey of Wren's churches concludes with his masterpiece, exceeded only by St Paul's Cathedral. Yet the exterior of St Stephen's, apart from the steeple, is not impressive (Fig 199). Bumpus,

(Fig 199) **St Stephen Walbrook** *The dome behind the tower.*

On entering, the visitor passes through the base of the tower, flanked by a vestibule and a vestry, and then through coffered arches into the church. Between the arches is a screen to exclude the noise from Ludgate Hill, and above is a gallery. The interior (see plan) is startling: four Corinthian columns support barrel-vaulted transepts, and as with the preceding church the crossing is groin-vaulted and the corner ceilings flat (Fig 197). In St Martin's, however, the entablatures which define the arms of the Greek cross terminate in pilasters against the walls. A large brass chandelier hangs from the middle. There is an abundance of seventeenth-century wood-work-gallery with fine door-cases, font-cover in his 'Ancient London Churches', wrote, 'Never was so rich a jewel in so poor a setting, so sweet a kernel in so poor a husk.' The tower and steeple, however, are fine (Fig 121, p 62), one of Wren's last and best creations.

The interior is overwhelming in its spatial effect, and ingenious in its arrangement of sixteen columns delineating the nave and aisles with a central dome (see plan). No photographs can do justice to the three-dimensional effects which Wren achieves apparently so effortlessly – the stamp of true genius. Approaching from the west, the visitor passes first a row of four columns, two on each side; and then the immense dome comes into view. At each corner, there is a group of three graceful Corinthian columns (Fig 200), and above are clerestory windows increasing the provision of light (Figs 201,202). The columns arise from high stone bases; previously these would have been hidden by the box-pews. Above the columns, the entablatures define the nave, chancel and transepts. The large coffered dome (Fig 201) of wood and plaster-work is lit by a central lantern; beneath are eight arches which spring from the points at which the entablatures of the columns make a right-angle turn (Clarke [a]). The north, south,

(Fig 200) **St Stephen Walbrook** *The dome and interior looking east.*

(Fig 201) **St Stephen Walbrook** *The dome and interior looking west.*

east and west arches run directly to the sides of the church, and the diagonal arches, with four more columns which complete the square within which the dome is described, supply support for four triangular groined vaults. The chancel and nave are groin-vaulted, but the transepts are barrel-vaulted. The ceilings in the four corners of the church are flat. The interior is an essay on the central theme with which Wren was wrestling in his design for St Paul's – the combination of nave, aisles and transepts with a central domed space (Summerson [b]). St Stephen's was built between 1672 and 1679; the foundation stone for the new St Paul's was laid on June 21st, 1675.

Beneath the dome now stands Henry Moore's controversial plain altar (Fig 7, p 12), made from a block of Italian travertine marble. To some, this appears now to belong

(Fig 203) **St Stephen Walbrook** *The font and cover.*

(Fig 202) **St Stephen Walbrook** *Corinthian columns and reredos.*

(Fig 204) **St Stephen Walbrook** *The organ case and door-case below.*

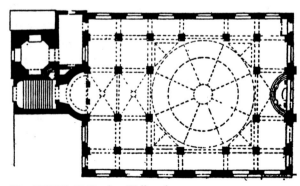

(Plan XXVIII) **St Stephen Walbrook.**

(Fig 205) **St Stephen Walbrook**
Wrought-iron sword-rest, from St Ethelburga Bishopsgate (1710).

naturally to its setting; but there are those who feel that to introduce a circle at the focal point on the ground level is incongruous (Hamilton). Around the altar are beech-wood benches carved by Andrew Varah. In addition to the modern altar, there are the original communion-table and rails with reredos in the conventional position at the east end of the church (Fig 207); also the pulpit (Fig 200), font and font-cover (Fig 203), all of which are distinguished examples of seventeenth-century woodwork. Later by about 75 years is the organ-case, with a splendid door-case below (Fig 204). The wrought-iron sword-rest (Fig 205) came from the wrecked church of St Ethelburga Bishopsgate.

Perhaps the best way to enjoy St Stephen's is to walk slowly around the building, absorbing the constantly changing spatial perspectives, and marvelling at the survival of this, the first dome to be built in any English church. The dome was damaged in an air-raid in 1941, but was superbly reconstructed after the war.

Yet St Stephen's is so much more than an architectural marvel: for here in 1953 the Samaritans were founded by Chad Varah to help the suicidal and desperate, and from this church the organisation has spread world-wide. Today, the church also ministers to London's needy, the poor, the homeless, the unloved.

Access: Nearest Underground station: Bank.

The Inheritance of Wren — the Eighteenth Century

BY THE time of the reign of James II (1685-88), Wren's task of rebuilding the churches lost in the Fire was virtually complete. No new churches were started after 1686, and by 1694 all were finished, saving only the crowning glory of the steeples, the last of which was not finished until 1717. Sir Christopher died six years later, at the age of 91.

For over 20 years after the Glorious Revolution of 1688, the Whigs were in power and any political impulse towards the building of further parish churches was not to be expected. The leading architects of the generation after Wren-Vanbrugh, Hawksmoor, Archer-turned their attention to the design of great houses for the aristocracy, above all Blenheim Palace. But in 1710 the political tide turned. The Tories returned to power, and with the backing of that devout Anglican Queen Anne the climate was ripe for change. Demographic and sociological factors supported the evident need for more churches in London: the population was growing apace, and the lower classes were becoming increasingly unchurched – or worse, turning to Dissent; new suburbs were being established without convenient places of worship even for the middle classes. The Church of England was widely seen as a desirable bulwark against a potentially disaffected populace.

As so often, the catalyst for political change was a chance event, in this case, the collapse of the roof of the medieval church of St Alfege, Green-wich. The parish applied to Parliament for funds to repair the building, but after a parliamentary enquiry it was seen that the situation in Greenwich was but a small part of the wider metropolitan problem. And so an Act was passed in 1711 providing for the establishment of a Commission to build 50 new churches in London, and the second spurt in church-building after the Reformation began. The members of the Commission included senior churchmen and government officers, Sir Christopher Wren (then aged 79), John Vanbrugh and Thomas Archer. Two surveyors were appointed, William Dickenson and Nicholas Hawksmoor (Downes). It was specified that the churches should stand free on an open site, with a handsome portico and a steeple with a peal of bells; inside, there must be a centrally planned, aisled and galleried auditorium, provided with a correctly orientated chancel.

It is interesting to compare these churches with those erected 40 years earlier after the Great Fire. Being situated (mostly) in the new suburbs, these were not the constricted sites that Wren and Hooke had had to contend with, and, at least in the early days of the Act, greater funds were available. So the churches of Hawksmoor and his fellow surveyors are on a much larger scale than all but the largest Wren churches (such as St James Piccadilly, likewise on a new site). But what they gain in grandeur, they of course lose in homely domesticity.

Events conspired to frustrate the aim of building 50 new churches: the political will was lost by the fall of the Tory government and the death of Queen Anne in 1714. And, an event which has a modern ring of familiarity, the expenditure of the Commission greatly exceeded its resources: by 1718, it had financially over-reached itself, and building had to slow down. By 1733, when the Commission was dissolved, only twelve churches had been built–but what churches – almost every one a masterpiece (see Table V).

Architects of the Fifty New Churches

Nicholas Hawksmoor (1661-1736)

Hawksmoor was born in Nottinghamshire in 1661, and by 1679 he had become clerk to Sir Christopher Wren, then deeply immersed in the rebuilding of St Paul's Cathedral and the city churches. It appears that he worked in Wren's office for about 20 years, gradually acquiring experience and expertise under the teaching of the great architect, and being given steadily more autonomy in various building projects. After the completion of the parish churches, he was closely involved with the work at St Paul's, and then with Christ's Hospital and Greenwich Hospital. From about 1699, he was working with John Vanbrugh (a playwright turned architect) first at Castle Howard in Yorkshire, and then at Blenheim. By 1711, he was 50, with years of experience behind him, and ready to break new ground in the design of parish churches.

(Fig 206) **St Michael Cornhill** *The tower by Hawksmoor.*

Table V
Churches built under the 'Fifty New Churches' Act

1712-14	St Alfege, Greenwich	Hawksmoor	1716-24	St Mary Woolnoth	Hawksmoor
1712-39	St Paul, Deptford	Archer	1716-31	St George, Bloomsbury	Hawksmoor
1714-17	St Mary-le-Strand	Gibbs	1717-33	St Luke, Old Street	Hawksmoor and James
1714-28	St John, Smith Square	Archer	1718-22	St Michael Cornhill (tower)	Hawksmoor
1714-29	Christchurch Spitalfields	Hawksmoor	1721-24	St George, Hanover Square	James
1714-29	St George-in-the-East	Hawksmoor	1723-33	St John Horsleydown	Hawksmoor and James
1714-30	St Anne, Limehouse	Hawksmoor			

Hawksmoor was responsible for six of the twelve churches built under the Fifth New Churches Act, and it is fortunate that all six survive today, though some have sustained severe damage and neglect. In addition, he combined with James to design St Luke, Old Street, which survives as a roofless shell (though the obelisk spire is worth seeing); and St John Horselydown (demolished in 1970). He also completed the tower of St Michael Cornhill, a Wren church (Fig 206); the style is Gothic, the top of the tower being replete with large corner pinnacles, with smaller pinnacles between.

In spite of the long tutelage and association with Wren, Hawksmoor's style is very much his own, and in some ways sharply differentiated from his great predecessor. He was a great admirer of Roman forms, and reminiscences of antiquity are frequent in his buildings. This classical leaning was strangely blended with a genuine feeling for Gothic, a very unfashionable sentiment in the early eighteenth century. And, even more than Wren, he was interested in the handling of space and geometrical forms: this pre-occupation enabled him to obtain many of his more striking effects. There is a massiveness in Hawksmoor's churches which is not found in Wren's. And, in one vital respect, he was more fortunate than Wren: apart from St Mary Woolnoth, and to a lesser degree, St George, Bloomsbury, Hawksmoor had extensive sites at his disposal, enabling him to provide grandiose effects which chimed happily with the powerful statements of Anglican faith which the Church demanded to aid its perennial two-front battles with Dissent and Rome.

The reputation of Hawksmoor has long been overshadowed by Wren, and, perhaps, even by James Gibbs. But since World War Two his genius has received belated recognition; this has not come a moment too soon-failure to accord greatness to Hawksmoor might well have doomed his finest work Christchurch Spitalfields when for many years its fate trembled in the balance.

St Alfege, Greenwich

The settlement of Greenwich dates back to Roman times; St Alfege was the archbishop who was captured by the Danes at the sack of Canterbury in 1011 and in the next year murdered when he forbade his people to pay a ransom for his release (Young [a]). There was another medieval dedication to him at London Wall in the City.

The medieval church was probably rebuilt in the thirteenth century; its most famous vicar was John Morton (1444-54), the originator of 'Morton's Fork', later Chancellor of England under Henry VII, Archbishop of Canterbury and Cardinal. The tower was rebuilt in 1617, and in 1710 in a severe storm, the roof collapsed. As it was this which led to the Commission for the Building of Fifty New Churches, it was only fair that Greenwich should have an early claim on the funds released by the Act. The result was Hawksmoor's first church, built between 1712 and 1714, a design which broke new ground in the development of English church architecture.

The most striking aspect of St Alfege's is the monumental east façade, where giant Doric columns support an entablature, and above is a huge pediment interrupted in the centre by an arch. In front of the portico are four Roman altars, decorated by drapery and cherubs' heads. At the four corners of the church, and at each end of the ridge of the roof, are giant urns. Doric pilasters are continued on the north and south façades (Fig 207), in the centres of which are projections leading to vestibules within.

The tower survived the collapse of 1710, and was simply recased by Hawksmoor. He originally designed a bold new tower which was to be surmounted by an octagonal lantern, similar to that built later at St George-in-the-East; unfortunately this was never built and the present tower

(Fig 207) **St Alfege, Greenwich.**

(Fig 208) **St Alfege, Greenwich** *View from the south gallery.*

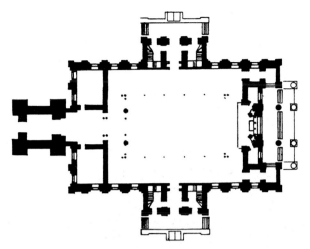

(Plan XXIX) **St Alfege, Greenwich.**

was added in 1730 by James; it is pretty (Fig 242, p 117), but comparison with Hawksmoor's other towers (Figs 210,213,217,221,225) confirms its inadequacy.

The interior (Fig 208, and see plan) was gravely damaged in the blitz, but has been skilfully restored. It is less imposing than the exterior, possibly the least interesting of Hawksmoor's churches, and unfortunately some fine furnishings by Grinling Gibbons and other have been lost. The external transeptal projections are not apparent within. There are galleries on three sides, supported by thin columns which do not rise to the ceiling. The flat ceiling is very wide and plain, and rises from corbels; it appears to float above the church, and is the best feature of the interior. At the east end is an apse, the altar flanked by Corinthian columns, the dome of the apse coffered, giving an illusion of greater depth. On either side of the sanctuary are eighteenth-century benefactions boards (Fig 209). *Access:* By train from

(Fig 209) **St Alfege, Greenwich** *Benefactions board.*

Cannon Street Station to Greenwich. Turn left out of the station, and a short walk brings you to St Alfege's.

St Anne, Limehouse

In the early eighteenth century, Limehouse was an expanding residential area within the parish of Stepney. A 'greenfield' site was obtained for the new church, and Hawksmoor's design was chosen. Building and furnishing lasted about twelve years from 1714, but St Anne's was not consecrated until 1730.

The approach to the church from the west must be reckoned one of the finest to any church in London. From Newell Street, the vista of the west front (Fig 210) – less forbidding than some of Hawksmoor's other churches – looks fine, flanked by attractive cottages. There is no portico, but instead a flight of steps leads to a semicircular 'apsidal' projection, crowned with a dome, and through which leads the main entrance. On either side are vestibules, with rusticated quoins and an attic storey above. The tower rises over the dome – firstly a square-set stage with paired corner columns, and then above the clock a narrower lantern diagonally; from this rises the top stage again placed diagonally compared with the stage beneath, and from which four spirelets arise. Pevsner remarks that this continual change of

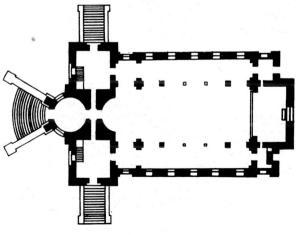

(Plan XXX) **St Anne, Limehouse.**

(Fig 210) **St Anne, Limehouse** *View from the west.*

(Fig 211) **St Anne, Limehouse** *The chancel.*

(Fig 212) **St Anne, Limehouse** *The chancel arch and part of the ceiling.*

longitudinal direction. The area delineated by the western columns is used for the western gallery, the side galleries being supported by the pedestals of the columns. Above the galleries, the columns support the ceiling at the corners. Above the central part of the nave is a circular ceiling (Fig 212), and marked beams define the ceilings of the corner rectangles. The ceilings are all of equal height (cf St George, Bloomsbury and St Mary Woolnoth). The chancel projects at the east end, the altar being flanked by paired Corinthian columns. There is good Victorian glass by Clutterbuck in the east window – a large portrayal of the Crucifixion which looks almost modern. Most of the furnishings were lost in a fire in 1852, and the font and pulpit date from the restoration by P.C. Hardwick and Morris after this.

Access: By Docklands Light Railway to Limehouse; or go to Mile End Underground station, and then by bus to Limehouse; or by bus 15 from the City or West End.

St George-in-the-East, Stepney

St George-in-the-East was built at virtually the same time as the preceding church, i.e. from 1715-23. It was a most original design, and the lovely exterior can still be admired (Fig 1, p 10). The interior was completely destroyed in World

direction gives a marked baroque effect. The north and south façades are rather plain, with square angle turrets at the eastern ends.

The interior (Fig 211, and see plan) is more complex than St Alfege's. Essentially, like St Mary-at-Hill, it is based on a Greek cross, with four columns placed to form, not a square within a square, but a rectangle within a rectangle; additional columns at the west and east ends give

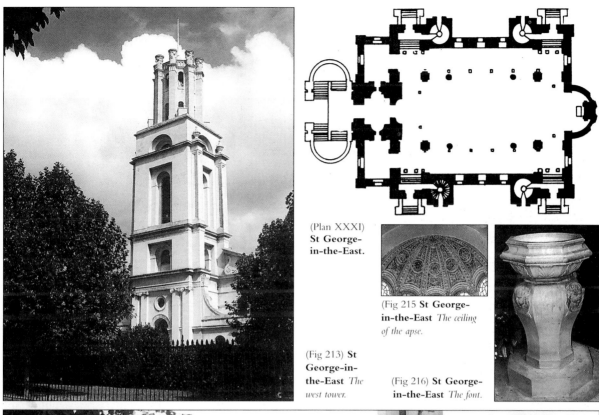

(Plan XXXI)
St George-in-the-East.

(Fig 215 **St George-in-the-East** *The ceiling of the apse.*

(Fig 213) **St George-in-the-East** *The west tower.*

(Fig 216) **St George-in-the-East** *The font.*

(Fig 214) **St George-in-the-East** *From the east, showing the apse.*

War Two. It has since been redesigned to provide a smaller church and containing within its walls a rectory and flats; and it is good to see that it still has an active worshipping congregation.

There is no western portico, and the tower rises sheer and uncompromising, four-square below and octagonal above (Fig 213). At the base of the tower are paired Doric pilasters on each side of the doorway, with scrolls connecting the tower to the vestibules on each side. Above is a massive square belfry stage, with pilasters on the north and south aspects. Finally, there is an octagonal lantern, with buttresses ascending to end in small round turrets. Behind the tower is an interrupted pediment.

The east end has a semicircular apse, and above a pediment with a round window within (Fig 214). On the north and south elevations are projections which contain the gallery stairs and the second and fifth windows, and above are four circular turrets with cupolas above, giving a fairy-tale atmosphere to the church. The effect is comparable to the contemporary St John, Smith Square by Archer (Pevsner).

Hawksmoor designed the interior on a Greek cross pattern, with a central space defined by four giant columns (see plan), the ceiling above being cross-vaulted, the ceilings in the corner squares being flat. The ceiling above the apse retains some original plasterwork (Fig 215), and the font from the old church has also survived (Fig 216).

Access: By bus from Tower Hill Station; St George's is at the corner of Cannon Street Road and The Highway.

St Mary Woolnoth

At St Mary Woolnoth, Hawksmoor was faced with the problem which regularly confronted Sir Christopher Wren – a very constricted site in the heart of the City of London. The medieval church had been damaged by the Fire, and had been repaired by Wren, but by 1711 it was in a dilapidated state, and the parishioners successfully

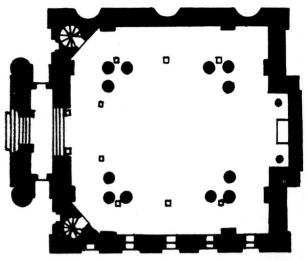

(Plan XXXII) **St Mary Woolnoth.**

applied for funds from the Commission to rebuild their church. Hawksmoor responded to the challenge with a church compact in size but intriguing both within and without.

Because of the pressure of surrounding buildings, the architect concentrated his external design on the west and north façades. The main doorway recalls, as Summerson [c] points out, the doorway at the base of the tower of St Mary-le-Bow (Fig 169, p 80), itself derived by Wren from Mansart's Hotel de Conti in Paris, though it is much plainer, without the columns, frieze and cherubs. There is heavy rustication across nearly the whole of the west front (Fig 217), embracing the pillars on each side of the doorway and the semicircular window above. At the belfry stage, a series of Corinthian columns supports an architrave from which arise twin rectangular turrets, with a balustrade between them, and a further balustrade on top of each.

Similar effects are obtained in the north elevation (Fig 218). Here the main doorway described above is transmuted into a series of three recessed window-like niches, each framed with small columns; above is a curved entablature. As with the west front, there is heavy rustication around and below the niches. There is no equal to this in baroque architecture in English churches.

(Fig 218) **St Mary Woolnoth** *The rusticated north elevation.*

(Fig 217) **St Mary Woolnoth.**

The boldness of the west façade and the unique design of the north elevation combine to make the exterior the finest of any church in the City.

The interior is superficially simple, but is even more memorable than the exterior. It is nearly square in plan (see plan), with a Greek cross (a square within a square) composed of twelve fluted Corinthian columns, three in each corner (Fig 219); these support a frieze and cornice, above which the plastered ceiling is lit by four large semicircular windows acting as a clerestory. Thus the central square is thrust up much higher than the surrounds (Fig 220), a new elaboration of the Greek cross design. Above the reredos, the cornice is interrupted by additional ornament, in the manner of a ceilure above a medieval rood-screen. The total design of the interior is pow-

(Fig 219) **St Mary Woolnoth** *The reredos and Corinthian columns.*

(Fig 220) **St Mary Woolnoth** *The ceiling and semi-circular windows.*

erful, but not overwhelming, for St Mary Woolnoth is not a large church.

Originally there were galleries, but these were removed by William Butterfield in 1875, the fronts of the galleries being placed against the walls. The original reredos survives, consisting of a canopy supported on each side by gold and black twisted columns enclosing under a richly carved and gilt choir of angels two panels of the Ten Commandments, written with flourishes of gold on red (Clarke [a]). The inlaid pulpit and organ-case are also original.

Access: Nearest Underground station: Bank

Christchurch Spitalfields

Many would claim that Christchurch Spitalfields vies with St Stephen Walbrook for the title of the finest parish church in London– the former for its prodigious west front, the latter for its subtle and elegant interior. Yet Christchurch is still not widely known among the general public – if people realised how close it was to Liverpool Street Station, visitors might come in greater numbers. For this tremendous church, Hawksmoor's masterpiece, broods over the East End with towering finality, the architect's last word in artistic terms, like Beethoven's ninth symphony or one of his late string quartets. And like those string quartets, it is not an easy work of art to assimilate immediately: the observer has to work to reap the appropriate reward. It is a sobering thought that Christchurch's very survival has until recently hung by a thread; but now at last its future seems assured.

This part of the East End, so close to the City, has witnessed enormous social change in the past

(Fig 221) **Christchurch Spitalfields.**

three hundred years. After the Revocation of the Edict of Nantes in 1683, the Huguenots migrated here in large numbers and built eleven chapels. The surviving Huguenot church at the opposite end of Fournier Street to Christchurch has been in turn a Methodist church, a Jewish synagogue and is now a mosque, reflecting successive changes in the inhabitants of the area. At the time of the reign of Queen Anne, the authorities were concerned that the Huguenots were spreading Dissent, and resolved to combat this with an overwhelming statement of Anglican establishment – hence Christchurch.

The scale of the church is astonishing (Fig 221): the spire is 225 feet high, dwarfing the surrounding houses. There is a large portico of four Tuscan columns, with a semicircular arch in the middle giving the Palladian effect of a large Venetian window. A similar effect on a somewhat smaller scale is in the belfry stage above, where the broadened tower, of the same width as the portico, has a prominent central arched window flanked with smaller windows (Fig 8, p 13). The tower then narrows, with concave scrolls on either side of the clock, above which peeps a smaller window; and even above this, on a still smaller scale, is a further square stage with a central arched window. Then rises a broach spire, which originally appeared Gothic, with three tiers of lucarne windows and crockets, removed in the nineteenth century. From the north and south sides, the belfry is seen to be hollowed out concavely, with a further series of vertically-placed windows. Compared with the west front, the north and south elevations are plain, with a series of seven round-headed windows, with circular 'portholes' above. The east end is gabled, with a Venetian window below.

The interior is dominated by giant Composite columns which rise directly to support the clerestory (Fig 222); these 'have a nobility seen in no other London church' (Summerson [b]). Counting from the west, the third and sixth columns are broader, with attached half-columns on the east and west aspects. These accentuate a central space (see plan – a rectangle within a rectangle again?). Between the two seventh columns, two further columns carry the architrave right across the church, providing a screen on which is placed the Royal Arms. Beyond, the east end curves inwards to form the sanctuary. There are similar columns at the west end between the two first columns of the arcade. The west gallery remains, but the original north and south galleries were removed in 1866. The coffered ceiling above the nave is flat and panelled (Fig 223). The entablatures over the columns run to the side walls, and above the aisles are coffered transverse barrel-vaults (Fig 222) as at St James Piccadilly and other Wren churches.

The most casual visitor cannot fail to note that the church is in great need of extensive repair. After a period of over 20 years when it was closed, it has reopened for worship, and it also functions, as it has for many years, as a home for alcoholics. It has been estimated that over £4m will be required for restoration by the year 2000, but with substantial grants from English Heritage, the National Heritage Memorial Fund and Sainsbury's Monument Trust the target is within sight, and Christchurch should soon be restored to its former splendour. There could be no worthier celebration of the millennium in London that this project. The Friends of Christchurch Spitalfields, a registered charity, have been formed to organise this work, and may be contacted on 0171 247 0165.

Access: From Liverpool Street Station, turn left into Bishopsgate, and after a short distance right into

(Fig 222) **Christchurch Spitalfields** *The interior, looking east.*

(Fig 223) **Christchurch Spitalfields** *The ceiling.*

(Plan XXXIII) **Christchurch Spitalfields.**

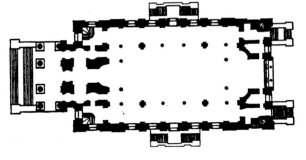

(Fig 224) **St George, Bloomsbury** *The portico – the finest in London?*

Rushfield Street, where the tower of Christchurch faces you at the end of the street.

St George, Bloomsbury

St George's, Bloomsbury, a most rewarding church, is at first sight a little confusing and not easy to describe. This stems from the geography of the site – not here a wide open space, but a site long from north to south and narrow from east to west – the converse of the requirement for a correctly orientated church. This in fact led to difficulties later, as we shall see.

But to begin with the exterior: the finest portico in London is reached up a flight of steps from Bloomsbury Way (Fig 224). There are six tall Corinthian columns, with an imposing pediment above. The 'portico has the depth and generosity which the functions of a portico demand; it has nobility without extravagance' (Summerson [a]). The portico is the south façade of the church; the

north façade is also impressive – here are two tiers of five arched windows, surmounted by a pediment; between the blind lower windows are pilasters, and between the upper ones columns. A second inner pediment supports the roof of the clerestory both on the south and north fronts.

To the west is the tower: this rises to belfry level, which consists of a miniature temple with colonnades and pediments on all four aspects (Fig 225). From this rises a steeply recessed and stepped spire, at the top of which is a Roman altar which serves as a pedestal for a statue of King George I as St George. For this conceit, which he executed without permission, Hawksmoor was reprimanded by the Commission and told that 'if he did that sort of thing again, he would have to pay for it himself' (Summerson [b]). At the foot of

(Fig 225) **St George, Bloomsbury** *The steeple, with statue of George I as St George.*

(Fig 227) **St George, Bloomsbury** *The altar was originally in the apse on the right (east).*

the spire, there formerly stood pairs of lions and unicorns embracing the Royal Crown. These animals were over ten feet high, but by 1871 they were unsafe, and were taken down by G.E.Street who replaced them with drapery on each side of the crown. The inspiration for the steeple comes from drawings of Pliny's description of the tomb of Mausoleus at Halicarnassus in Turkey – one of the seven wonders of the ancient world. The top of the mausoleum was adorned with a chariot drawn by four horses, and Sacheverell Sitwell conjectures that this may have inspired Hawksmoor to place the lion and unicorn at the base of his pyramid.

With all this external grandeur, it is natural to wonder whether the interior may be an anticlimax. Not so: in fact, here one encounters Hawksmoor's spatial ambivalence at its most confounding. The visitor enters from the south through a vestibule and then between Corinthian columns to face the high altar under a depressed arch and flanked by further columns on each side (Fig 226). To the right is a semicircular apse (Fig 227) with some lovely plasterwork by Isaac Mansfield

in the ceiling. The position of the apse is surprising until one realises that this is the east end, where the altar originally was situated, and that only later, in 1781, was the altar moved to its present situation on the north to accommodate extra seating for the growing population.

Having digested this, the time is ripe for further analysis. The interior is basically again a square within a square (see plan), as in other churches by Wren and Hawksmoor. But the architect's ingenious use of space introduces further refinements. The east-west axis, from the apse to the corresponding bay on the west wall is essentially a vertical perspective, with the apse and bay flanked by heavy columns which rise to support the clerestory without any horizontal emphasis. In contrast, the north-south axis is full of horizontal stress, provided mainly by the entablatures of the two rows of columns which are extended laterally, complementing the depressed arch over the present altar (Fig 226). On the south wall (Fig 228), the gallery, organ-case, entablature and depressed arch again provide horizontal emphasis. As Professor Downes points out, 'The spectator enters, from whatever direction, on an axis, and the building makes complete spatial sense only from the centre, the point at which the two axes cross, and where the two most different readings of the interior are combined'.

The nave ceiling is raised above the ceilings of

(Fig 226) **St George, Bloomsbury** *The interior, looking north.*

(Fig 228) **St George, Bloomsbury** *The apse (on the left), and south gallery with organ-case and Royal Arms.*

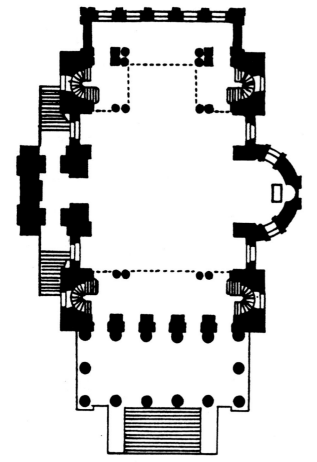

(Plan XXXIV) **St George, Bloomsbury.**

(Fig 229) **St George, Bloomsbury** *The ceiling.*

spectator. The mahogany pulpit is the original one, as is the font.

Access: Nearest Underground station: Holborn or Tottenham Court Road.

Thomas Archer (1668-1743)

Thomas Archer was born in comfortable circumstances in Warwickshire, and was very much a 'gentleman architect'. After leaving Oxford, he travelled abroad for several years, and in Rome encountered the works of the great Italian baroque architects, Bernini (1598–1680) and Borromini (1599–1667). Signs of their influence (particularly the latter's) can be found in his work. In 1705 he was appointed Groom-Porter to Queen Anne, a lucrative post which licensed all gambling activities. He developed his architectural ideas at Chatsworth, where he designed the north front, and at the parish church (now the cathedral) of St Philip at Birmingham.

the rest of the church (Fig 229) and this again reinforces the north-south axis. The height of the central square provided by the series of clerestory windows introduces a third vertical axis to the

In 1711 he was appointed a Commissioner under the 'Fifty New Churches' Act. He designed two outstanding churches for the Commission, both of which are reviewed here. After these, he designed little more, so his professional career was not long (*c*.1700–1720), and coincided with the brief heyday of English baroque.

St John, Smith Square, Westminster

Among parish churches, St John's is, perhaps, the most extreme example in England of the baroque, and as this style has never been much beloved by English people the church has always been undervalued. Add to this the accidents of severe fire in 1742, twelve years after its completion, and bombing in 1941, and its very survival is a wonder.

The church stands on an island site in Smith Square, and because of the proximity of buildings, and more recently of large trees, its complex exterior is not easy to appreciate and even harder to photograph! Walk all round the square to appreciate its varied forms. Basically St John's is a Greek cross plan, i.e. four equal limbs radiating from a central square. The angles between the limbs are concealed by convex rusticated projections. The north and south façades have impressive porticos, with Tuscan columns rising to a pediment which is interrupted by a central colonnade. The east and west façades are simpler, with a large Venetian window and a series of pilasters; above the architrave is a raised pediment with a central niche (Fig 230). At the four corners are prominent rounded towers (Fig 231) each with four columns set diagonally, with a lot of superficial decoration. These towers were apparently lightened by Archer to prevent St John's from subsiding into a marsh. The whole external edifice is a *tour de force*, an uninhibited extravaganza which compels admiration.

The original interior also had a Greek cross pattern of twelve columns (as at St Mary Woolnoth), with a central groin-vaulted ceiling; this was lost after the fire of 1742, when the columns which formed a square within the square were not renewed. There were also galleries supported on Ionic columns. After the bombing in 1941, the church survived as a roofless shell for over 20 years, but then was restored in the 1960s for use as a concert hall.
Access: Nearest Underground Station: Wesminster.

(Fig 230) **St John, Smith Square** *From the west.*

(Fig 231) **St John, Smith Square** *The north-west tower.*

(Fig 232) **St Paul, Deptford**
The steeple and south elevation.

St Paul, Deptford

This, the finest church in London south of the river, is also Archer's greatest, less quirky than St John's, more mature than Birmingham Cathedral. It has recently acquired some fame as the church in which the erring Lydia Bennett married Mr. Whickham in the BBC's production of *Pride and Prejudice*. The church was built between 1712 and 1730; it is raised on a masonry platform, and is set in an impressive churchyard.

Approaching St Paul's from the west, the visitor sees the semicircular portico approached up a flight of stone steps (Fig 2, p 10). The portico is based on the church of S. Maria della Pace in Rome, by da Cortona (1667). Four Tuscan columns support the roof, above which is a balustrade. There is no pediment, allowing the round tower to rise straight from behind the portico – an excellent solution to the problem of the

(Fig 233) **St Paul, Deptford** *The interior, looking east.*

(Fig 234) **St Paul, Deptford**
The ceiling.

combination of English tower with Italian portico, which vexed many eighteenth-century architects and defeated some! Above the balustrade are four circular openings in the tower, and an urn is placed in front of a higher arched opening. The pattern is repeated on a smaller scale above the clock and then the spire tapers to end in a copper vase and gilded weathervane (Fig 232). The steeple is pretty, rather than impressive – certainly quite unlike the massive structures which Hawksmoor was designing at the same time. On the north and south elevations, flights of re-entrant steps lead to an arched doorway in the centre of a three-bay projection, above which is an imposing pediment At the east end, the apse has a large curved Venetian window, and above is a pediment.

The enormously impressive interior is derived from Borromini's S. Agnese in Rome (Summerson [b]). There is a central square, flanked by giant Corinthian columns. Between the columns are galleries which towards the apse project forwards like a box at the theatre (Fig 233). The apsidal chancel provides the focal point, and the Venetian window contains eighteenth-century glass showing the Ascension flanked by the figures of St Michael and St Gabriel. Above the whole nave is a flat ceiling with exquisite plasterwork (Fig 234). *Access:* By train from London Bridge or Cannon Street to Deptford Station, or by bus to Deptford Broadway.

James Gibbs (1682-1754)

The great architects of the English baroque, Hawksmoor, Archer, Vanbrugh, were all born in the 1660s; by 1720 their best work was done, and the baroque was giving way to the Palladian movement (p 120), headed by Burlington, Kent, Campbell, none of whom designed churches in London. Between these two groups, and adhering to neither, is James Gibbs.

Gibbs was born of a good family in Aberdeen in 1682, and by 1703 he was in Rome, where he stayed for six years, studying baroque and mannerist architecture. He returned to England in 1709, and four years later he was appointed Surveyor to the Commission for the Fifty New Churches instead of Dickenson, working therefore alongside Hawksmoor. He quickly obtained the commission for building St Mary-le-Strand (1714-17), but by 1714, the political tide had turned, the Tories were out of power, the Queen was dead, and Scots were not popular in London, especially if suspected of Jacobite sympathies. Gibbs was a Scot, a Tory, and a covert Catholic-and quite suddenly he was on weak political ground. He lost his Surveyorship, and henceforth worked alone, often for the Tory aristocracy. For the Earl of Oxford, he designed the church of St Peter, Vere Street (1721-24); and at almost the same time, for a Whig vestry, he obtained his most important commission, on which above all his reputation rests, that of St Martin-in-the-Fields. Outside London, he built the nave of All Saints, Derby (now the cathedral) in 1725, and the church of St Mary, Patshull, Staffordshire in 1743.

Favouring neither baroque nor the Palladians, Gibbs remained closest to the legacy of Sir Christopher Wren, especially after the building of St Mary-le-Strand. He was immensely influential throughout the rest of the eighteenth century, mainly because of his *A Book of Architecture* published in 1728. Countless churches in England and in colonial America were designed according to the precepts laid down by Gibbs. If he perhaps showed a little less originality than Hawksmoor or Archer, he was always competent; and Summerson [b] describes him as 'one of the most individual of English (sic) architects; Not a profound innovator like Wren or Vanbrugh, or a man of great imaginative power, he was a superlative technician and possessed an ability to select and combine the characteristics of other architects and fuse them into a style of his own, independent of the trend of fashion.'

St Mary-le-Strand

The medieval church dating from the twelfth century was demolished by Lord Protector Somerset in 1549, and the parishioners had to move to the Savoy chapel. However, after over 150 years, they seized the opportunity to rebuild under the Fifty New Churches Act, and their application was successful, the design of Gibbs being ultimately chosen. The church was built between 1714 and 1717 and the architect was not long back from Rome; and St Mary's, more than any other church in London, shows the influence of Italian architecture of the sixteenth century, especially in the use of florid decoration both externally and internally. The style soon fell out of favour, and Gibbs did not repeat it in his later churches–either out of prudence for the sake of his career, or because of a genuine change of heart. No doubt many felt St Mary's to be too popish for England!

Standing on an island site at the east end of the Strand, its west front is prominent and appealing (Fig 235). It is a narrow church, with markedly vertical thrusts. There is a semicircular Ionic entrance porch, and above this the upper storey of the west front shows an arched window flanked by twin Corinthian columns and above a pediment; on each side are smaller windows, each with their own pediment. The tower rises above in diminishing square stages, with columns and urns and at the top a gilded weathervane. The apsidal east end matches the west porch, and has panels of fruit, foliage and books. The side elevations are equally rich. The windows are disposed in two storeys (Fig 236), the lower ones blind to exclude the noise. There is rustication round the ground floor windows, with alternate curved and pointed pediments above each, and pilasters between. The arched upper windows are separated by columns, and above the second, fourth and sixth windows are large pediments, the outer ones pointed, the central one curved.

(Fig 235) **St Mary-le-Strand.**

(Fig 237) **St Mary-le-Strand** *The apse.*

(Fig 238) **St Clement, Danes** *The steeple, by Gibbs.*

Between the pediments are balustrades and urns.

Architecturally speaking, the interior is simple, without aisles and lateral galleries. Two tiers of Corinthian pilasters on the sides lead the eye upwards to the ceiling. The chancel is framed by two tiers of twinned columns, and above is a large pediment enclosing the Hanoverian Royal Arms. Both the apse (Fig 237) and the ceiling over the nave are richly decorated in an Italian manner. There is a carved and inlaid pulpit, and there is fine carving also on the altar-rails and vestry door-cases.

Not long after the completion of St Mary-le-Strand, Gibbs designed the steeple for Wren's St Clement Danes, a short distance eastwards along the Strand. The steeple is rather similar to that of St Mary's, but the successive stages are octagonal instead of square (Fig 238; cf Fig 235).
Access: Nearest Underground station: Aldwych or Temple.

St Peter, Vere Street, St Marylebone
This little church deserves to be much better known, for it is a real gem. It was designed to serve a new area of London developed by Lord

(Fig 236) **St Mary-le-Strand** *The south elevation.*

(Fig 239) **St Peter, Vere Street** *The sanctuary and ceiling.*

open on all sides and crowned with a dome, from which springs a ball and vane (Thomas Smith, 1833, quoted by Baker).

The elegant interior is notable for the ceiling (Fig 239), where there is lovely plasterwork by Bagutti (who also worked at St Martin's). There are galleries on three sides, with giant columns rising to the ceiling. There are some excellent pre-Raphaelite windows by Burne-Jones; the east window shows Christ with the woman of Samaria at the well, with angels on each side. On the south side is a two-panelled window showing (above) the Entry into Jerusalem, and (below) the Reception of Souls into Paradise. On the north side, the upper window shows two angels, and below St James and St John healing the lame man.

St Peter's is now associated with All Souls, Langham Place, and is the headquarters of the Institute for Contemporary Christianity (Christian Impact).

Access: Nearest Underground station: Bond Street. From there, turn right (east) along Oxford Street, and Vere Street is the fourth turning on the left.

St Martin-in-the-Fields

Several reasons have conspired to make St Martin-in-the-Fields the most famous parish church in London. Firstly, there is the quality of Gibbs' design-though, as we shall see, it is not without alleged blemishes, particularly in the eyes of architectural purists. Secondly, there is the influence of Gibbs' book, *A Book of Architecture,* which established his reputation at home and overseas. And thirdly, and quite fortuitously, the laying out of Trafalgar Square in 1826 brought the church, previously sited obscurely in St Martin's Lane, into the most prominent situation in London; since then its popularity has never flagged, and excepting only St Paul's and Westminster Abbey, it must be the most photographed church in London.

St Martin's dates back at least to the thirteenth century; and the small medieval church was rebuilt,

Harley, extending from what is now Marylebone Lane to Berners Street, and was built between 1721 and 1724. It was a proprietary chapel and was originally known as the Marylebone or Oxford Chapel (Lord Harley became the second Earl of Oxford on his father's death); it was dedicated to St Peter only in 1832.

The church was memorably described by Summerson (a) as a 'miniature forecast' of St Martin-in-the-Fields. Built of brick with stone quoins, it has two tiers of windows on each side. The west front has a modest Tuscan portico, with pediment above, and at the east end is a Venetian window, also with a triangular pediment. 'The steeple springs from the centre of the roof at the west end and consists of three stages, a square tower of brick, above which is an octagon tower,

(Fig 240) **St Martin-in-the-Fields** *From Trafalgar Square.*

and doubled in size, in 1607. A hundred years later, this building was again decayed and inadequate for the expanding parish, and it was hoped that a replacement would be provided by the Commission established under the Fifty New Churches Act. But no progress was made, so the parishioners obtained an independent Act for the rebuilding of the church at their own expense; and Gibbs won the appointment as Surveyor in 1720.

The architect had come a long way in the few years since the design of St Mary-le-Strand. Gone were the exuberantly baroque features of that church – the decorative pediments, the Italianate flourishes, deemed to be too Mediterranean, too Catholic, for sober, Protestant London – especially, perhaps, as St Martin's was the parish church for the royal palace of Whitehall. So the church, though built indeed on a grand scale, is conservative and undemonstrative, 'perfectly attuned to the climate of English eighteenth-century Protestantism' (Smith, Cook and Hutton).

The west portico (Fig 240) is designed to impress – six giant Corinthian columns, with a large pediment above enclosing the Royal Arms. The north and south sides have recessed pairs of columns at the corners, and Corinthian pilasters between the series of five windows in two storeys, with rustication around the windows. At the east end is a large Venetian window, flanked by further windows and Corinthian pilasters.

But it is Gibbs' treatment of the tower which has raised the hackles of the architectural establishment. The problem was the relationship between the classical portico and the Christian tower. At St Martin's the tower rises boldly through the roof behind the pediment, so that it appears to ride on the pediment, and this pattern was repeated a hundredfold in both the Old and the New Worlds. 'Integration this procedure can hardly be called' (Pevsner). 'The spire sits uneasily on the roof' (Hutton). 'The incongruity of the temple-like church and the steeple which rushes up through its roof is undeniable' (Summerson [b]). Yet all acknowledge the splendour of the steeple itself (Fig 240): the belfry has twin pilasters at each corner, and above the clock is an octagonal lantern, and then a superb spire punctuated with four rows of fenestrations. Here Gibbs rivals his hero Wren with a design never surpassed for grace and vitality.

Having assimilated the wonders of the exterior, what awaits the visitor within? The auditorium has four giant columns on each side, each carrying its own entablature from which arise semicircular arches (Fig 3, p 10 and Fig 241), There is no clerestory, the nave being barrel-vaulted. The ceiling has lovely plasterwork by Artari and Bagutti; they bring the only touch of rococo permitted in this Anglican temple. There are galleries on three sides, less prominent than in Wren's churches (cf St James Piccadilly). At the east end, the entablatures curve towards the chancel, allowing a royal box on each side. The sanctuary itself is plain, with clear glass in the large Venetian window compensating for the absence of a clerestory.

Opinions about St Martin-in-the-Fields vary hugely. 'Aesthetically the most successful of all London churches' (Sitwell). But Elizabeth and Wayland Young compare it unfavourably with its contemporary Christchurch Spitalfields: 'It is sad to reflect on the decay of …that lily of a golden age Christchurch Spitalfields, when this begonia

(Fig 241) **St Martin-in-the-Fields** *Nave, arcades and ceiling.*

(i.e. St Martin's) flourishes so well'. But changing the metaphor from botany to music: if the Hawksmoor can be likened to a late Beethoven string quartet, then perhaps St Martin-in-the-Fields is a Schubert equivalent–less strident, more tuneful, equally moving.

But this church is of course more than an architectural *tour de force*: it is a living church. It makes a distinguished contribution to the musical life of the capital, and since the days of its great vicar Dick Shepherd, (1914 -26), it has been in the forefront of work among the poor, with a social care unit which serves up to five hundred homeless people each week. Some may think that *this* is the real St Martin's.

Access: Nearest Underground station: Charing Cross.

John James (c.1672-1746)

John James, the last of the architects who designed churches under the Fifty New Churches Commission, had been employed as clerk of works at Greenwich under Wren and Vanbrugh. He succeeded James Gibbs as Surveyor in 1715, and is remembered as the designer of just one church, St George's, Hanover Square. He was also responsible for the tower at Hawksmoor's St Alfege's, Greenwich (Fig 242), a pretty enough structure ,but unlike any of Hawksmoor's own towers and inadequate in comparison with them.

James was a competent architect, but lacked the originality of Hawksmoor, Archer or Gibbs. Yet at St George's he is credited with the earliest full-scale Corinthian portico in London, anticipating Hawksmoor's St George's, Bloomsbury and Gibbs' St Martin-in-the-Fields. Like these two churches, the west front has a grand portico with six Corinthian columns and pediment above. James' chief claim for architectural distinction is that his design appears to be a little earlier than the others; although Pevsner states that both Gibbs and Hawksmoor had devised such a portico several years earlier.

(Fig 242) **St Alfege, Greenwich** *The steeple by James.*

St George, Hanover Square

'If all the best people are married at St Margaret, Westminster, all the next best people are married at St George's …Theodore Roosevelt was married here; so were we', add Elizabeth and Wayland Young engagingly. And indeed it is as the scene of fashionable weddings that St George's Hanover Square is best known to the London public. Yet the church, set in the heart of the West End, does not generally get a favourable press. It is an attractive building, designed by John James and built in 1721-24. The west front has a grand portico with six Corinthian columns and pediment above (Fig 243). Behind the portico, the tower of St George's rises, like that of St Martin's, but here the resemblance ceases. Gibbs' steeple is graceful and worthy of Wren; James's is more solid, not quite so inspired: a square belfry

(Fig 243) **St George, Hanover Square** *The portico and tower.*

(Fig 244) **St George, Hanover Square** *The sanctuary and east window.*

Unknown architect: Grosvenor Chapel

Of the many humbler versions of St Martin-in-the-Fields built in Britain and North America, Grosvenor Chapel in South Audley Street is a good example. Its homeliness appeals after the visitor has been sated by the larger and more formal churches which have just been reviewed. Said to be in the New England style (is this what made it appeal to the American servicemen in London who worshipped here during World War Two?), it was built as a proprietary chapel and is one of the few such that survive. Even its architect

stage with twin Corinthian columns at the corners (as at St James Garlickhythe, Fig 120, p 62); and over the openings are festoons of drapery. Above is a cupola, a tiny lantern and a weather-vane.

Inside, there are the conventional galleries on the north, south and west sides, supported by square columns; Corinthian columns support the ceiling (Fig 244). The nave has a tunnel-vault above, the aisles are transversely vaulted, as at St James Piccadilly. The Venetian east window is imposing: the central window is flanked by paired Corinthian columns, and the outer lights have a further column and a pilaster on each side. The finest artefact in the church is in the centre of the east window where Flemish glass of the sixteenth century was brought from a convent in Malines in the 1840s; the theme is a Tree of Jesse, with the Virgin Mary in the centre. Below is the reredos, with an original Last Supper painting by Kent. On each side, the reredos has canted ends, with paired Corinthian columns. The pulpit stands on six columns, and is reached by a wrought-iron stair-rail.

Access: Nearest Underground station: Oxford Circus.

(Fig 245) **Grosvenor Chapel.**

is uncertain, but the builder was Benjamin Tim-brell; the church was completed by 1731 (just five years after St Martin's) and became a chapel of ease to St George, Hanover Square in the next year.

The west front has a modest porch with Tuscan columns, with a series of five windows above (Fig 245). The tower is plain, square below where it is flanked by a broken pediment, and octagonal above, with a short spire. The elegant interior has galleries on three sides, with high-sided box-pews. The nave is roofed with a barrel-vault, the aisles groin-vaulted. The east end was transformed by Sir Ninian Comper in 1912: he interposed between the nave and chancel a screen on Ionic columns, converting the chancel into a Lady Chapel. This retains the original reredos, and above is a fine plaster ceiling. The wrought-iron communion rails were brought forward into the body of the church and now enclose a new sanctuary with the altar against the screen. The pulpit is original.

Access: Nearest Underground station: Marble Arch or Bond Street.

The Palladians

The Palladians were a group of architects under the influence of Lord Burlington who brought about the early demise of English baroque, and whose taste prevailed from about 1720 to 1760. Palladio (1518-80) harked back consciously to ancient Roman architecture as interpreted by Vitruvius, and his work *I quattro libri dell'archi-tettura* was a seminal influence on Inigo Jones. By 1715, *I quattro libri* had been translated into English and exerted a crucial influence on the development of the Palladian movement in England. The chasteness of Palladio's designs struck a chord in the architectural puritanism of the English psyche, and ensured that the floridities of continental baroque and rococo would not prevail in this country. Instead we see the con-

scious reinterpretation of classical forms and proportions, often combined with rustication. By this is meant the art of according special emphasis to parts of buildings by the use of large blocks of rough or smooth masonry separated by sunken or chamfered joints; we have met this previously in churches by Wren (Fig 169, p 80) and Hawksmoor (Fig 218, p 103). Palladian architects, such as Kent, Campbell and Burlington himself, concentrated on domestic architecture and designed few churches – certainly none in London. Nevertheless both Henry Flitcroft and the elder George Dance were on the periphery of the Palladian movement, and both designed important churches in the capital.

St Giles-in-the-Fields

Henry Flitcroft (1697-1769), son of one of William III's gardeners, was taken on by Burlington as a draughtsman in 1725, but his church of St Giles-in-the-Fields owes much more to Gibbs and to Wren than to any of the Palladians. Only the extensive use of rustication in the lower storey is a recognisable Palladian motif. Otherwise, St Giles closely resembles St Martin's. Apart from this church, Flitcroft was probably responsible for the parish church of St John, Hampstead, and he also designed parts of Woburn Abbey and Wentworth House.

St Giles-in-the-Fields traces its origin to the foundation in 1101, in fields to the west of London, of a hospital for lepers. The hospital, and associated monastic establishment, lasted until 1539 when it was dissolved by Henry VIII. The chapel of the hospital served both the patients and the people of the village which developed around the hospital; the earliest reference to a parish of St Giles dates from 1222. The chapel survived the Dissolution and became a parish church in 1547. The church was rebuilt by Flitcroft in 1731-33, independently of the Fifty New Churches Commission.

St Giles is rather hemmed in by surrounding

(Fig 246) **St Giles-in-the-Fields**
The south elevation.

buildings, but there is a churchyard to the south. There are two tiers of windows on the north and south sides, and the lower storey is heavily rusticated (Fig 246). Flitcroft dispenses with the portico, and thus avoids the incongruity of temple and tower which bedevilled Gibbs at St Martin's. The west façade is pedimented, and above rises the tower. The steeple is closely modelled on that of St Martin's (compare Figs 246 and 240), the only differences being the rather insignificant balustrade at belfry level, and the transverse bands instead of the openings on the spire.

The interior is again similar to St Martin's, with galleries on three sides, an arcade of square columns beneath, and Ionic columns (Fig 77, p 42) above, the gallery. The nave is tunnel-vaulted, the aisles groin-vaulted (Fig 247) as at St Andrew Holborn. The entablatures are continued round

(Fig 247) **St Giles-in-the-Fields** *The Ionic arcades and sanctuary.*

the east wall, where Ionic pilasters flank the east window. There is a fine seventeenth-century inlaid pulpit, from which John Wesley preached on more than one occasion. The reredos is simple, and is flanked by paintings of Moses and Aaron. The organ, built by Father Smith in 1671, is in its original case in the west gallery. Of the monuments, the most notable is that to George Chapman, famous as the translator of Homer; it is in the form of an upright tombstone, and is said to have been designed by Inigo Jones.

St Giles' ministry has always been to the poor and dispossessed (Taylor) from its foundation as a hospital for lepers to the eighteenth and nineteenth centuries when the parish was notorious for poverty and squalor. That ministry continues today in an area with a diminished residential population but no shortage of social problems in the heart of London's theatreland.

Access: Nearest Underground station: Tottenham Court Road.

St Botolph Bishopsgate

With George Dance the Elder (1700-68), we virtually come to the end of the architects who designed in the tradition of Wren and Gibbs. He became Clerk of the City Works in 1735, and is best known as the architect of the Mansion House (1739-52). He designed four churches in London-the three that follow, and lastly St Matthew, Bethnal Green (1743-46; Fig 248). His churches are perceptibly less original than Wren, Hawksmoor or Gibbs, but they are all competent and his best, St Leonard's, Shoreditch, is impressive.

The present church of St Botolph Bishopsgate, which dates originally from medieval times, was built in 1727-29, and was apparently designed jointly by Dance and his father-in-law James Gould. Its walls of warm red brick (Fig 249), with the neighbouring early Victorian school, sit very happily in the grassy churchyard, itself a relief in the streets of the City. The east front, facing

(Fig 248) **St Matthew, Bethnal Green.**

(Fig 249) **St Botolph Bishopsgate.**

(Fig 250) **St Botolph Bishopsgate** *The north arcade, ceiling and sanctuary.*

Bishopsgate, is of stone, with the east window flanked by twin Doric pilasters. The tower most unusually rises from the east end, and has a circular lantern, with cupola and urn above. The sides are built of brick, with stone quoins and dressings.

The spacious interior is light and elegant, with galleries supported by giant Composite columns which ascend without an entablature to the coved ceiling (Fig 250). In the centre of the nave is a glass dome, dating from 1820, increasing the light within. The chancel is longer than in most Georgian churches, giving greater dignity to the building. The pulpit and lectern are original. Cachemaille-Day restored the church in 1947-48. *Access:* Nearest Underground station: Liverpool Street.

St Leonard, Shoreditch

St Leonard's has a commanding position on Shoreditch High Street; it was built of red brick, the front being of Portland stone, in 1736-40, the architect being the elder Dance. There is a portico with four tall Tuscan columns and pediment above (Fig 251). Behind the portico, the tower rises in the manner of St Martin-in-the-Fields. The steeple (Fig 14, p 14) issues from the top of the tower, a familiar landmark in east London. It is slender, gracile in form. Above the clock is a square belfry, with columns at the angles and above this an octagonal stage with free-standing columns. This is crowned by a cupola from which rises a tall lantern and then a needle-thin spire. The whole composition is said to be based on the steeple of St Mary-le-Bow (compare Figs 14 and 114, p 58), but 'surpassing it for its Classic elements are more defined and clearer (Sitwell).

The interior is light and airy, lofty and impressive. The original side galleries were removed in 1857, leaving the Doric columns to soar up to the interrupted entablature from which spring the arches carrying a low clerestory and a flat ceiling (Figs 76, p 42 and 252). A rood-beam at the east end is an incongruous feature in a Georgian Protestant church; it was added in 1923. Plans are afoot to reinstate the galleries to restore historical authenticity; if so, surely the rood-beam should be removed on the same grounds?

(Fig 251) **St Leonard, Shoreditch.**

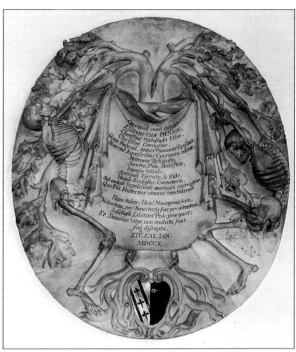

(Fig 253) **St Leonard, Shoreditch**
The rather ghoulish memorial to Elizabeth Benson (1710).

(Fig 252) **St Leonard, Shoreditch** *The nave and sanctuary.*

There are some attractive furnishings: best is the pulpit, eighteenth-century with sounding-board, and a lovely clock on the front of the west gallery. Note also the rather ghoulish memorial to Elizabeth Benson (1710, Fig 253) showing skeletons, drapery and oak trees. Medical visitors will be intrigued to see the tablet to James Parkinson who worshipped here for many years and whose paper 'On the shaking palsy' in 1818 first described the disease which bears his name.

Access: By bus 22b or 67 from Liverpool Street Station.

St Botolph Aldgate

Here the City of London and the East End meet; here the well-heeled denizens of the financial world may encounter the homeless, the have-nots, the vagrants, the alcoholics, the mentally ill-all those, shunned by the respectable, who belong to the underclass of our society. Yet here, in St Botolph's, the lonely are given fellowship, the bruised comforted, the hungry fed, the rejected

(Fig 255) **St Botolph Aldgate** *Tuscan columns, Venetian east window and 'Arts and Crafts' ceiling.*

accepted. For in the crypt is a Day Centre where up to 60 people come. On five days a week, three hundred homeless people find shelter in the evenings. Five residential hostels offer high-quality accommodation and care to women and men in need.

The parish is ancient, dating from Anglo-Saxon times, and during the Middle Ages the church was rebuilt more than once. The fifteenth-century church survived the Fire, but had to be demolished in 1739 because it was unsafe. It was rebuilt between 1741 and 1744 to the design of George Dance the Elder.

The church is built of brick, with stone quoins and dressings. The south tower is surmounted by a simple octagonal spire with fenestrations. The other elevations all have a central Venetian window (Fig 254).

The interior is more impressive: on three sides galleries, from which rise tall Tuscan columns to the flat ceiling, now store an enormous quantity of canned foods given at harvest festivals in more affluent churches for the poor to whom St Botolph's ministers. The carved ceiling and plasterwork were designed by J.F. Bentley, architect of Westminster Cathedral, in 1887 and are a good example of the Arts and Crafts style of that period (Fig 255). The striking east window, with glass in dark hues depicting Rubens' Descent from the Cross, is early Victorian. The

(Fig 254) **St Botolph Aldgate** *The south elevation.*

(Fig 256) **St Botolph Aldgate** *Carving: King David with musical instruments, from St Mary, Whitechapel.*

elegant wrought-iron altar-rails date from the eighteenth century. A moving statue of the Virgin Mary holding the crown of thorns stands opposite the pulpit; it is by Connie Cook, and was given to St Botolph's in 1979; perhaps more than anything else it epitomises the work of this church among the needy. In the south aisle is the greatest treasure of St Botolph's–an exquisite carving in wood of King David surrounded by musical instruments; though not claimed to be by Grinling Gibbons, it is of his style and period (Fig 256). It came from St Mary Whitechapel which was destroyed in 1941.

Access: Nearest Underground station: Aldgate.

St James, Clerkenwell

Clerkenwell Green is an attractive enclave just a short walk north from the City and St Paul's, and there are two ancient churches in the vicinity. St John's was originally the Priory Church of the knights of St John of Jerusalem, and of this the very fine crypt remains. St James, Clerkenwell traces its origins to a Benedictine nunnery founded around 1100; at the Dissolution under Henry VIII, the site of the nunnery was granted

(Fig 257) **St James, Clerkenwell.**

to the Duke of Norfolk, but the nuns' church became the parish church of Clerkenwell. By 1788 the medieval church, with various post-Reformation accretions, was becoming dilapidated, and it was decided to replace it with the present church built to the design of James Carr. Carr was a local architect, not to be confused with his contemporary and namesake of York. The end of the eighteenth century was not a good time for church-building, but Carr knew his Wren and his Gibbs and the result of his work is a building out-of-date from the moment of its inception maybe, but pleasing nonetheless.

The central part of the striking west façade is built of stone, the outer parts of brick (Fig 257). There is rustication around the doorway, and a pediment above the first-floor windows. From this rises a square tower, topped with balustrade and vases, and from this rises a steeple which is very much in the Wren-Gibbs tradition. The east end has a large Venetian window, with pediment above.

The interior (Fig 258) is notable for the pairs of galleries, rounded at the west end, and for the staircases which ascend to them; here are assembled a series of monuments, including that to Thomas Cross (1729) by Roubiliac (*c.*1705-62), a cartouche to Elizabeth Partridge (1702) and a decorated obelisk to Henry Penton (1714). The church itself is spacious, with a good flat ceiling and Victorian glass in the large east window. The communion-table is of mahogany, inlaid with box-wood.

Access: Nearest Underground station: Farringdon.

Neo-classicism

From about 1750 the influence of Palladianism began to wane. The feeling grew that the art of the Palladians was essentially derivative-that they were interpreting Roman forms through an intermediary, namely Palladio, rather than at first hand. This feeling was enhanced by the experience of a new generation of architects, such as Robert Adam, Sir William Chambers and George Dance the Younger, all of whom spent years in Rome studying antiquities. Linked with this was the philosophy of the

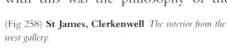
(Fig 258) **St James, Clerkenwell** *The interior from the west gallery.*

Enlightenment, the Age of Reason, the desire to return to basics, a feeling for simplicity, perhaps derived ultimately from John Locke. And it was not only Roman antiquities that were studied: Etruscan remains had recently been uncovered, and as we shall see later, there was renewed interest in things Greek. Thus a more eclectic selection of classical sources came to be made, resulting in an ability to combine elements from various styles. Adam and Chambers designed no churches in London, so their work is peripheral to our story: but the younger Dance produced one masterpiece, the one London church of the first rank in the second half of the eighteenth century, and to that we now turn.

All Hallows London Wall

This was a medieval church which survived the Great Fire but by the 1760s required rebuilding. The commission was won by George Dance the Younger (1741-1825), son of the Clerk of the City's Works; he had just returned from travelling in Italy, and was still only 24 years of age. The building established Dance's reputation, and he became one of the first four Royal Academicians in 1768. Later, he rebuilt the church of St Barth-

(Fig 259) **All Hallows London Wall.**

olomew the Less (p 131), and his finest work was judged to be Newgate Prison, now destroyed. He was said by Sacheverell Sitwell to be the most interesting personality of his time, a consummate technician whose interests bordered on the coming Romantic era.

The exterior of All Saints London Wall (Fig 259) is plain to the point of austerity, built of

(Fig 260) **All Hallows London Wall** *The elegant interior from the west gallery.*

brick except for the western tower, and with no windows except for the high semicircular lunettes. The west façade has a Tuscan doorway, with frieze and pediment above, and then the tower rises to a cylindrical stone lantern surmounted by a cupola.

But any thoughts of mediocrity are banished by the entrancing interior: a restrained design of nave and apsidal east end, without aisles (Fig 260). Fluted Ionic pilasters on each side rise to support the barrel-vault, with only a frieze running along the sides, and no cornice. This omission flouted the conventions of the time, and the theme was developed later by Sir John Soane (who in his younger days was Dance's pupil). The marvellous ceiling is lit by the lunettes on each side, revealing a flower pattern; the apse is crowned by a coffered half-dome. The plain pulpit is entered from a vestry on the north wall. The cool elegance of All Hallows makes this one of the loveliest of the City churches.

Access: The church is usually closed, but the nearest Underground station is Liverpool Street.

St Botolph Aldersgate

Like the preceding church, this medieval foundation was by the mid-eighteenth century falling into decay, and it was rebuilt to the design

(Fig 261) **St Botolph Aldersgate** *The western tower from Postman's Park.*

of Nathaniel Wright in 1788-91. The design shares many features with All Hallows London Wall, including the apsidal east end with a half-dome above, the high semicircular lunettes, and the barrel-vaulted ceiling.

The church is built of plain brick, and a western tower, with a square wooden cupola above (Fig 261), is set at an angle to the church. The classical stuccoed east end, with a Venetian window set between paired Ionic columns, dates

(Fig 262) **St Botolph Aldersgate** *The classical east end dates from 1831.*

from 1831 (Fig 262). On the south side is Postman's Park, a welcome open space in the City, and a plaque on the railings commemorates the conversion of John and Charles Wesley in 1738 at a house just north of the churchyard.

Inside, the church is gorgeous, quite different in atmosphere from the chasteness of All Hallows London Wall in spite of the similarities noted above. It is dominated by the warm brownness of the furnishings, the pews, the pulpit, the galleries, the organ-case. Galleries on three sides are supported by square pillars below, and above Corinthian columns rise to the beautiful ceiling decorated with beads and flowers and lit by the high clerestory windows (Fig 263). The east window is outstanding — the sole example of painted glass in the City, a portrayal of the Agony in the Garden by James Pearson (1788). The link with Methodism is again stressed by a window showing John Wesley preaching in Moorfields after his conversion (Fig 264). The pulpit is contemporary with the church, and used to have a

(Fig 264) **St Botolph Aldersgate** *The Wesley window.*

sounding-board; it is hexagonal, and made of oak inlaid with king-wood; it is sup-ported on a carv-ed palm tree. The organ, built in 1778, has elegant casing, and is situated in a western apse.

Access: Nearest Underground station: St Paul's.

(Fig 263) **St Botolph Aldersgate** *The apse with the painted east window, and the exquisite ceiling lit by semi-circular lunettes.*

There remain two churches, which, though built by Thomas Hardwick in the early nineteenth century, really hark back to the fashions of the eighteenth. Hardwick (1752-1829) had been a pupil of Sir William Chambers (1726-96), a

(Fig 265) **St Johns Wood Chapel.**

leading exponent of Neo-classicism, and he designed St John's Wood Chapel (Fig 265) at the same time as St Marylebone; St Bartholomew the Less followed about ten years later.

St Marylebone, Marylebone Road

Marylebone Parish Church is the fourth building on the site which is now just south of Mary-lebone Road. In the eighteenth century, the population of the parish burgeoned, and after a lot of political uncertainty it was decided to build a new chapel for the area. Later the plan was changed into a project for the rebuilding of the parish church, on a scale large enough to seat 3,000 people, and to the design of Hardwick.

The church has a noble exterior, with a portico of six Corinthian columns above which is a giant pediment, the whole façade facing north. Behind rises the steeple, as at St Martin-in-the-Fields; above a square base is a circle of free-standing columns, then a smaller upper stage with caryatids and a cupola above. When John Nash was laying out Regent's Park, he arranged York Gate to open immediately opposite the church, which adds immeasurably to the grandeur of the parish church. At the south end, towards Marylebone High Street, two wings project diagonally (Fig 266), and between is an apse which was added by Thomas Harris in 1885.

The interior (Fig 267) is rather conventional, the very image of a prosperous parish church. There are galleries on three sides, supported by

(Fig 266) **St Mary, Marylebone** *From the south-east.*

St Bartholomew the Less

This tiny church is unique in that the parish is confined to the hospital of St Bartholomew, established by Rahere in 1123. From the medieval period survives the church tower (fifteenth century), and added to the tower is an octagonal nave. The design of this goes back to George Dance the Younger, who built in 1789-93; this was replaced by the present nave in 1823, built by Thomas Hardwick. The interior (Fig 268) is attractive, and is well lit by lunette windows. The plaster ceiling is ribbed with bosses.

Ionic columns, and above a flat ceiling. Beneath is a crypt, which now houses a health centre.

It is not surprising that many famous people have had connection with the church. Thus Francis Bacon, the philosopher, was married here in 1606; Lord Byron was baptised in 1788; and Lord Nelson's and Lady Hamilton's daughter Horatia was baptised here in 1801. Samuel Wesley, the Catholic son of the Methodist hymn-writer Charles, was organist here. And on 12 September 1846 was celebrated that most romantic of Victorian marriages between the poets Robert Browning and Elizabeth Barrett.

Access: Nearest Underground station: Regent's Park or Baker Street.

The greatest treasure of the church is the brass in the vestry to William Markeby and his wife (1439). To a medical visitor, however, there is probably greater interest in the memorials to a series of Barts physicians and surgeons who have made their name in medicine, the most famous probably being Sir James Paget

(Fig 268) **St Bartholomew-the-Less** *The octagonal nave.*

(1814-99), who gave his name to Paget's disease of bone. But I was moved most by the memorial to an unknown junior hospital doctor, one Lancelot Andrews, who died in 1895 aged 31, 'for two and a half years a member of the resident staff of this hospital' – and doubtless as overworked and stressed as his successors a century later. A touching footnote records the passing of his wife, Sister John, 39 years after.

Access: Nearest Underground station: Barbican.

(Fig 267) **St Mary, Marylebone** *The nave and chancel.*

The Swing of the Pendulum — From Italian to Greek and Gothic 1810-1840

Commissioners' Churches

The influence of Wren and his successors was waning in the second half of the eighteenth century, a time when relatively few churches were being built. Then came the French Revolution and the Napoleonic wars, and for a generation, church-building in London virtually came to a halt. But all the time, social problems in the big cities were growing: because of industrialisation, people flocked from the countryside to new cities in the Midlands and North-Birmingham, Manchester, Leeds-and also to London, which grew rapidly. The establishment, both government and ecclesiastical, looked nervously across the Channel to the fate of the nobility and Church in France and were keen to avoid similar troubles at home. And if, in Queen Anne's reign, Dissent was seen as a threat by the Church of England, the situation was far worse one hundred years later. For in the intervening time, John Wesley had preached up and down the land, and although he and his brother Charles remained priests of the Church of England all their days, after their deaths in 1788 and 1791 the Methodists moved steadily away from the established church, increasing enormously the strength of non-conformity. Both

the government and the Church had a problem: how to stem the tide of political disaffection and religious dissent? And alongside these rather worldly motives, there was also of course a deep concern for the spiritual and physical needs for the new multitudes of urban poor-a recurring theme in British politics throughout the nineteenth century.

The solution offered by both government and Church was the same: the building of new parish churches would lessen political disaffection, rally the working classes to the Church of England and away from non-conformity, and bring the light of the gospel to people who walked in darkness. So, the Church founded the Church Building Society in 1818 and in the same year Parliament passed the Church Building Act. This provided one million pounds to be spent by Commissioners, and the churches resulting from the Act were known as Commissioners' Churches. This was the last time that substantial government aid would come to the established church.

The impetus that the Society and the Act gave to church-building was impressive: it is estimated that between 1818 and 1833, six million pounds were spent, and two hundred and fourteen churches built throughout the country (Clark). This is in great contrast to the meagre results of the Fifty New Churches Act of 1711, which resulted as we have seen in only twelve churches, and was in any case confined in its operation to London. The Commissioners' churches were on a substantial scale, and each was intended to hold 2000 people. Yet money was generally in short supply, and the average amount spent on each new church was in the region of £15-20,000; it is not surprising that many of the churches appeared skimped, and few could compare with the magnificent edifices built after 1711. But in what style would the new churches be built? There were two candidates-Greek and Gothic.

The Greek Revival

We have seen how, under the influence of Neo-classicism, there was a deeply-felt desire to return to primitive models; previously, this had meant the antiquities of Rome, but now this became supplanted in men's minds by those of Greece. This was seen as more basic, simpler, and above all earlier than Rome, and the three Greek orders (Doric, Ionic and Corinthian) were added to the five Roman orders in the vocabulary of many architects. The Greek orders were similar to the Roman, but tended to be simpler and less ornate, the mouldings less decorated, the proportions subtler.

The relatively short-lived Greek Revival dates back to a visit to Athens (then part of the Ottoman Empire) between 1751 and 1755 by two young architects James Stuart (Athenian Stuart) and Nicholas Revett. There they studied ancient Greek architecture, and after their return they published *Antiquities of Athens* in successive volumes. They themselves designed a few buildings in Greek style; in particular, Revett designed the front of the church of Ayot St Lawrence, Hertfordshire in 1778. Enthusiasm for the Greek style was rather slow in developing, until late in the eighteenth century when established archi-

tects such as George Dance the Younger and Henry Holland became interested. Lord Elgin, British Ambassador at Constantinople from 1799 to 1803, studied the ruins of the Parthenon in Athens, and brought the Elgin marbles back to England because they were in great danger of neglect and destruction. This augmented the interest in all things Greek, and encouraged leading architects such as Soane and Smirke. Later, in the 1820s, the Greek struggle for independence caught the public imagination, especially when Lord Byron became involved; he died during the Greek war of independence in 1824; and by 1830, the Greek revival was over.

During this time (from about 1810 to 1830), Greek churches were built up and down the land, and in London, one masterpiece was produced-St Pancras, Upper Woburn Place, without doubt the finest church in the capital since St Martin-in-the-Fields, nearly one hundred years earlier. Most of the early churches built by the Commissioners were in the Greek style: churches were contributed by Nash, Soane and Smirke (the three architects on the Board of Works who advised the Commissioners), and others in the same style included the four so-called 'Waterloo' churches-St John, Waterloo Road, St Luke, West Norwood, St George, Camberwell, all by Francis Bedford, and St Matthew, Brixton by Charles Porden.

St Pancras, Upper Woburn Place

The old village of St Pancras had a medieval church which may still be seen in St Pancras Gardens, off Pancras Road, half a mile north of St Pancras Station. By the early nineteenth century, the area to the south of Euston Road was being built up, and a new church was deemed necessary. The result was the building in Upper Woburn Place, a church which broke decisively with the Wren/Gibbs tradition which had held sway for nearly 150 years.

For this was the first, and easily the greatest, church built in a neo-Grecian style, in 1819-22. The architects were W. and H.W.Inwood (father and son). 'The son, H.W.Inwood (1794-1843) submitted designs for the new church and received, in a limited competition, the first award in June 1818. In 1819, he was in Greece and the church must have been begun in his absence' (Summerson [b]). The inspiration came from the temple of the Erectheum on the Acropolis, via the engravings of Stuart and Revett and the booty of Lord Elgin. It proved an expensive choice, the initial sum of £40,000 awarded by Act of Parliament being more than doubled by the time of completion. *Plus ça change…!*

(Fig 269) **St Pancras, Upper Woburn Place** *The steeple.*

(Fig 270 **St Pancras, Upper Woburn Place** *The four caryatids on the south 'transept'.*

The church is built of brick, faced with Portland stone, and from Upper Woburn Place there is an impressive portico, with six Ionic columns. Above the entablature is a pediment, and then the tower rises from the top of the portico, having two octagonal stages circled with columns, surmounted by a short obelisk (Fig 269). The design is adapted from the Tower of the Winds and the monument to Lysicrates in Athens. Both these tower-like structures were of immense help to British architects seeking to combine Greece with the British church tradition (Hamilton). Even more startling in a Christian church are the 'transepts'-one-storeyed projections on each side towards the east end of the

nave, above which are four draped females (caryatids) looking north and south (Figs 12, p 14 and 270). These very pagan ladies were made of terracotta around cast-iron columns by Rossi. It is not surprising that Pugin disapproved!

Behind the entrance portico is a vestibule which leads into the nave. There are galleries on three sides, but the most imposing structure is the series of six Ionic columns of scagliola (an imitation marble) at the east end of the church which surround the apse and which rise to the full height of the flat ceiling (Fig 271). The octagonal pulpit (Fig 272) has mahogany

(Fig 271) **St Pancras, Upper Woburn Place** *The apse, girt with Ionic columns.*

(Fig 272) **St Pancras, Upper Woburn Place** *The pulpit, standing on Ionic columns.*

(Fig 273) **St Pancras, Upper Woburn Place** *The font (1887).*

(Fig 274) **St Pancras, Upper Woburn Place** *Modern wooden crucifix carved by F.Lawson.*

veneers, and is supported by four Ionic columns; it is reached by a graceful iron stairway. Also notable is the marble font of 1887 (Fig 273) and a modern wooden crucifix (Fig 274) carved by F.Lawson for the University Church of Christ the King.

Access: Nearest Underground station: Euston Square.

St Luke, West Norwood

Francis Bedford (1784-1858) travelled in Greece and around 1822 designed three churches in the Greek style for the Commissioners. St Luke's, West Norwood, looks impressively down from its eminence above Norwood Road; the exterior is good, with a portico of six Corinthian columns, surmounted by a pediment and tower (Fig 275).

The interior (Fig 276) was drastically remodelled by G.E.Street in the 1870s: he installed arcades in an Italian Romanesque style, and a chancel which is now blocked off.

Access: Nearest station West Norwood.

(Fig 276) **St Luke, West Norwood** *The interior, remodelled by G.E.Street (1878).*

(Fig 275) **St Luke, West Norwood** *The tower and steeple.*

St Matthew, Brixton

This church again dates from 1822, and is by Charles Porden (1790-1863); it is perhaps one of the best of the Greek revival churches of the 1820s. Porden offers an unusual solution to the problem of combining portico and tower – he moved the tower to the east end, thus freeing the imposing west portico of four Doric columns

(Fig 277) **St Matthew, Brixton.**

(Fig 277). The tower rises from the ground; its first upper stage has Doric columns, and the second is an octagonal lantern surmounted by a cupola.

The interior was designed on a grand scale, with three galleries; unfortunately it has now been drastically remodelled, providing a small chapel for worship at the west end.

Access: Nearest Underground station: Brixton.

All Souls, Langham Place

John Nash's familiar church, at the north end of Upper Regent Street, is a good deal more interesting from the exterior than within. It was built in 1822-24 to complete the ambitious design of

(Fig 278) **All Souls, Langham Place.**

Regent Street, Portland Place and Regent's Park which had recently transformed the West End; and it was supposed to conform with the neo-Grecian movement of the 1820s. Nash ingeniously arranged the circular portico of ten giant Corinthian columns in such a manner that it both provided a façade for the church and also terminated the view up Regent Street, which is at an angle to it. Above the portico is a balustrade, and above this a circle of columns from which rises a needle-sharp spire (Fig 278). The façade was mocked when it was built, but is now a much loved part of the London scene, which has gained in prominence since Broadcasting House was built in a rather incongruous style almost next-door, thus ruining the effectiveness of the silhouette one used to get.

The interior of All Souls is more conventional: galleries on three sides; Corinthian columns from the galleries to the ceiling.

Access: Nearest Underground station: Oxford Circus.

St Mary, Bryanston Square (Wyndham Place), St Marylebone

Sir Robert Smirke (1781-1867) is today remembered mainly as the architect of the British Museum. In London he designed two Commissioners' churches in the Greek manner, St Anne's, Wandsworth, and St Mary's, Bryanston Square. Both have a prominent circular tower in two stages, but the porticos beneath are different: at Wandsworth, the Ionic portico is straight, and at Bryanston Square semicircular. The towers have been much criticised; thus Sir John Summerson (a) wrote, 'Smirke evidently felt that if Greek Ionic must keep company with a tower, the tower should exhibit no trace of Wren or Gibbs. A very proper point of view; but Smirke's mere evasion is

(Fig 279) **St Mary, Bryanston Square** *The semi-circular portico of Ionic columns, and 'pepperpot' tower above.*

put to shame by Inwood's clever results at St Pancras and Camden Town.'

The church was built in 1823 to serve the recently developed Portman estate (Young [a]). In spite of the 'pepper-pot' tower, the view north from Wyndham Place is undeniably impressive. The semicircular portico of unfluted Ionic columns has a balustrade above (Fig 279), and then the cylindrical tower rises in two stages, surmounted by a cupola. The rest of the ext-

(Fig 280) **St Mary, Bryanston Square** *The interior from the west gallery.*

erior is plain – two tiers of windows on each side. The interior (Fig 280) is rather dull: galleries on three sides, with Greek Doric columns above rising to a low segmental coffered ceiling.
Access: Nearest Underground station: Marylebone.

St Peter, Walworth

Of the three leading architects of the Regency period – Nash, Smirke and Soane – it was Sir John Soane (1753-1837) who ultimately designed churches of the greatest originality. The active professional careers of these three coincided, as we have seen, with a period of dearth as far as

(Fig 281) **St Peter, Walworth.**

church-building was concerned; for it was not until the energies (and funds) released by the Church Building Act of 1818 that a concerted

(Fig 282) **Holy Trinity, Marylebone Road.**

attempt to build churches for the expanding population was made. By this time, Soane was 65 and had behind him a distinguished career characterised especially by his subtle interior designs of houses and public buildings, notably the Dulwich Art Gallery and the Bank of England.

It was not until 1822 that he turned his attention to London churches, and then he produced three – St John, Bethnal Green (1825-28), Holy Trinity, Marylebone Road (1823), and St Peter, Walworth (1823-25). All three survive, but the interior of St John's was completely altered in 1871, though the vestibule and staircases retain their original character. Holy Trinity is now the headquarters of the Society for the Promotion of Christian Knowledge and is no longer used for services. The south front facing Marylebone Road has a handsome portico with four Ionic columns (Fig 282); the tower has a lower square stage with paired columns at the angles, and above a circular stage surmounted by a cupola.

(Fig 283) **St Peter, Walworth** *The Ionic columns of the portico.*

St Peter's, Walworth is approached from the west (Fig 281) and again presents an attractive face, with a portico of four Ionic columns (Fig 283) supporting the balustrade and tower; again the tower has a square lower stage, then a circular stage ringed with Composite columns, and a dome above (Fig 284). The gracious interior (Figs 13, p 15 and 285) has galleries on three sides supported by Doric columns; above are thinner octagonal columns which rise to arcades and a flat ceiling. At the east end, thin

(Fig 284) **St Peter, Walworth** *The steeple.*

(Fig 285) **St Peter, Walworth** *The south and west galleries.*

segmental arches separate the chancel and nave in a manner typical of Soane.

St Peter's has had a full share of tragedy: 84 people sheltering in the undercroft were killed in an air-raid during the war; ironically the damage to the church was not extensive.

Access: Nearest Underground stations: (St Peter, Walworth) Elephant and Castle, then by bus. (Holy Trinity) opposite Great Portland Street.

Gothic Revival

The Greek revival lacked staying power and was finally swept away by enthusiasm for Gothic – a choice which would have seemed unaccountable to Wren and his immediate successors. For in general during the seventeenth and eighteenth centuries, Gothic styles were held in low regard by architects, certainly from the time of Wren onwards. But from about 1750, choice spirits such as Thomas Gray (of the famous Elegy) and Horace Walpole were growing dissatisfied with classical forms, and were beginning to regard medieval architecture with greater enthusiasm than their contemporaries. Walpole (1717-97) bought a former coachman's cottage near Twickenham and gradually converted it into the stuccoed and battlemented Strawberry Hill. This influential building started a fashion for Gothic amongst some aristocrats, who delighted in building sham castles, follies, and sometimes more substantial edifices. A unique venture was Fonthill Abbey in Wiltshire, a Gothic extravaganza on a large scale, built by Wyatt for William Beckford between 1795 and 1807. It was planned as a cruciform building, with a gigantic central tower 276 feet high. It was a crazy composition, and the tower collapsed in 1825. But "Gothick" in the last half of the eighteenth century was not the preserve only of eccentric plutocrats – a handful of churches were built in the picturesque style which had evolved, but none in London; they include Shobdon (Herefordshire) and Coombe d'Abitot (Worcestershire).

At the same time, more serious study of Gothic building was being undertaken, and in 1817 Thomas Rickman published his *Attempt to discriminate the Styles of English Architecture*, which for the first time analysed medieval buildings in terms which, though perhaps not ideal, have stood the test of time and have survived until the present day. As a result of this, architects began consciously to look back to medieval styles, now formally described as Norman, Early English, Decorated and Perpendicular, and especially after the influence of Pugin, a revolution in taste was rapidly accomplished.

During the 1820s, however, Gothic was still lagging behind Greek, and at the start of the Commissioners' work, relatively few churches in London were Gothic. Quite the best was the first, St Luke's, Chelsea; others built during this decade included three churches in Islington by Sir Charles Barry (none of them nearly as good as his church at Brighton, St Peter's), Holy Trinity, Brompton, and St Barnabas, Addison Road, Kensington.

As a footnote to the Gothic revival may be noticed a short-lived fashion for the revival of Romanesque styles, either Norman or Italian. Neo-Norman churches are nowhere frequent, but dotted around the country are a number of such buildings, such as Llanymynech, Shropshire and Armitage, Staffordshire; nearly all were built in the 1840s. In a vaguely Italian Romanesque style may be included the two churches built around 1840 which are mentioned below –– All Saints, Ennismore Gardens, Kensington, and Christchurch, Streatham.

St Luke, Chelsea

St Luke's, Chelsea, the earliest church of the Gothic Revival in London (designed 1819), came only two years after Rickman's publication, at a time when serious knowledge of Gothic style was still immature. The adjective 'serious' i[s] important, implying a contrast between churche[s] such as St Luke's and its successors with the rather frothy confections built in the romantic Gothick fashion of the previous century (e.g. Shobdon) So, although compared with later Victorian Gothic, when there was much more accurate knowledge of medieval building, St Luke's appears a little naïve, a little tentative, a little mechanical, it is nevertheless a fine building, far exceeding in quality any Gothic building in the succeeding 20 years. This is a measure of the architect's achievement. And it is interesting in view of later developments that Perpendicular was the Gothic style that was adopted.

Like its Greek contemporary, the new St Pancras, it was a very expensive church, costing £40,000, constructed of Bath stone, and vaulted throughout in stone – a rarity in a parish church. The architect, James Savage (1779-1852), was later responsible for two other churches in London, Holy Trinity, Sloane Street (destroyed later in the nineteenth century to make way for the present church) and St James, Bermondsey, built in the Greek style in 1827-29. He was also involved in restoration work at St Mary-at-Hill and at the Temple Church.

The exterior is striking, with the tower entrance flanked by a two-bay open porch, all with ogee arches (Fig 286). There is a certain monotony about the exterior, with the nine regular string-courses on the buttresses of the tower, and the series of identical windows on the north and south elevations. But these are quibbles: the ashlar stonework looks well, and the vaulting is supported by a series of flying buttresses. The church guide points out that this

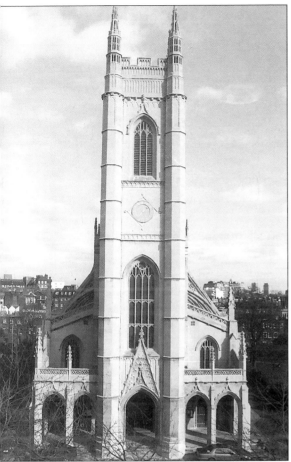

(Fig 286) **St Luke, Chelsea** *View from the west.*

was the first time for 300 years that stone vaulting and flying buttresses had been used.

The interior is formal, with slender Perpendicular arcades, and above a triforium and clerestory (Fig 287). The east window is an impressive seven-light, five-tiered Perpendicular structure, and below is a stone-panelled reredos. In contrast to genuine Perpendicular churches, Savage's original chancel was shallow, just a recess to contain the altar, in conformity with post-Reformation usage; it has since been extended into the body of the church. Galleries on both sides bring the seating capacity up to 2,500 persons.

Access: Nearest Underground station: South Kensington; the church is in Sydney Street.

Holy Trinity, Brompton Road

Holy Trinity, Brompton, is chosen as a typical example of Commissioners' Gothic, a style that has received a very poor press. Thus Kenneth

(Fig 287) **St Luke, Chelsea** *Perpendicular arcades and east window.*

(Fig 288) **Holy Trinity, Brompton** *A plain Commissioners' church.*

Clark: '…the grubby Gothic of the Commissioners' churches – perhaps the most completely unattractive style ever employed'. The architect was T.L. Donaldson, and building started in 1826. Three-quarters of the cost of £10,734 came from the Commissioners, the remainder being provided by the parish of Kensington.

The church is constructed of stock brick, with a west tower, nave and aisles. Lancet windows are used, plain in the clerestory and paired lancets under a common hood-mould in the aisles. The interior is more interesting; the best feature is the roof of the nave, a handsome ribbed wooden vault dating from 1882. There are galleries on three sides, and arcades of slender piers (Fig 288). The chancel was altered by Sir Arthur Blomfield in 1879, when the present east window of five stepped lancets was installed. The reredos is Italian, and shows Christ in glory.

The visitor cannot fail to be impressed by the life of 'HTB': this powerhouse of evangelism must be one of the most successful Anglican churches in the country, and has an influence far and wide through the courses it organises for prospective believers. This just shows that there is little relation, if any, between architectural excellence and spiritual vitality – but surely we knew that already!

Access: Nearest Underground station: South Kensington or Knightsbridge.

St Barnabas, Addison Road, Kensington

Lewis Vulliamy (1791-1871) had been articled to Sir Robert Smirke and had travelled in Italy and Greece; he designed a large number of churches in London, and was said by Clarke (b) to design in any style that was required. Confirmation of that versatility may be offered by the two of his churches here illustrated.

The church of St Barnabas, Addison Road is a miniature of King's College Chapel, Cambridge. It is a Commissioners' church, built of stock brick in 1828. The west front (Fig 289) has a large Perpendicular window, and there is a turret in each corner of the building but not along the sides. Inside there are the usual galleries supported by cast-iron columns and a flat ceiling (Fig 290).

By contrast, the former church of All Saints, Ennismore Gardens, Kensington (now the Russian Orthodox Cathedral) is built in a round-arched style based on Early Christian and Italian Romanesque sources. The striking west front (Fig 291) has a pediment above the doorway, and above this is a wheel window. Vertical pilaster

(Fig 289) **St Barnabas, Addison Road** *King's College Chapel in miniature.*

(Fig 290) **St Barnabas, Addison Road** *The interior from the west gallery.*

strips modify the squat symmetry of the façade. The church was built in 1837-44, but the south-west campanile was added in the 1870s. The original internal decoration was by Owen Jones (see p 144).

Access: Nearest Underground stations: (St Barnabas) High Street, Kensington; (All Saints) Knightsbridge.

(Fig 291) **All Saints, Ennismore Gardens** *(now the Russian Orthodox Cathedral).*

St Dunstan-in-the-West

Walking westwards along Fleet Street from Ludgate Circus, the visitor is immediately attracted to St Dunstan's by the remarkably pretty tower. Said to resemble a scaled-down version of the Boston stump, it was in fact modelled on the church of All Saints Pavement, York. St Dunstan's has a very ancient lineage, dating probably from the eleventh century; the medieval church escaped the Great Fire, but gradually became unsound and it was pulled down in 1829. The present church was built in the Gothic style by

(Fig 293) **St Dunstan-in-the-West** *The octagonal nave, with the chapels dedicated to the Romanian Orthodox church (left) and the Anglican church.*

John Shaw senior in 1829-33, and was the last church to be built in the City of London. The upper part of the tower is octagonal, and it is crowned with pinnacles (Fig 292). The clock overhanging Fleet Street dates from 1671, and is said to be the first to have a minute hand. To the right is a statue of Elizabeth I from Ludgate, dating from 1586.

The octagonal theme is continued within, for the nave is a regular octagon (Fig 293), with a central star-ribbed vault, and seven radiating chapels, alternately groined and wagon-vaulted. These are dedicated to major branches of the Christian church; on entering the church, turn left, and these are in turn the Old Catholics, the Assyrian Church, the Romanian Orthodox Church (a gorgeous iconostasis), the Anglican Church, the Oriental Churches, the Protestant Churches (a very poor showing!), and lastly, and again rather inadequately, the Roman Catholic Church.

(Fig 292) **St Dunstan-in-the-West** *The tower and steeple.*

(Fig 294) **Christchurch, Streatham.**

Access: Nearest Underground station: Aldwych or Temple.

Neither Gothic nor Greek

Christchurch, Streatham

This is a building that resists classification: it is impossible to pigeon-hole a church that is not classical, not Norman, not Gothic. As at All Saints, Ennismore Gardens, Early Christian and Italian Romanesque sources are apparent, but German, Byzantine and Islamic influences have been identified; and indeed the architect, James Wild (1814-94), later became an authority on Islamic architecture, even risking his life to enter in Arab disguise the mosque at Damascus. But although so difficult to pin down, the importance of Christchurch as an influence on modern building is being increasingly recognised; it is probably true to say that its reputation at the end of the twentieth century is higher than it has ever been. It is pleasing to know that English Heritage is helping in some much-needed restoration.

The church was built in 1841 and is a basilica of yellow brick with an apse and a very tall Italianate campanile at the south-east (Fig 294).

(Fig 295) **Christchurch, Streatham** *The nave and chancel.*

The campanile is divided vertically on each face by four thin pilasters which run right up to the tall and narrow belfry windows; above is a simple spire. Over the doorways and windows, voussoirs of red and yellow brick are laid alternately, providing welcome variety to the façades, an early example of polychromy in brick that later became so popular.

The nave (Fig 295) has very tall columns supporting semicircular arcades; lesser arcades support the gallery, with two arches to each bay of the main arcade. The apse has a series of tall windows and is not divided from the nave. As at All Saints, Ennismore Gardens, much of the interior decoration was done by Owen Jones, brother-in-law of the architect: note especially the ceiling of the apse and the capitals of the columns. The paint and gold leaf are presently deteriorating and expert conservation is planned. Owen Jones was the celebrated author of *A Grammar of Ornament*; he was superintendent of works of the Great Exhibition of 1851 and director of decoration for the Crystal Palace.

This remarkable church, which exhibits influences from so many countries, now has a multiethnic Anglican congregation, and on Sunday afternoons accommodates the charismatic, black-led Elijah Tabernacle Church; in addition it ministers in an Urban Priority Area to the homeless and the mentally ill.

Access: By bus from Brixton Underground station.

The Victorian Era: Gothic Triumphant

Augustus Welby Northmore Pugin

A.W.N.Pugin (1812-52) was born in London, the son of a French refugee from the Revolution and an English Presbyterian mother. His father became a draughtsman in John Nash's office, and specialised in the study of Gothic architecture. Pugin junior early developed a passion for Gothic, and this became an *idée fixe* throughout his short and tumultuous life. It led him in 1833 to convert to the Roman Catholic Church, then newly emancipated, in which he doubtless hoped to be able to express his love for Gothic. Not the least irony of Pugin's life is that his ideas made little headway in the Roman church, which by and large remained wedded to Italianate forms, yet they were taken up uncritically and enthusiastically by the church he had forsaken, the Church of England.

Pugin was not merely content to advocate Gothic architecture in general: he analysed the various styles of Gothic, and decided that in the Decorated style, Gothic had attained perfection. After initial experimentation with Early English, this was later held to be immature, while Perpendicular was regarded as 'decadent', or worse, tinged with Protestantism.

It was Pugin whose passionate advocacy of Gothic wrought a cultural revolution which persisted into the twentieth century. And it was he who first propounded an idea which seems incomprehensible to us, that good architecture can come only from good men – a thesis that was taken up by a greater writer than Pugin, John Ruskin. Kenneth Clark divided the Gothic Revival into two phases – the picturesque (such as Strawberry Hill and its imitators) and the ethical – and asserts that it was Pugin who was responsible for the great break between the two phases. Yet a building such as St Luke's, Chelsea antedated the influence of Pugin and is neither picturesque nor ethical; realistic or serious might be the better adjective to apply to the Gothic churches of the 1820s (with one or two exceptions: Barry's St Peter's, Brighton and even Vulliamy's St Barnabas, Addison Road could certainly be described as picturesque).

Pugin's influence was incalculable, but his direct legacy of buildings, especially in London, is rather sparse – just the church of St Thomas of Canterbury, Fulham and St George's Catholic Cathedral, Southwark. Outside the capital, his finest churches are probably the great Catholic churches at Cheadle, Staffordshire, and next to his home at Ramsgate, Kent. In recent years, his reputation as a designer and architect has grown as appreciation for Victorian building has matured. A recent exhibition in London gave many the opportunity for a more just appreciation of his many-sided genius (Atterbury and Wainwright, 1994).

The Oxford Movement and the Cambridge Camden Society

But in the same year that Pugin converted to Roman Catholicism, life began to stir in the established church. It cannot be denied that the Church of England at this time was at a low ebb. Morale had suffered as its earlier monopoly of religious belief was assailed by Methodists and other dissenters on the one hand and by the newly emancipated Roman Catholics on the other. But regeneration was at hand which ensured that by the end of the nineteenth century, much of the lost ground would be reclaimed; the Anglican church in 1900 was much more confident of its future than it had been 70 years earlier – in fact, over-confident, in the light of the century that was to follow! The vehicles for this transformation were the Oxford Movement and the Cambridge Camden Society.

In Oxford, in 1833, John Keble preached a famous sermon on National Apostasy, and he was joined by Pusey, Newman and others in launching the Oxford Movement, which published Tracts for the Times, the movement becoming known as the Tractarians. They were intent on reviving Anglican worship by a greater insistence on correct liturgical and sacramental observance, and in this they were extraordinarily successful, leading to the dominance of the 'high-church' party within the Church of England which lasted well into the twentieth century, and easily surviving the later defection of Newman and others to Rome. Their beliefs also led them to favour Gothic architecture in contrast to classical forms. As Kenneth Clark wrote: 'The Tractarians ...arrived at Gothic architecture by reversing Pugin's position. He had said: To revive Gothic architecture you must also revive old forms of worship. They said: To revive old forms of worship you must revive Gothic architecture. His impulse had been primarily architectural, theirs was primarily religious.'

But if the Oxford Movement was the prime instigator of liturgical change in the established church, it was at Cambridge that the trend towards Gothic architecture became most effectively underpinned. There, in 1839, a group of undergraduates, including J.M.Neale (now remembered chiefly for his hymns), formed the Cambridge Camden Society, dedicated to the reform of church architecture and ritual. In 1841, they started to publish the monthly magazine *The Ecclesiologist* which lasted until 1868 and which achieved a dominating, some would say a tyrannical, influence over the design of churches. In its pages, new churches were regularly reviewed, and every detail of architectural and liturgical significance was assessed. The aim throughout was to influence the building so that it could readily express high-church ritual which was held to be essential to the gospel.

The dominance of the high-church movement did not, of course, go unchallenged. As early as 1844, the Reverend Dr Close, later Dean of Carlisle, attacked the Cambridge Camden Society in a sermon at Cheltenham under the title, 'The restoration of churches is the restoration of Popery', prompting the metamorphosis of the Society into the Ecclesiological Society and exhibiting a low-church paranoia which is not perhaps quite dead, even in our own day.

It is easy today to mock the beliefs that *The Ecclesiologist* so piously propagated for over a quarter of a century. But the fruits of their labours ensured the creation of such masterpieces as All Saints, Margaret Street, St James the Less, Westminster, and St Augustine, Kilburn, and had a direct effect on the internal arrangements of almost every parish church in England. They ensured that until the First World War almost every new church was built in the Gothic style. And there is little doubt that, largely because of their labours a nearly moribund Church of England had been splendidly revitalised.

St Giles, Camberwell

Sir George Gilbert Scott (1811-78) is by far the best known of the Victorian architects. The sheer volume of his output ensures that his name is most frequently encountered; after 1847 he was said to have been concerned with 476 churches (Clark). And of course he was a great populariser of Gothic. Moreover, in his reading of Pugin in 1840 he experienced something akin to a religious conversion. Kenneth Clark quotes Scott: 'I was awakened from my slumbers by the thunder of Pugin's writings. I well remember the enthusiasm to which one of them excited me, one night when travelling by railway, in the first years of their existence. I was from that moment a new man. What for fifteen years had been a labour of love only, now became the one business, the one aim, the one overmastering object of my life. I cared for nothing as regarded my art but the revival of Gothic architecture.' John Wesley could not have phrased it better.

And yet, in spite of the earnestness of his conviction, he fails to convince us of the grandness of his vision. His reputation today is probably less than that of his contemporaries, Butterfield, Street and Pearson; all three had a streak of originality which was denied to Gilbert Scott. Competent though his churches usually are, he seldom quickens our pulse.

Scott's first London church after his conversion was the rebuilding of St Giles, Camberwell. The former church was burnt down in 1841, and the design of Scott and Moffatt was chosen. St Giles established him as the leading Gothic architect of the day. There is a freshness and spontaneity about the design which contrasts with his later, more mature, but perhaps less inventive style exhibited, for instance, at St Mary Abbot's (p 159). The style at Camberwell is Early English, and the design was welcomed by *The Ecclesiologist*; Eastlake, writing 30 years after its building, was also enthusiastic.

The cruciform church is large, with a nave of five bays, deep chancel of three bays (a deep chancel was a *sine qua non* for the ecclesiologists), transepts, and tower and broach spire over the crossing. The capitals of the piers are foliated (Fig

(Fig 296) **St Giles, Camberwell** *The south arcade.*

296), and there is an open timber roof. The original galleries have gone, and the interior was whitened, and apparently improved, after World War Two. Unfortunately, rows of ugly radiators and strings of light bulbs now obscure the arcades. In the chancel, the fourteenth-century sedilia and piscina from the previous church are preserved. There is some good glass in both east and west windows (the former by Ruskin and Oldfield). *Access:* By bus from Victoria Station.

St John of Jerusalem, South Hackney

This church was begun in 1845, when the Gothic Revival was getting into its stride, but a little before the time when the Decorated style, as espoused by Pugin and *The Ecclesiologist* was *de rigueur* in Gothic building. Thus the architect of St John's (E.C.Hakewill 1812-72) was at liberty to follow his bent, and here he erected a large church in Early English.

But it is a rather florid Early English. The west portal (Fig 297) is ornate and impressive-it is safe to say that no thirteenth-century church had a portal like this. Above it is a sculpture of Christ walking on the water, and then the tower rises impressively; originally it was

(Fig 297) **St John of Jerusalem, South Hackney** *The ornate west portal.*

(Fig 298) **St John of Jerusalem, South Hackney** *The nave and chancel.*

(Fig 299) **St Stephen, Rochester Row** *In the Decorated style.*

surmounted by a broach spire which was removed and replaced by the present structure by Cachemaille-Day. The church is cruciform, and the tall clerestory is supported by flying buttresses.

The interior (Fig 298) is spacious, with slender columns in the arcades and intricately carved capitals. The arches at the crossing on either side of the chancel are multishafted. There is blind arcading in the polygonal apse. The lancet windows are in pairs in the aisles, and in clusters of three in the clerestory. Overall, the design is bold, original, a little naïve by later Victorian standards–but a good church and still much-loved.

Access: By bus 26 from Liverpool Street Station.

St Stephen, Rochester Row, Westminster

Benjamin Ferrey (1810-80) was a pupil of Pugin senior, and subsequently wrote *Recollections of A.N. Welby Pugin* (1861). With this background it is not surprising that all his churches show great attention to detail, with a concern to reproduce accurately Gothic (or occasionally Norman) architecture. He is not, however, an architect of genius, nor can we look in his churches for striking innovation.

His best London church is St Stephen's, Rochester Row, Westminster. This was built in 1847-49 in a poor district at the expense of Baroness Burdett-Coutts, and it shows Ferrey's devotion to Pugin's teaching. The church is built

in Bargate stone from Surrey, with quoins and dressings of Morpeth sandstone. The tower is placed unusually at the east end of the north aisle.

St Stephen's is in the favoured Decorated style and it received the approval of *The Ecclesiologist*. It is elegant and stylish: nave, chancel, arcades and clerestory are all beautifully accomplished (Fig 299). There is a certain formality about it all; perhaps this is unfair, for nearly all Ferrey's decoration has gone, and it is impossible now to recapture the intended effect. Even so there are good things to see: the pulpit of Caen stone; the font carved with scenes from the life of Christ; the carving on the capitals of the piers showing birds and beasts; the bosses on the chancel roof showing scenes from the Creation. St Stephen's remains one of the best churches of its date in London.

Access: Nearest Underground station: Victoria.

St Mary Magdalene, Munster Square, St Pancras

Richard Carpenter (1812-55) is best remembered today for the superb chapel at Lancing College, Sussex, which was built to his design after his early death; but his most seminal work, which continued to influence architects throughout the nineteenth century, was this church in Munster Square, built in 1849-52. Carpenter had early become interested in Gothic building, and was a friend of Pugin and an associate of the Cambridge Camden Society. No practitioner of

(Fig 300) **St Mary Magdalene, Munster Square** *The arcades from the south aisle.*

(Fig 301) **St Mary Magdalene, Munster Square** *The chancel and east window.*

his day, wrote Eastlake, understood so thoroughly as Carpenter the *grammar* of his art; and, unlike Butterfield and Street, his work remained free from foreign influences. St Mary Magdalene was an early product of the scholarly phase of the Gothic revival, and like St Stephen, Rochester Row, was designed in the Decorated style; *The Ecclesiologist* said it was 'the most artistically correct new church yet consecrated in London'. Begun in the same year as All Saints, Margaret Street, and with both churches favoured by *The Ecclesiologist*, the contrast between them is striking and unexpected; St Mary Magdalene is thoroughly English in its antecedents, All Saints continental in its polychromy. If the latter church had the greater impact at the time, it could be argued that Carpenter's was the more influential in the long run: for medieval Italian and French

influence had a vogue in the 1850s and 1860s, but later declined.

Built of Kentish ragstone, denied the tower and spire which Carpenter originally intended, and invested on the south side by other buildings, St Mary Magdalene's exterior is not especially impressive. But within, Carpenter's cool design has worn well and continues to excite admiration. The nave and aisles are of almost equal height, without a clerestory, a frequent pattern in English fourteenth-century churches before the introduction of Perpendicular. The nave is separated from the aisles by arcades and piers of four shafts in the Decorated style (Fig 300), and the tracery of the windows is in accordance. The chancel (Fig 301) is nicely ordered, and there are parclose screens at the east ends of both aisles, designed by J.T.Micklethwaite. Originally the east window contained stained glass designed by Pugin but, sadly, this has been destroyed. The reredos is by Sir Charles Nicholson (1933).

Access: Nearest Underground station: Great Portland Street.

St Barnabas, Pimlico

It is ironic that this church, built like the preceding one to serve the urban poor, became instead a fashionable Anglo-Catholic church of Belgravia society. After its opening, it was the scene of riots and was spurned by the masses because of its supposed association with popery (its opening coincided with the re-establishment by the Pope of the Roman Catholic hierarchy in England).

Yet it was the first church to be built in accordance with the principles and precepts of the Ecclesiological Society, and *The Ecclesiologist* waxed lyrical about it, describing it as 'the most complete and sumptuous church'. Though later overshadowed by All Saints, Margaret Street, it remains an impressive and beautiful church. The architect was Thomas Cundy ('the Younger';

(Fig 302) **St Barnabas, Pimlico** *The first interior inspired by the Ecclesiological Society.*

1790–1867), surveyor to the Grosvenor Estate, who designed several other churches in Pimlico and elsewhere in London.

St Barnabas was built between 1847 and 1850; Cundy's earlier churches had followed the 'politically incorrect' Gothic style favoured by the Commissioners, but in the design of St Barnabas he broke new ground. The church was built of Kentish ragstone, and is in the Early English style (Fig 302); it was part of a group of buildings including a rectory and school. The interior has been enriched by some notable furnishings: Pugin designed the altar plate and ornaments, and later there was the reredos by

(Fig 303) **St Barnabas, Pimlico** *The font of Purbeck marble.*

Bodley and Garner (1893), a Madonna and Lady Chapel by Comper (1900), and a baptistry by F.Hunt. The font (Fig 303) is of blackened Purbeck marble, with a wooden cover; the pulpit and lectern are the original designs by Cundy. A striking series of Italianate mosaics graces the north and south walls.

Access: Nearest Underground station: Sloane Square.

(Fig 304) **All Saints, Margaret Street** *The tower and broach spire.*

All Saints, Margaret Street, St Marylebone

All Saints, Margaret Street is arguably the first great Victorian church, some would say the greatest church, of the Gothic Revival. It arose directly out of the Tractarian movement and the church was the centre of a Tractarian lay brotherhood which numbered William Gladstone among its members (Jenkins); the foundation stone was laid by Pusey on All Saints' Day 1850. It was built to the wishes of the Ecclesiological Society to embody their ideas of a church fit for sacramental worship. Their president A.J.Beresford Hope supplied many of the ideas, and a high proportion of the money. The architect, William Butterfield, had been closely associated with the Society for several years.

Butterfield (1814-1900) was born in London; he had been apprenticed to a builder, and remained a builder-architect. He was a friend of Benjamin Webb (one of the co-founders of the Cambridge Camden Society) and All Saints was his first famous church. Later he built other London churches, St Matthias, Stoke Newington and St Alban, Holborn (both badly damaged during the war), and St Augustine, Queen's Gate, Kensington (p 156). He was forceful, innovative, and was the first to introduce 'structural polychromy' into churches, bringing back colour to the interior of English churches for the first time since the Reformation. As a restorer of medieval churches, however, he was less successful, being widely felt to be rather harsh and unsympathetic. But there is no doubting the greatness of his accomplishment at All Saints.

It is difficult to appreciate the church from the outside because it is hemmed in by adjacent buildings. The site was cramped, and the architect showed great ingenuity in fitting church, choir school and vicarage round an open courtyard within such a small compass. In the courtyard,

(Fig 306) **All Saints, Margaret Street** *The north arcade and chancel.*

the eye is immediately drawn upwards by the great verticality of the tower and the lead and slate broach spire, 227 feet high (Fig 304). A large pinnacle rises from a prominent buttress next to the porch of the church. The church is built basically of red brick, with liberal use of black brick to create polychromatic effects.

As one steps inside, even on a sunny day, the dim light is all-enveloping, the silence profound, the sense of holiness awesome. And as one's eyes become accustomed to the light, the first impression is of overpowering colour: every square inch of every surface is coloured to

glorious effect. Not all have been impressed: Pevsner wrote in 1952: 'The interior is indeed dazzling, though in an eminently High Victorian ostentatiousness or obtrusiveness.

(Fig 307) **All Saints, Margaret Street** *A capital: stiff-leaf foliage carved in alabaster.*

(Fig 305) **All Saints, Margaret Street** *The north (left) and south arcades.*

It is by no means tasteful... The motifs are without exception big and graceless.' Today such an adverse reaction would be less frequent, as Victorian art, so long derided, has at last become accepted.

The church is not large, though the decoration makes it appear larger than it

(Fig 308) **All Saints, Margaret Street** *The chancel: reredos by Sir Ninian Comper (1909).*

(Fig 309) **All Saints, Margaret Street** *The Lady chapel.*

(Fig 310) **All Saints, Margaret Street** *Marble pulpit on granite columns.*

(Fig 311) **All Saints, Margaret Street** *Marble font.*

really is. The nave is short, of three bays, (Figs 305 and 306), the columns of red granite on black marble plinths. The capitals exhibit florid stiff-leaf foliage, carved in alabaster (Fig 307). There are no windows in the north wall, which is taken up with a tile picture, erected in 1873 as a memorial to William Richards, the first vicar of the church. There is no screen, the chancel being separated from the nave by a low marble wall inlaid with colours, so that, according to Tractarian principles, the altar is visible throughout the church. On either side of the chancel are iron grilles of excellent workmanship (Fig 9, p 13). The reredos (Fig 308) now consists of painted panels by Sir Ninian Comper dating from 1909; these replace earlier panels by William Dyce which had by that time deteriorated. The panels are contained in a framework of painted and gilded alabaster. Comper also decorated the vault of the chancel, and designed the lovely Lady Chapel (Fig 309) in gilded wood and alabaster.

The pulpit (Fig 310) is made of various coloured marbles, and stands on a cluster of pink granite columns. The marble font is also very fine (Fig 311). At the west end is a Jesse window, and below a further painted tile composition in memory of the second vicar, Berdmore Compton.

John Ruskin, greatest of nineteenth-century critics, wrote in *The Stones of Venice* not long after

All Saints was built: 'It is the first piece of architecture I have seen, in modern days, which is free from all signs of timidity or incapacity. In general proportion of parts, in refinement and piquancy of mouldings, above all, in force, vitality and grace of floral ornament, worked in a broad and masculine manner, it challenges fearless comparison with the noblest work of any time. Having done this, we may do anything.'

A formal description of this wonderful church fails to do justice to the church as a whole. For it is an *integrated* composition – every feature is totally dedicated to the provision of an ambience wherein the worship of God can be conducted with seemly reverence. Those of the high-church persuasion will need no encouragement to visit their shrine; but others are urged to go as well, for this church is not only an architectural experience but a religious one also.

Access: Nearest Underground station: Oxford Circus. From the station, turn east along Oxford Street; take the third turning left (Titchfield Street); Margaret Street is then the second turning on the right.

John Ruskin

The last influence moulding and endorsing the Gothic Revival, even though he turned against it in later years, was John Ruskin (1819-1900). This many-faceted genius, art critic, ethical champion, social reformer, achieved by the 1850s tremendous authority over the building designs of the period, largely by his two seminal works, *The Seven Lamps of Architecture* (1848) and *The Stones of Venice* (1851-53). His chapter in the latter book 'On the Nature of Gothic' made his reputation as the foremost critic of the day, and widened his range to include moral and ethical issues. With his enthusiasm for Venetian Gothic, he might have been thought to be another potential convert to Catholicism; but in fact his unbending Protestantism acted as a counterweight to the Catholicism of Pugin and the high-church tendencies of the ecclesiologists, and made appreciation of Gothic architecture acceptable to a much wider range of Victorian churchmanship. Like Pugin, he detested the Renaissance, and strongly disliked classical buildings. It is interesting that from diametrically opposite religious viewpoints both Ruskin and Pugin should have concluded that early Decorated Gothic was the ideal style for church building. And like Pugin and the ecclesiologists, he concluded that good architecture could be produced only by good men.

The influences advocating Gothic were by 1850 overwhelming. Pugin had provided the genius, the vision and the passion; the Tractarians and Camdenians harnessed and buttressed high-church opinion; Ruskin brought his exquisite aesthetic sensitivity and reassured the low-church faction; and for over half-a-century (with few exceptions) no other style was used. The other side of the coin was that in such a climate, classical buildings were disparaged, and, as we have seen, during the last 30 years of the Victorian era, Wren's City churches were being demolished at the rate of one every two years.

St James the Less, Vauxhall Bridge Road, Westminster

G.E. Street (1824-81) was an outstanding Victorian architect, and this is his first and best church in London. Later he designed St John the Divine, Kennington and St Mary Magdalene, Paddington (p 158). Street was an assistant to Sir George Gilbert Scott in early life, but outshone his

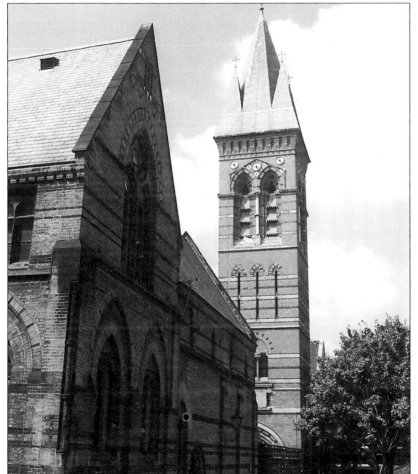

(Fig 312) **St James the Less, Vauxhall Bridge Road** *The Italianate tower.*

master in originality and boldness of effect. In the early 1850s, he travelled in France, Germany and Italy and in 1855 he published *Brick and Marble Architecture in Italy*. Both Street and Butterfield were associated with the Ecclesiological Society, and Street had clearly been influenced by All Saints, Margaret Street, where he worshipped and was a churchwarden for many years (Goodhart-Rendel). His design of St James the Less shows his imaginative use of brick to brilliant effect, and reflects his appreciation of Italian styles.

The church was built in 1859-61, and, at that time, the area was very poor. It was built at the expense of the three daughters of Dr James Monk, late Bishop of Gloucester and Bristol. From the outside, the church is seen to be part of an homogeneous group of buildings with the parish hall and school. The churchyard has excellent iron railings on its northern and eastern sides. The tremendous tower (Fig 312) is separate from the church, and has been likened to an Italian campanile (Eastlake). Built of red brick, with horizontal patterning of black brick, the belfry is surmounted by a slated pyramidal roof with an octagonal spire and pinnacles at the corners.

From the base of the tower, the church is entered via a columned porch, and then the grand spectacle of the nave, the Doom over the chancel arch and the apsidal chancel unfolds (Figs 10, p 13 and 313). Like All Saints, Margaret

(Fig 315) **St James the Less, Vauxhall Bridge Road** *The chancel.*

Street, the church is not large, the arcades again being merely of three bays. In contrast to the slender, clustered columns of All Saints, which give an effect of height, the marble columns here are short and solid (Fig 314), emphasising the horizontal plane; they support arcades of patterned brickwork with serrated edges. The roof above the nave is painted with the Tree of Jesse. The Doom is of mosaic, and is by G.F. Watts, and shows Christ with the four evangelists. The chancel (Fig 315) is richly decorated. The stone pulpit (Fig 316), by Thomas Earp, is beautifully carved, though unfortunately some of the stone has worn. At the west end of the church, the marble font (Fig 317) has an unusual iron canopy. Some excellent stained glass by Clayton and Bell can be seen in the windows of the aisles.

(Fig 316) **St James the Less, Vauxhall Bridge Road** *Stone pulpit carved by T. Earp.*

(Fig 313) **St James the Less, Vauxhall Bridge Road** *The serrated brick north arcade and the chancel.*

(Fig 314) **St James the Less, Vauxhall Bridge Road** *A capital on a short sturdy marble column.*

(Fig 317) **St James the Less, Vauxhall Bridge Road** *Marble font.*

Access: Nearest Underground station: Pimlico, or by bus from Victoria; the church is just off Vauxhall Bridge Road, on the south side.

St Peter, Vauxhall

John Loughborough Pearson (1817-98) is the third member of the trio of great architects who, apart from Scott, dominated London church-building in the 1850s and 1860s. Three years younger than Butterfield, and seven years older than Street, he differed from these two by maintaining a discreet detachment from *The Ecclesiologist* which stood him in good stead. He was thus freer to express and develop his own personality without being constrained by an approach to church architecture which was fast becoming doctrinaire. As a result, he gained inspiration from a variety of sources, both English and continental. His greatest work is probably Truro Cathedral, but in London his masterpiece is St Augustine, Kilburn (p 160); he also built St Peter, Vauxhall, reviewed here, and St John's, Red Lion Square, Holborn, which was destroyed by bombing.

Basil Clarke (b) well summarises his gifts: Pearson's 'earliest churches are in a simple fourteenth-century style: then he had an early French Gothic period (St Peter, Vauxhall): and he ended by using a thirteenth-century style (St Augustine, Kilburn)… Pearson's large churches

(Fig 319) **St Peter, Vauxhall** *Vaulting of the nave and chancel.*

are distinguished for their planning and for their construction: most of them are vaulted, and there was no nineteenth-century architect who understood vaulting better, and constructed it with more ingenuity.'

St Peter, Vauxhall was founded as part of a group of buildings intended to serve the urban poor-church, school, orphanage, a clothes workshop and soup kitchen. Pearson built it in an early French Gothic style, and it subsequently became the model for James Brooks' churches in the East End and Battersea (q.v.). It is built of stock brick, with stone dressings. The west front has a three-bay narthex and above is a rose window.

The nave (Fig 318) is divided from the aisles by low arcades; the piers are round, and the capitals intricately carved. The clerestory (Fig 319) is tall, with paired lancet windows and a circular window above each bay. The chancel (Fig 320) is apsidal, and there is a triforium stage below the lancet windows. A north chapel of two bays flanks both nave and chancel. The whole church is vaulted throughout-the ribs in stone and the cells

(Fig 318) **St Peter, Vauxhall** *The north arcade and chancel.*

(Fig 320) **St Peter, Vauxhall** *The sanctuary.*

in brick. Below the glazed triforium in the chancel are a series of paintings of the Passion executed by Clayton and Bell, who were also responsible for some of the stained glass. The reredos is very fine-made of alabaster and studded with mosaic by Salviati of Venice. Notice also the iron grille over the choir-stalls, which was highly praised by Eastlake in 1872.

St Peter's continues today to serve the local community, now vastly changed from that of the 1860s but still with an abundance of challenge. One of the church's attractions is that the Anglo-Catholic furnishings of the 1860s survive virtually unaltered (Stamp and Amery).

Access: Nearest Underground station: Vauxhall.

St Augustine, Queen's Gate, Kensington

Twenty years after the epoch-making All Saints, Margaret Street, Butterfield designed this church and again demonstrated his power by the vigor-ous use of polychromy both without and within. The west façade is bold and uncompromising: four tall lancet windows flanked by turrets on columns, and above twin bell-turrets. Horizontal bands of stone contrast with the red and yellow brickwork.

The interior is more difficult to assess. Originally it was as polychromatic as Margaret Street, but the colour was obliterated in 1925 when the church was whitened with lime wash. Fifty years later the

(Fig 321) **St Augustine, Queen's Gate** *The north arcade and chancel.*

(Fig 322) **St Augustine, Queen's Gate** *The nave and west end of the church.*

(Fig 323) **St Chad, Haggerston.**

whitewash was removed and as much as possible of the architect's polychromy was restored.

The arcades (Figs 321,322) are low, the aisles narrow and windowless. Light comes from an exceptionally tall clerestory. In the spandrels of the arcades are large stone quatrefoils. The chancel arch dominates the nave, and above it are twin internal windows which open into the roof of the chancel. The chancel floor is of coloured marble and the ceiling above is painted and gilded. In the sanctuary itself, the gilded reredos was designed by Martin Travers in southern baroque style in 1928. The alabaster pulpit, cast-iron lectern and marble font are all designed by Butterfield.

St Augustine's is perceptibly a maturer work than Margaret Street, but it has never caught the public imagination in quite the manner of the earlier church. In view of the severe damage which affected Butterfield's other two London churches (St Alban, Holborn and St Matthias, Stoke Newington) we must be grateful for its survival, and for its near restoration to Butterfield's original concept.

Access: Nearest Underground station: South Kensington.

St Chad, Haggerston

The Shoreditch and Haggerston Church Extension Fund was started in 1862 to promote the building of impressive churches for the teeming masses of London's East End-a deliberate Anglo-Catholic mission to the poor. James Brooks (1825-1901), a High-Churchman himself, designed several churches, working within a tight budget which precluded inessentials. He had a notable ability to construct churches of large capacity with very cheap materials and yet achieve satisfying results, without producing any feeling of starvation, such as may be found in some of the poorer Commissioners' churches. He built in the style of the French thirteenth century, using brick in a restrained manner, without polychromy; and in densely built-up areas he relied on tall clerestories for lighting. In Haggerston, St Columba and St Chad are his work; the former is now used by Pentecostalists, but the latter has remained true to its high-church foundation. Later, he designed the church of The Ascension, Battersea (p 161), and All Hallows, Gospel Oak (p 175), widely regarded as his finest.

Viewed from the west (Fig 323), the height of St Chad's is undoubtedly impressive, accentuated by tall clerestory windows consisting of twin lancets with a circular window above; in addition the gable of the west wall has a further round window above the clerestory. There is no tower, just a short timber spire at the crossing.

(Fig 324) **St Chad, Haggerston** *The nave and chancel.*

(Fig 325) **St Chad, Haggerston** *The chancel.*

(Fig 326) **St Chad, Haggerston** *The south chancel chapel.*

The church inside (Fig 324) is dignified and lofty. Stone columns separate the nave from the narrow, windowless aisles, and above is a timber roof. The chancel (Fig 325) is of two bays with an apse, and is divided from the nave by an iron screen; both the chancel and the south chancel chapel (Fig 326) are vaulted in brick, with stone shafts and ribs. The stained glass is by Clayton and Bell.

Access: By bus from Liverpool Street Station.

St Mary Magdalene, Warwick Estate, Paddington

A few years after the building of St James the Less, Street was asked to

design a church in Paddington by worshippers who attended All Saints, Margaret Street, and who wanted a similar church nearer to their home. A constricted site became available, and the result was St Mary Magdalene – a building more restrained, mellower, less strident than St James the Less, but equally original and exciting. Building proceeded in stages between 1867 and 1873.

(Fig 327) **St Mary Magdalene, Paddington.**

In contrast to the earlier church, the emphasis throughout is on verticality, perhaps dictated by the narrowness of the site. This is shown above all by the south-east tower (Fig 327), tucked into a corner between the south transept and chancel, which soars up to a striking octagonal belfry conspicuously marked by alternating bands of brick and stone; above rises the stone broach spire. The chancel is tall and polygonal, and its gabled west end terminates in a small bell-turret. The building is generally in the Early English style, as shown by the lancet windows, single in the aisles, paired in the chancel, and arranged in triplets in the clerestory, but continental influences, especially Italian, still remain.

The nave is unusual because of the asymmetry

(Fig 328) **St Mary Magdalene, Paddington** *The west windows and north arcade from the chancel.*

(Fig 329) **St Mary Magdalene, Paddington** *The vaulted chancel and south arcade.*

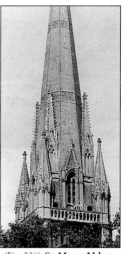

(Fig 330) **St Mary Abbot, Kensington** *The base of the spire.*

of the aisles; the south is spacious, the north reduced to a vestigial passage-way. This narrowing of the north aisle is compensated for by extra elaboration of the arcade-massive octagonal piers alternate between narrow cylindrical ones (Fig 328). In contrast, the south arcade (Fig 329) has widely spaced multishafted piers. Above both arcades are a series of statues in canopied niches. The clerestory is tall, and above is a wagon roof, the ceiling painted by Daniel Bell.

The vaulted chancel is eight steps higher than the nave, and is divided from it by a low screen. The reredos and the statues in the nave were carved by Thomas Earp, and there is some excellent stained glass by Henry Holliday. Below the south aisle is a crypt, with the chapel of St Sepulchre, decorated by Comper in 1895.

Access: Nearest Underground stations: Warwick Avenue or Royal Oak.

St Mary Abbot, Kensington

St Mary Abbot's, the parish church of Kensington, is so called because the abbey of St Mary, Abingdon acquired land in Kensington after the Norman Conquest, and the medieval church remained in the hands of the abbey until the Dissolution. The church was rebuilt in 1697, but by the 1860s it was decided that a new edifice was required-and who should build it but the foremost architect of the day?

And so Gilbert Scott built this church nearly 30 years after St Giles, Camberwell (p 146). In the interval had come the great churches built by Butterfield, Street and Pearson, but Scott had remained immune to influences from his great, but slightly younger, contemporaries. As a result, St Mary Abbot's remains a rather conventional middle-class church, neither high nor low, for a comfortable middle-class suburb. Undoubtedly, the finest part of the church is the spire (Fig 330), 278 feet tall, an entrancing confection of crockets and pinnacles, said to be based on St Mary Redcliffe at Bristol. Another external feature which has been widely praised is not by Scott at all-the vaulted cloister leading to the south porch. This was added in 1889-93 by Micklethwaite and Somers Clarke.

The church is faced in Kentish ragstone, with the interior of Corsham stone and shafts of Irish marble. It is built in a correct Early English style (Fig 331), with nave, chancel, and double transepts projecting from the east end of the nave. The altar and reredos are by Clayton and Bell. The hexagonal pulpit has inlay panels in carved frames, and dates from 1697. The best monument (Fig 332) is that to the Earl of Warwick and Holland (1721), step-son of Joseph Addison,

(Fig 331) **St Mary Abbot, Kensington** *In the Early English style.*

(Fig 332) **St Mary Abbot, Kensington** *The Earl of Warwick and Holland (1721) by Guelfi.*

(Fig 333) **St Augustine, Kilburn.**

St Augustine, Kilburn

'Is there anywhere a Victorian church which is entirely harmonious, which is pleasing without and within, which lacks neither prettiness nor grandeur, which invites the eye both to dwell and to proceed, which is in short quite beautiful? There is, and this is it!' Thus E. and K. Young (b) describe St Augustine's, Kilburn,

showing his lordship seated languidly in Roman costume; it is thought to be by Guelfi, who had been brought from Rome by Lord Burlington (Whinney [b]).

Access: Nearest Underground station: High Street, Kensington (almost opposite).

and I endorse their judgment — this is, I think, the most beautiful Victorian church in London.

(Fig 334) **St Augustine, Kilburn** *The spacious and magnificent interior.*

(Fig 335) **St Augustine, Kilburn** *The rood screen and chancel.*

(Fig 336) **The Ascension, Lavender Hill** *The nave and screen.*

St Augustine's was designed by J.L.Pearson in 1870, and the body of the church was complete by 1877; the tower and spire followed 20 years later. The west façade is dominated by a large rose window, set above four lancets; on either side are short turrets with small stone spires. At the north-west corner rises the very tall (254 feet) brick-built tower (Fig 333), with stone spire and corner pinnacles. The total effect is majestic, and decidedly more French than English in inspiration.

The interior is breathtaking, and again French influences abound. Derived from the cathedral at Albi is the internal arrangement of the buttresses which are pierced with double aisles (Fig 11, p 13). The arcades are low, with simply carved capitals, but above is a gallery which all but circumnavigates the church (Fig 334), bridging over the north and south transepts; again the galleries are divided into compartments by the pierced buttresses. The transepts are spacious, and on the south side there is an apsidal chapel of St Michael. The chancel is separated from the nave by an elaborate stone screen with five arches and much sculpture (Fig 335); and there is also a stone reredos. Above are two tiers of lancet windows. Both nave and chancel are superbly vaulted (Figs 11, 334, 335) in the architect's finest manner.

Access: Nearest Underground station: Kilburn Park. From here, proceed south along Cambridge Avenue, and the church will soon appear ahead on Kilburn Park Road.

The Ascension, Lavender Hill, Battersea

James Brooks' church of the Ascension, built in 1873, five years after St Chad's, shares many similarities with his churches in the East End (p 157). All are large, lofty, brick-built churches, employing a style which leans heavily on early French Gothic, with short and rather wide lancet windows. At Lavender Hill, Brooks was grappling with a site on steeply sloping ground, and a large portion of his budget was expended on the foundations. This so upset the authorities that Brooks was relieved of his responsibilities and the church was completed by Micklethwaite, but still to Brooks' design.

The external appearance is imposing, especially the apsidal east end. The lofty interior is lit by exceptionally tall clerestory windows which more than compensate for the complete absence of windows in the aisles (as at St Chad, Haggerston). The nave is tall, with a wagon-roof. The arcades in the nave are low (Fig 336), the capitals uncarved. In contrast, the piers in the chancel are much closer to each other than in the nave (Fig 337), and the capitals have stiff-leaf foliage. The imposing rood-screen was added in 1914.

Access: Nearest Underground station: Clapham Common; from here, walk along Long Road, turn right into Cedars Road, and then left into Lavender Hill.

(Fig 337) **The Ascension, Lavender Hill** *The chancel.*

Low-church architects

The Ecclesiological Society did not always get its own way, and throughout the mid-Victorian period there was considerable demand for new churches from the low-church or Evangelical wing of the Church of England. Architects who catered for this market (called 'rogue architects' by Goodhart-Rendel) were much less constrained by *The Ecclesiologist's* demand for 'correct' interpretation of Gothic styles, and were freer (sometimes too free!) to indulge their own idiosyncrasies. As Stamp and Amery observe, 'The Evangelicals had no use for an ecclesiological 'correct' Gothic church with a deep chancel. They needed a large space to contain a large congregation within earshot of the pulpit. They were, however, prepared to use the Gothic style and even those mannerisms employed by architects such as Butterfield and Street.' So their churches are primarily for preaching after the eighteenth-century mode, but transformed into the elaborate Gothic of the high Victorian era. The churches of Joseph Peacock, S.S. Teulon and E.B. Lamb are the finest of this group. For many years it was fashionable to ignore or deride their efforts; and it is fair to say that no low-church building can compare with the glories of All Saints, Margaret Street, St James the Less or St Augustine, Kilburn. Nevertheless, as a group they exhibit many fascinating aspects, and a just appreciation of them is long overdue.

St Simon Zelotes, Chelsea

Joseph Peacock (1821–93) designed this and the following church in 1859 and 1865 respectively, and much later Holy Cross, Holborn (1887). St Simon Zelotes is built on a rather narrow site of Kentish ragstone, with dressings of Bath stone; and the exterior has a rugged appeal, the eye being drawn mainly to the west front (Fig 338). Here twin lancet windows, separated by a central

(Fig 338) **St Simon Zelotes, Chelsea.**

(Fig 339) **St Simon Zelotes, Chelsea** *The nave, north arcade and transept.*

buttress, are surrounded by diaper decoration within the arch which supports a rather too tall bell-gable.

The interior consists of nave, aisles, transepts, and a chancel not deep enough for the ecclesiologists but possibly dictated by the constraints of the site. 'Never can there have been more architecture in less space', wrote Goodhart-Rendel. 'Peacock was determined that no visitor should be dull for a single moment.' In spite of the ragstone exterior, structural polychromy is obtained inside through the brickwork, which, though basically white, is enlivened with red and black brick. Marble columns, with carved capitals, separate the nave and aisles, and there are unusual arcades of differing heights in the transepts (Fig 339). Marble is also used in the pulpit and reredos and in the shafts of the east window. The quality of the furnishings is high, and the overall effect is pleasing and homely, without any conscious striving after grandeur.

Access: Nearest Underground station: Sloane Square. From here, walk along Sloane Street and take the first turning left (Cadogan Gardens) leading into Cadogan Street; the third turning right is Moore Street, and the church is at the end on the right.

(Fig 342) **St Stephen, Gloucester Road** *The font.*

(Fig 340) **St Stephen, Gloucester Road** *The nave and north arcade.*

(Fig 341) **St Stephen, Gloucester Road** *The reredos and south wall of the chancel.*

St Stephen, Gloucester Road, Kensington

This church, also by Peacock, was one of the many churches carved out of the parish of Kensington during the incumbency of John Sinclair, vicar of St Mary Abbot's from 1842-75 (Brooks and Saint). It started life as a low-church foundation, but later moved towards the high-church wing.

Outside it is faced in stone, and originally the interior, like the preceding church, had polychromatic brick; this has now been whitened, giving an impression within of brightness and cheerfulness-a welcome contrast to some of the more overpowering mid-Victorian churches. The church consists of nave and aisles (Fig 340), double transepts, and a chancel with lateral projections. Later, when the church became Anglo-Catholic, the chancel was lengthened and a fine reredos was added by Bodley and Garner in 1903 (Fig 341). At the west end are paired very tall lancet windows with a round window above; and a notable font (Fig 342), with an extraordinary painted wooden font-cover. This now soars heavenward behind the font, the mechanism for lifting it having become suspect.

Access: Nearest Underground station: Gloucester Road. From the station, turn left, cross Cromwell Road, and the church is immediately on the left.

(Fig 343) **St Mark, Dalston.**

(Fig 344) **St Mark, Dalston** *The chancel and south aisle. Note the capitals on the cast-iron pillars.*

St Mark, Dalston

Of the churches in this group, none is more remarkable than St Mark's, Dalston. Chester Cheston junr., the architect, was apparently a relatively inexperienced young man whose project became beset with difficulties. Design started in 1860, but the church was not consecrated until ten years later. The tower (Fig 343) was built in 1877 to the design of E.L. Blackburne (1803-88) in a style reminiscent of Teulon (Symondson [a])-compare Figs 343 and 348. St Mark's tower is both broad and tall, a massive brick edifice with stone dressings, large corner pinnacles at balustrade level, and a squat spirelet. The style of the body of the church is

Early English, with lancet windows paired in the aisles and arranged in groups of three in the clerestory. There is a prominent wheel window at the west end.

The interior is impressive: a large auditorium with multishafted cast-iron pillars separating nave and aisles (Fig 344), and the liberal use of notching and polychromy in brick after the manner of Street. Note the intricately carved capitals on the pillars. There is much stained glass, and a unique feature is the pair of angel windows in the roof at the junction of transepts and nave. The total effect is awesome-a low-church extravaganza which has to be seen to be believed. Visitors are positively encouraged-the church is open every day, and a notice at the door informs the congregation that the Authorised Version of the Bible and the services from the 1662 Book of Common Prayer are used.

Access: By bus 149 from Liverpool Street Station to Dalston Junction; then walk north along Kingsland High Street for a short distance, and turn right into Sandringham Road which leads to St Mark's Rise.

St Mary, Ealing

Ealing parish church was first mentioned in the twelfth century, but it is very probable that a Saxon church preceded this building. In the fourteenth century Thomas de Bradwardin was rector of Ealing for ten years from 1337; later he became Archbishop of Canterbury but died of the plague within a week of taking up the office. The medieval church collapsed in 1729, and was replaced six years later by a plain Georgian preaching-box. By the middle of the nineteenth century, it was felt that Ealing, the newly fashionable 'queen of the suburbs', deserved something better, and in 1863 the architect S.S.Teulon was appointed virtually to rebuild the church; he transformed it into the building which we see today.

Samuel Sanders Teulon, (1812-73), a devout Evangelical, pursued his architectural career in an idiosyncratic manner, oblivious to the stylistic preferences of the ecclesiologists. He was innovative and eclectic, drawing inspiration from several sources, including Norman, French Flamboyant, and even Islam (Saunders). His churches have been criticised as harsh and unsympathetic, but recently he has gained a more favourable press; how ironic, therefore, that his greatest work, St Stephen's, Rosslyn Hill, is on the point of abandonment.

St Mary's Ealing has received extravagant praise and denigration in perhaps equal measure–a sure sign that 'love him or loathe him', Teulon cannot be ignored. The exterior is dominated by the tower (Fig 345) described by Pevsner–never a fan of Teulon's–as 'elephantine'. There are large corner pinnacles, and on each side a lower staircase turret. It was originally intended to provide a spire, but funds never became available for this.

Internally, the church is dominated by the complex cast-iron roof structure, supported by an arcade of cast-iron columns (Figs 346, 347). There are galleries on each side, and below these are a series of longitudinal brick horseshoe arches

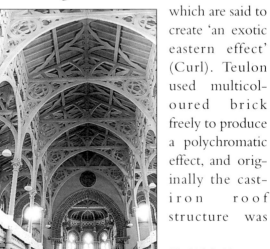

which are said to create 'an exotic eastern effect' (Curl). Teulon used multicoloured brick freely to produce a polychromatic effect, and originally the cast-iron roof structure was

(Fig 346) **St Mary, Ealing** *The cast-iron columns and roof structure, and the brick chancel arch.*

(Fig 345) **St Mary, Ealing.**

(Fig 347) **St Mary, Ealing** *The nave looking west.*

also vividly coloured; this was toned down in 1955.

Access: Nearest Underground station: South Ealing. From the station, turn left along South Ealing Road, and the church is a short distance along on the right.

St Stephen, Rosslyn Hill, Hampstead

In a book published by English Heritage as recently as 1995 (*Victorian Churches* by J.S.Curl), there is a fine photograph of St Stephen's, showing 'the polychrome interior, tough roof construction, and massive west window'. Yet when I visited St Stephen's in the same year, the church was desolate indeed: all the lower windows were boarded, pieces of masonry were flaking off, the signs of vandalism and decay

unmistakable. But disheartening though the exterior is, the shock when one goes inside is palpable: totally unexpected was the stench pervading the building, due presumably to animal remains; the nave full of clutter of every conceivable type, heaped higgledy-piggledy in utter confusion. But if the visitor holds his breath, ignores the floor and looks upward to the roof, the arcades, the west window, something of the majesty of Teulon's finest church may yet be appreciated (Fig 4, p 11, taken in May, 1996).

Can anything be done to rescue St Stephen's? Time is running out, and if decay persists for much longer the point of no return will be reached, and demolition will be inevitable. Restoration would be vastly expensive, but restoration for what purpose? There is clearly no congregational need for St Stephen's as a church; the priest who has titular responsibility for St

(Fig 348) **St Stephen, Rosslyn Hill** *Crumbling into ruins?*

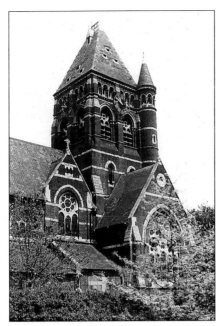

(Fig 349) **St Stephen, Rosslyn Hill** *The nave and west window.*

Stephen's also cares for the excellent and much-loved All Hallows, Gospel Oak (p 175), just a short distance away. Yet all who care for Victorian churches should clamour for something to be done soon to rescue this church from its present disgraceful state before it is too late.

The quality of St Stephen's, built in 1869, was immediately recognised by Eastlake, who three years later wrote a lyrical account in his great work, *A History of the Gothic Revival*, and accompanied it with a woodcut illustration. 'The walls are mainly built of fine hard brick ranging in colour from pale gray to Indian red, the admixture of which tints gives them at a little distance a rich stippled texture which is very agreeable. Stone and granite are also largely employed for the quoins and dressings... The interior is sumptuously decorated, especially at the east end, where the apse is groined, and its walls are inlaid with gilt mosaic work. The chancel arch is corbelled out on panelled blocks enriched with sculpture in high relief, illustrating the life and death of St Stephen. The pillars of the nave arcade are cylindrical, supported on high plinths, and crowned with boldly carved capitals varying in design. The arches are admirably proportioned to the height and plan of the church... though fastidious critics may object to the notched and billet-moulded edges of the brickwork introduced... The open-timbered roof over the nave is an excellent example of constructive skill.'

Teulon built this church in the style of muscular French Gothic which was in vogue in London in the 1860s, but which thereafter rapidly fell out of favour. The architect's brusqueness, stark contrasts and uncompromising originality later gave way to a gentler style. The tower (Fig 348) over the chancel has a steep capped pyramidal roof. Internally, the roof has massive trusses of arched braces, queen-posts and collar purlins (Fig 349). In the spandrels of the arcades are alabaster roundels commemorating among others, Latimer (said by Clarke [a] to be there as a protest against romanising practices in the Church of England). There is a short polygonal apse behind the chancel, and both these are vaulted (Fig 4).

Access: There is no access to the interior. Nearest Underground station: Belsize Park; from here, turn right up Haverstock Hill and St Stephen's is a short distance along on the right.

St Martin, Gospel Oak

Few London churches have aroused more conflicting critical opinion than St Martin's, Gospel Oak. It was built at the expense of a wealthy Evangelical philanthropist, John Derby Allcroft,

(Fig 350) **St Martin, Gospel Oak.**

(Fig 351) **St Martin, Gospel Oak** *The nave and chancel, with four square piers supporting the roof.*

specifically to bring the gospel to the poor. The architect was Edward Buckton Lamb (1806-69), who throughout his career remained immune to the gospel according to Pugin. And the style chosen was a very idiosyncratic form of Perpendicular-not fashionable in the 1860s and not favoured by the high-church party. It is not surprising that the church was ignored by *The Ecclesiologist* and that for decades it languished in obscurity.

St Martin's rehabilitation began with a paper by Goodhart-Rendel on *Rogue Architects of the Victorian Era* (1949); and in 1970 it was furthered by Sir John Summerson in his stimulating account of two Victorian churches (St James the Less and St Martin's), in which he analysed why the former had won universal acclaim and the latter opprobrium or neglect (Summerson [d]). He awarded considerable praise to Lamb for his originality and stubborn inventiveness, and as a

result it is now possible to appreciate St Martin's at its face value, perhaps for the first time in 130 years.

The church is built of Kentish ragstone, and the most obvious external feature is the tower (Fig 350) which, though not especially tall, is distinctly unusual. At the base is the entry porch; at the first stage, the three-light belfry windows are tall, and above is the clock-face. Then follows a prominent string-course and an upper stage leads to a parapeted, formerly pinnacled, summit, with the stair-turret projecting higher. The interior is unorthodox and enormously impressive: basically a cruciform church, with a central space in which four square piers support a hammer-beam roof (Fig 351). The piers themselves are unique-from each face rises a shaft which extends up to a

(Fig 352) **St Martin, Gospel Oak** *The octagonal chancel.*

capital which supports the beams of the roof. From this central area, the nave is prolonged westwards without aisles, and to the east is an octagonal chancel (Fig 352), austere in a low-church manner, and with the Lord's Prayer and Ten Commandments flanking the chancel arch. The transepts are wider with Tudor windows. 'Lamb inserts a spacious rectangular bay into each of the angles formed by the intersection of the cross-axes. The result is that the church seems to centre, like a nine-square plan, on the crossing. There is an almost magical flow and interpenetration of spaces, and this is emphasised by the magnificently daring timber roof, with its sinewy rafters and web-like surfaces.' (E.N.Kaufman in Howell and Sutton, 1989).

More than enough time has now elapsed for a fresh evaluation of St Martin's: the passions and prejudices of earlier generations have passed away, and today's visitor, and worshipper, can make his or her own appreciation of Lamb's forceful and unconventional design. It is a church that is difficult to describe: go and see it!

Access: Nearest Underground stations: Belsize Park, Chalk Farm and Kentish Town. By bus, take the 24 from Victoria or 46 from King's Cross; alight at Malden Road outside the Priory RC Church, and St Martin's is a short distance away in Vicars Road.

Eastlake and the later Victorian and Edwardian Eras

During the 1840s and 1850s, as we have seen, the principles upheld by Pugin, the ecclesiologists and, later, Ruskin predominated, and after initial experiments with Early English, most architects settled for the Decorated style of the first half of the fourteenth century as the ideal for Christian buildings. During the 1850s, influenced by the travels and writings of Ruskin and Street, there was greater emphasis on foreign, especially Italian, Gothic styles, readily detected in such churches as St James the Less. From about 1860 onwards, French medieval styles became fashionable, following the publication in France of the works of Viollet-le-Duc. These produced more massive churches, e.g. St Peter, Vauxhall and the East End churches of James Brooks, described as 'muscular' Gothic. After about 1870, the French influence waned, but even as late as 1884 St Cuthbert, Philbeach Gardens was built in a solid Burgundian style.

By 1870, the first phase of the Gothic Revival may be said to be over; Pugin had been dead for 20 years; Ruskin was turning his attention increasingly to social issues; *The Ecclesiologist* had ceased publication . In 1872, Charles Eastlake (1836-1906), Secretary of the Royal Institute of British Architects and later Keeper (but never Director) of the National Gallery, published *A History of the Gothic Revival*, which has since become a classic. Tracing the Revival from its origins in the eighteenth century, Eastlake carries the story to 1870 and, considering that he was writing when the Revival was still in full swing, it is remarkable that his judgment of recently erected buildings has been largely endorsed by posterity. In the specific field of London churches, his account of Gothic edifices from St Luke, Chelsea (1820) to St Stephen, Rosslyn Hill (1869) has stood the test of time.

The publication of Eastlake's work conveniently divides the Victorian Gothic Revival into two nearly equal halves; and from his time until just before the First World War, Gothic continued to reign unchallenged. From about 1880 onwards, and extending into the Edwardian coda of the Gothic era, the Arts and Crafts movement began to influence not so much the design of churches as their furniture and fittings. The work of William Morris and the Pre-Raphaelites revolutionised attitudes to art and design, and stained glass in particular retrieved a vigour which it had not known for several centuries; although much Victorian glass is insipid and sentimental, the best achieved a standard which has not since been excelled. In London, the churches of St Cuthbert, Philbeach Gardens, Holy Trinity, Sloane Street and St Cyprian, Clarence Gate are perhaps the best examples of this flowering of late Victorian inspiration; here, the Arts and Crafts devotees endeavoured to recapture the delicate craftsmanship of English wood- and stone-work of the late Gothic period. It was not surprising that hand in hand with this should come the rehabilitation of Perpendicular, despised in the 1840s but now highly regarded by late Victorian architects such as Bodley, Sedding and Comper. The finest example of Victorian Perpendicular is Bodley's Holy Trinity, Prince Consort Road, perhaps the only late Victorian or Edwardian church which ranks with the earlier giants of the Gothic Revival by Butterfield, Street and Pearson. The wheel of the Revival had ironically come full circle, since it was Perpendicular that Savage had somewhat naively used way back in 1820 for St Luke's, Chelsea.

St Mary of Eton, Hackney Wick

George Bodley (1827-1907) was related to Sir George Gilbert Scott by marriage, and he became Scott's first pupil (Clarke [a]). He developed a restrained style of architecture, less fussy than some of his predecessors, and although he favoured the Decorated style, as Pugin and *The Ecclesiologist* enjoined, it was late Decorated, almost Perpendicular, and in his later churches Perpendicular prevailed. Apart from the church in Prince Consort Road (p 176), his best works are outside London – e.g. the Church of the Holy Angels, Hoar Cross, Staffordshire, St Augustine, Pendlebury, Lancashire and St Mary the Virgin, Eccleston, Cheshire. In the capital he was also responsible for St Mary of Eton, and St Michael, Camden Town. For over 25 years, he worked in

(Fig 353) **St Mary of Eton, Hackney Wick** *The church is by George Bodley (1890), the tower by Cecil Hare (1912).*

partnership with Thomas Garner, and it is not easy to apportion responsibility for features of the design.

The church of St Mary of Eton is not, as some may imagine, dedicated to a hitherto unknown Buckinghamshire saint, but was founded by Eton College as a mission to one of the poorest parts of east London. The mission began in 1880, and lasted until 1965, an exceptionally long association for a charitable endeavour. The church followed ten years later, being built between 1890 and 1892.

St Mary's is built of brick, with dressings of Bath stone, and the east end faces the main road (Fig 353). The tower was not completed until 1912, and is by Cecil Hare. The church forms part of an attractive group of mission buildings designed by Bodley. The interior is plain but not austere, 'bearing the marks of expensive simplicity' (Symondson [a]). The nave and chancel are continuous, and the piers of the arcades rectan-

(Fig 354) **St Mary of Eton, Hackney Wick** *The 'expensive simplicity' of nave and chancel.*

gular and without capitals (Fig 354). The nave roof is boarded and of the wagon type, and the tracery of the east window is Decorated verging on Perpendicular, so typical of Bodley. There is a south-east chapel.

Access: By 26 bus from Liverpool Street Station.

St Michael and All Angels, Bedford Park

Richard Norman Shaw (1831-1912) was a pupil of G.E.Street and built two notable London churches, St Michael and All Angels, Bedford Park, and Holy Trinity, Latimer Road, Paddington. Outside London he designed All Saints', Leek, Staffordshire, and All Saints', Batchcott, Shropshire. He blended with great freedom an interest in Gothic, particularly Perpendicular architecture, and, especially in his domestic buildings, features of the seventeenth and early eighteenth centuries (the 'Queen Anne' style); and echoes of this can be found in his churches, especially St Michael's.

The concept of Bedford Park, the 'first garden suburb', planned to appeal to middle-class families with aesthetic pretensions but limited means, was the creation of a property speculator, J.T.Carr. In 1877, he asked Norman Shaw to design some dwellings there and the church of St Michael and All Angels followed shortly afterwards.

The church is unique in its combination of styles from the fifteenth and seventeenth centuries – it is almost as if St Anne and St Agnes (p 90) had a Perpendicular interior! The exterior is very pretty, though now so heavily shaded with trees that it is difficult to assess, yet alone photograph. Above the trees are the timber lantern and white balustrades (Fig 355) reminiscent of the seventeenth century; below, Gothic takes over with large Perpendicular windows and, internally, Perpendicular arcades.

Inside, the dominant feature is the woodwork, all painted a rather dull green: the roof timbers, the screen, the benches, the bases of the columns. Yet the proportions of the building are most satisfying (Fig 356); the arcades have a rhythmic sweep which carries the worshipper onwards (and upwards) to the chancel. The pulpit, dating from 1894, is also in the style of two hundred years earlier.

(Fig 356) **St Michael, Bedford Park** *The roof timbers and north arcade.*

Access: Nearest Underground station: Turnham Green.

(Fig 355) **St Michael, Bedford Park** *The lantern and east end, glimpsed between the trees.*

St Cuthbert, Philbeach Gardens

St Cuthbert's is another church which was carved out of the parish of Kensington in the nineteenth century. The architect was H.R.Gough (1843-

(Fig 357) **St Cuthbert, Philbeach Gardens.**

1904), and he designed a lofty brick-built church in a Cistercian style of Gothic, said to be based on Tintern Abbey (Harwood and Saint). The church was built between 1884 and 1887 (Fig 357); note the unusual flèche on the roof.

Inside, the nave is separated from the aisles by piers of polished Torquay marble (Fig 358). The interior is made memorable because of the sumptuous furnishings and fittings in the style of the Arts and Crafts Movement. Many of these were the work of members of the early congregation, who were organised into guilds, some with professional guidance. Gough himself designed the pulpit (Fig 359), sedilia, rood-loft and font. Many of the other fittings are by W.Bainbridge Reynolds, especially the metal screens, the altar rails and the elaborate lectern of wrought-iron and copper. The gigantic

(Fig 358) **St Cuthbert, Philbeach Gardens** *The highly-ornate interior.*

(Fig 359) **St Cuthbert, Philbeach Gardens** *The pulpit, and north arcade and aisle.*

reredos was designed by the Reverend E.Geldart in a medieval Spanish style, and installed just before World War One.

Access: Nearest Underground station: Earl's Court. Take the Warwick Road exit, and turn right and then left into Philbeach Gardens.

Holy Redeemer, Exmouth Market, Clerkenwell

This church, built in 1887-88, could fairly claim to be the greatest non-Gothic Anglican church

built in London during the reign of Queen Victoria. It is thoroughly Italian in inspiration and style, both within and without; its only rival might be Christchurch, Streatham,

(Fig 360) **Holy Redeemer, Clerkenwell** *The vaulted nave and Corinthian columns.*

(Fig 361) **Holy Redeemer, Clerkenwell** *The ciborium above the high altar.*

built nearly 50 years earlier.

The architect of Holy Redeemer is John Dando Sedding (1838-91), one of the most inventive of the late Victorian architects. In his youth, he was a pupil of G.E. Street, and then he worked in the West Country. He moved to London in 1874, and became one of the leaders of the Arts and Crafts Movement, being influenced by John Ruskin and William Morris. Like Street, like Pugin, he was much interested in good craftsmanship, and this is apparent in the furniture and fittings of his churches. The two major stylistic influences which are apparent in his churches are the Renaissance (which predominates at Holy Redeemer) and a free rendering of English Perpendicular (as at Holy Trinity, Sloane Street); it is remarkable that these two churches, so different in style and inspiration, were built within a year or so of each other. Underlying all Sedding's work was an intense belief in the redemptive value of art, and he was above all dedicated to bringing beauty and light into the benighted lives of the urban poor.

And so at Clerkenwell he designed a building so unorthodox by contemporary Anglican standards that it is usually mistaken for a Roman Catholic church. The church is closely invested by neighbouring buildings so that it is easy to overlook the grandeur of the design. The west front has a round-headed doorway; above, a horizontally striped façade encloses a circular window, and higher still is a large pediment. To the right is an Italian campanile, in the lower storeys of which is the clergy house, and to the left a parish hall; these were designed by Henry Wilson, Sedding's associate, and were completed in 1906.

The interior is startling – dominated by a series of giant Corinthian columns on each side which rise from panelled pedestals direct to an unbroken entablature (Fig 360); the capitals of the columns were carved by F.W.Pomeroy. Above is a groined vault. There is no screen or sanctuary reserved from the common gaze: the nave opens to a ritual area where the High Altar is surmounted by a gigantic ciborium or baldacchino (Fig 361), closely modelled on that in the church of San Spirito in Florence. Behind the High Altar is a Lady Chapel, built in 1895 to the design of Henry Wilson.

Access: Nearest Underground station: Farringdon. Turn left out of the station, then right into Farringdon Road. After crossing Clerkenwell Road, Exmouth Market is the sixth turning on the right.

Holy Trinity, Sloane Street, Chelsea

Holy Trinity quickly followed the preceding church, being built between 1888 and 1890. Although generally in Perpendicular style, medieval features are not slavishly followed, and Sedding's originality keeps breaking through; certainly no English church of the fifteenth century looks at all like Holy Trinity! From the opposite side of Sloane Street, the west front (Fig 362) is dominated

by the huge west window flanked by turrets. Above the window, an ogee-curved moulding supports a statue of Christ.

The interior is tremendously impressive. Immediately one's eye goes to the great east window (Fig 363), filled with stained-glass by the Pre-Raphaelite Sir Edward Burne-Jones. Here are 48 figures of apostles, patriarchs, kings, prophets and saints, and above are depicted the Fall, the Crucifixion and the Annunciation – a vast panorama of colour. Further excellent stained glass is in the windows of the north and south aisles.

The wide nave is separated from the narrow aisles by octagonal pillars which soar up to the vault without interposed capitals, something never seen in genuine Perpendicular. The original vaulted wooden roof was destroyed in the war, and has been replaced by a plaster structure. The impressive marble pulpit stands on a circular alabaster shaft, with four smaller columns of porphyry. Equally rich is the font (Fig 364) at the west end; the bowl is fashioned from a single piece of Mexican onyx, and behind is a relief designed by Henry Wilson.

Wilson was Sedding's pupil and successor, and he completed the church after Sedding's death in 1891. He was responsible for the altar-rail (destroyed in an air-raid in 1940), and the railings outside the church in Sloane Street. He also was

(Fig 363) **Holy Trinity, Sloan Street** *The great east window.*

(Fig 362) **Holy Trinity, Sloan Street** *The west window and twin turrets.*

(Fig 364) **Holy Trinity, Sloan Street** *The font of Mexican onyx, with behind a relief by Henry Wilson.*

(Fig 366) **All Hallows, Gospel Oak** *The tall arcades and west window.*

(Fig 367) **All Hallows, Gospel Oak** *The vaulted chancel by Giles Gilbert Scott.*

(Fig 368) **All Hallows, Gospel Oak** *The low arcades dividing the chancel from the side chapels.*

involved in the design of much of the fittings in the choir-stalls. The chancel (Fig 365) is separated from the nave by a green marble parapet; to the north of the chancel is the Lady Chapel, and on the south side is the Memorial Chapel, or Chapel of the Resurrection. The Lady Chapel has a baldacchino on four Ionic columns of red porphyry; this is said to be the first Anglican church to have a baldacchino over the altar (Symondson [b]). Throughout the east end of the church, the richness of the furniture and fittings is clearly apparent; and the work of many of the leading members of Arts and Crafts Movement is represented.

Holy Trinity is rather engagingly described as 'the Cathedral of the Arts and Crafts Movement', and its importance as a repository of some of the finest work in this tradition is now well recognised. In fact, this recognition was in the nick of time, for it is not long since closure and demolition of the church were

(Fig 365) **Holy Trinity, Sloan Street** *The south wall of the chancel.*

contemplated. Fortunately, a campaign led by the Victorian Society and Sir John Betjeman was successful, and in the past seven years a major programme of restoration, aided by grants from English Heritage and the diocese of London, has preserved this glorious church for posterity.

Access: Nearest Underground station: Sloane Square. The church is in Sloane Street, a few yards north of Sloane Square.

All Hallows, Gospel Oak

Some 20 years after his East End churches (p 157s), in 1889, James Brooks designed All Hallows, Gospel Oak in a mellower, maturer style. Pevsner described it as Brooks' masterpiece. The exterior is imposing: the great circular west window, flanked by stunted towers; the central gable of the nave above the window; and separate gables of the aisles rising on each side of the towers. The north and south elevations are replete with enormous buttresses which ascend to the eaves.

The interior is clean and light, the nave being divided from the aisles by very tall columns without capitals (Fig 366); at the top may be seen the beginning of vaulting ribs which were never completed. The aisles are as tall as the nave. The vaulted chancel (Fig 367) was completed just before World War One by Giles Gilbert Scott (1880-1960); it is lower than the nave, and there are side-chapels, separated by lower arcades (Fig 368). The design is restrained and dignified. Altogether, this is one of the finest of the late Victorian churches.

Access: Nearest Underground station: Belsize Park.

St Luke, Kidderpore Avenue, Hampstead

Even in 1872, Basil Champneys (1842-1935) had been mentioned by Eastlake as one of the up-and-coming architects of the later Gothic Revival, apparently on the basis of his design for the church of St Luke, Kentish Town, built in 1868-70. St Luke's in Kidderpore Avenue is 30 years later (1898), and the difference between the

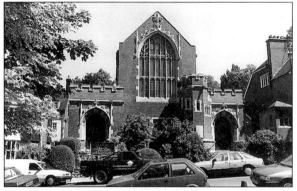

(Fig 369) **St Luke, Kidderpore Avenue.**

(Fig 370) **St Luke, Kidderpore Avenue** *The east end of the north arcade and the chancel.*

two is instructive. The earlier church is notable especially for its bold tower, very much in the 1860s fashion (see Figs 343, p 164 and 348, p 167) the church, perhaps, of a young man making a statement; St Luke's, Kidderpore Avenue is prettier, softer, more modest, and has no tower. Also, by the 1890s there was a perceptible lessening of the strict Gothic historicism which had prevailed 30 years earlier, allowing architects

to be much freer in their adaptation of Gothic styles for the *fin de siècle*.

So at Kidderpore Avenue, Champneys' design is less rigorous, more engaging: the west front (Fig 369) is positively picturesque, and the interior (Fig 370) is correspondingly undogmatic. The piers are polygonal, and rise without capitals to support the clerestory, which has two three-light windows in each bay. Nave and chancel are not divided.

Access: Nearest Underground station: Finchley Road; then by bus.

Holy Trinity, Prince Consort Road, Kensington

This church claims lineal descent from a chapel known as Holy Trinity, Knightsbridge, which was attached to a leper hospital founded by Westminster Abbey in the early sixteenth century. In succeeding centuries, the chapel was rebuilt, repaired and extended several times, until at the

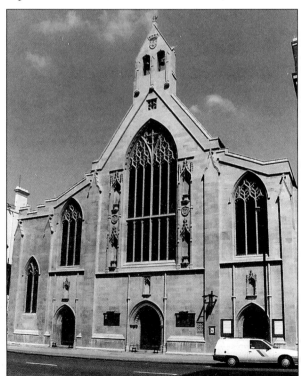

(Fig 371) **Holy Trinity, Prince Consort Road.**

end of the nineteenth century the site in Knightsbridge was sold and the church rebuilt in Prince Consort Road near to the Royal Albert Hall. Bodley was appointed architect, and this was Bodley's last church, and his finest in London. It was built between 1901 and 1903, and can fairly be claimed to be the capital's finest Edwardian church.

It was built on a rather cramped site, and the orientation of the long axis is north-south. It is built of Bath stone, now gleaming after a recent cleaning (Fig 371). It is in the Perpendicular style, Bodley's favourite in his later years, and the window tracery of the triple-gabled façade is very fine.

The interior is immediately impressive (Fig 372), one of the finest interiors in London. The great height of the Perpendicular arcades, and the intricate tracery of the chancel window give nobility, and the overall colours of brown and gold provide artistic unity. The stained glass in the chancel window is by Burlison and Grylls. The reredos (Fig 373) below depicts the Crucifixion, with figures of the Virgin Mary and St John; on each side are angels, and below scenes of the Nativity and Annunciation. The oaken pulpit, designed by the architect, has carved figures of the Evangelists and Fathers of the early church.

Bodley died not long after the building of Holy Trinity; and the reredos was installed in his memory; his formal memorial by Edward Warren is to

(Fig 373) **Holy Trinity, Prince Consort Road** *The sanctuary.*

the left of the pulpit. But in a greater sense, the whole of this marvellous church is his memorial, and his legacy to the people of London. *Access:* Nearest Underground station: South Kensington.

St Cyprian, Clarence Gate, St Marylebone

Sir John Ninian Comper (1864-1960) was a Scot, and one of the leading architects of the first part of the twentieth century. He was articled to Bodley and Garner, and like Bodley was much attached to Perpendicular styles expressed in a modern idiom. Indeed, referring to St Cyprian's, he wrote of Perpendicular as 'the last manner of Gothic architecture which for us in England is the most beautiful of all' (quoted in Bumpus). Like Street and Bodley, he took infinite pains with interior furnishings, believing that the purpose of a church is 'to move (people) to worship', not to express the age in which it was built or the individuality of the designer (quoted by Clarke [b]). His exquisite furnishings have already been noted at St Barnabas, Pimlico and St Mary Magdalene, Paddington and elsewhere, but here at St Cyprian's is the finest Comper interior in the country.

The church was founded in 1866 by the Reverend Charles Gutch who laboured in what was then a poor part of London for over 30 years in temporary premises – the landlord, Lord Portman, disapproved of Gutch's high-church leanings, and it was only after Gutch's death in 1898 that a site for a permanent building was made available. Comper designed the church, which was opened in 1903.

The exterior is not imposing, as with a good

(Fig 372) **Holy Trinity, Prince Consort Road** *The north arcade and chancel.*

(Fig 374) **St Cyprian, Clarence Gate** *The Perpendicular arcades and rood-screen.*

many other London churches; the plain brick building, with buttresses and late Perpendicular windows, scarcely prepares one for the splendour within. On entering, the visitor is immediately struck with the tallness and simplicity of the arcades (Fig 374); but the crowning glory is the gilded and fan-vaulted rood-screen which stretches across the east end of the church (Fig 375); similar parclose screens demarcate the chapels on each side of the chancel. The tall font-cover, similarly gilded, stands sentinel at the west end (Fig 376). *Access:* Nearest Underground station: Baker Street; the church is in Glentworth Street.

All Saints, Tooting Graveney

Tooting is first mentioned in 666 as one of the

(Fig 375) **St Cyprian, Clarence Gate** *Looking through the screen to the west end of the church.*

(Fig 376) **St Cyprian, Clarence Gate** *The font and font-cover.*

(Fig 377) **All Saints, Tooting Graveney.**

(Fig 378) **All Saints, Tooting Graveney**
The south aisle.

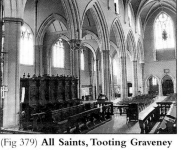

(Fig 379) **All Saints, Tooting Graveney**
The nave, looking westward from the choir.

(Fig 380) **All Saints, Tooting Graveney**
The nave, looking east.

(Fig 381) **All Saints, Tooting Graveney**
The chancel.

properties of the Abbey of Chertsey founded in that year. In the Domesday Book (1086), 'Totinges' is described as belonging to the Abbey of St Mary's of Bec in Normandy – hence Tooting Bec.

'Graveney' derives its name from the Lord of the Manor of Gravenel, who held the manor of Lower Tooting from Chertsey Abbey.

All Saints' church was built in 1904-06 at the expense of Lady Augusta Brudenell-Bruce in memory of her late husband, and she nominated her husband's friend, Canon John Stephens, as trustee. He chose to build in this area of south London, which at that time was rapidly expanding, and Temple Moore was appointed architect.

Temple Lush-ington Moore (1856-1920) had been trained in the office of George Gilbert Scott, son of Sir George Gilbert Scott, and succeeded to his practice around 1890. Moore designed many churches, both urban and rural, over half of them in his native Yorkshire, and restored and sensitively preserved a number of others (e.g. Hexham Abbey). His greatest church in London is All Saints', Tooting, a spacious building of noble proportions dwarfing its surroundings of semi-detached suburbia.

The church is built of stock brick, with a south-western tower. In general, it is designed in the Decorated style, at least as far as the window tracery is concerned. The external appearance is a little austere (Fig 377) in contrast to the highly impressive interior.

The nave is flanked by double aisles (Fig 378), giving great breadth to the church. The columns of the main arcade are multishafted (Fig 379), and in each aisle is a secondary arcade of slender columns of Forest of Dean stone, the arches being displayed transversely. Both nave (Fig 380) and aisles are vaulted in timber. The chancel (Fig 381) is richly furnished and expensively laid out, and beyond is a simple Lady Chapel. Many of the furnishings were imported from Italy by Canon Stephens; he introduced the walnut choir-stalls from Bologna, the Florentine candlesticks and the medieval wrought-iron chancel grille from a church near Lake Como. The reredos in the Lady Chapel is French work of the sixteenth century. Canon Stephens' insistence on the tall reredos behind the high altar, interrupting the view of the eastern windows from the west wall, led to the resignation of Temple Moore. This altarpiece contains a copy of Velasquez' *Christ Crucified*. Other furnishings, font, pulpit etc. were by Sir Walter Tapper, who took over after Temple Moore's resignation.

Access: Nearest Underground station: Tooting Bec.

The Annunciation, Bryanston Street, St Marylebone

With the building of the church of The Annunciation just before World War One, the long series of churches of the Gothic Revival in London comes to a fitting conclusion. The church was built on the site of the former Quebec chapel, which dated back to 1788 and

(Fig 383) **The Annunciation, Bryanston Street** *The east window, reredos, altar and sedilia.*

was one of a number of proprietary chapels in St Marylebone (Young [a]). For its date, The Annunciation decidedly looks back to the Revival that was then ebbing: there is no trace of modernism, no hint of the twentieth century which was thirteen years old at the time of its design. Yet the quality of the building and its furnishings command our appreciation.

The architect was Sir Walter Tapper (1861-1935), who had worked with Bodley and Garner, and signs of Bodley's influence are not hard to find; and it is built in the early Perpendicular style which Bodley favoured. The south façade towers above Bryanston Street (Fig 382), with windows only in the clerestory stage; there is an elaborate Perpendicular east window and a small rose window.

Inside, the church impresses by its dignity; it is not large, but gains tremendously from its height and by the vaulting. There is a north aisle only, divided from the nave by an arcade. Excellent woodwork abounds: especially impressive is the rood-screen, intricately carved in each aspect. The church has been lovingly furnished and the chancel (Fig 383) is especially notable; in the floor is a fine brass to the Reverend Bernard Shaw, the first incumbent.

Access: Nearest Underground station: Marble Arch.

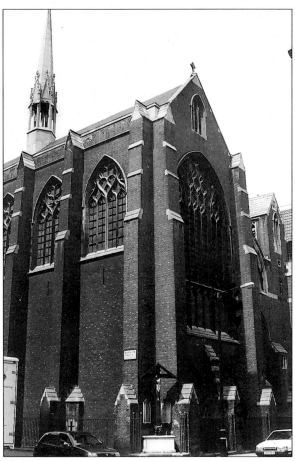

(Fig 382) **The Annunciation, Bryanston Street.**

The Twentieth Century

THE catastrophe which overwhelmed Europe in August, 1914 had the most far-reaching effects in church architecture, as in almost every other field of human endeavour. Indeed consciously or not, we have all been living in the shadow of those events ever since. In the much-quoted words of Sir Edward Grey, 'The lamps are going out all over Europe; we shall not see them lit again in our lifetime.' It was not only the appalling scale of the casualties which afflicted every country involved: not only the flower of a generation that was lost: the survivors, or many of them, lost something as precious as life itself – religious faith. So the churches emerged from the deluge permanently weakened, and this became reflected in the scale, the style and the reputation of church architecture.

Even before 1914 the force of the Gothic Revival was flagging; after the war, Gothic was dying – even though several of the churches built between the two World Wars exhibit features which might be described as 'stripped' or 'reduced' Gothic (e.g. St Gabriel, North Acton; St Thomas, Hanwell). Gradually a genuinely new style emerged, although the Modernism of Le Corbusier and Gropius hardly arrived in England before 1950, and had remarkably little impact on church architecture in London. That new style, neither classical nor Gothic, is still with us, and will evolve in the third millennium in directions which none can foresee.

The reaction against everything Victorian was, of course, profound, and lasted until well after World War Two. Gone were the vast auditoria built in the eighteenth and nineteenth centuries; a more intimate style of worship suited the mood and the need of the times. The new architecture was spare and functional, decoration sparse or non-existent; churches were modest in size, as was appropriate for reduced congregations and lessened expectations. And, for the first time in three hundred years, many leading architects just did not design churches: they turned instead to domestic, public, industrial architecture. Sir Edwin Lutyens' St Jude-on-the-Hill (1908) is possibly the last London parish church designed by an architect of international renown; in the twentieth century, architectural reputations were made elsewhere. A further factor inhibiting the design of outstanding churches was sheer lack of funds: government aid was out of the question, and none of the churches could afford buildings of the scale and luxuriance of previous centuries.

During the inter-war years, and in the early years after World War Two, churches continued to be built in a traditional longitudinal design of nave and chancel. Thus when, in 1951, the competition for the new Coventry Cathedral was held, Sir Basil Spence's successful design was of this type. The Liturgical Movement, which had its origins in Lutheran Germany, was advocating that for modern congregational worship the altar should be at the centre, visible and accessible all round – a complete reversal of the ecclesiologists' position a century earlier. In the 1950s, the movement gained ground, and the first London church fully to reflect this was St Paul's Bow Common, built in 1958, though some of Cachemaille-Day's churches show tentative signs of the influence of such ideas. By 1959, when the competition for the new Catholic cathedral of Liverpool was held, it was clear that only a central plan would win (Pevsner: South Lancashire). So in the space of a decade, there was a complete change in the prevailing style of new parish churches: it is notable that of the churches reviewed here built since 1958, all are more or less 'in the round', with the exception of St Paul's, Harringay.

In the Church of England, some years after the Second World War, at last the tide turned: the high-church party dominant since the days of the Oxford movement and the Cambridge Camden Society lost impetus, and the Evangelicals gained ground. The decision after prolonged debate to ordain women was the most obvious result of this change, and led some to convert to Rome, as Pugin and Newman had done a century and a half earlier. Was the ascendancy of the low-church party a further factor limiting the desire for large and impressive churches?

It is hard to make a selection of twentieth-century churches which the visitor may find rewarding. In many cases, we are too close to the situation to make a definitive judgment. Few churches have been built in central London since 1918, but there are hundreds in the outer suburbs, and it is here that we must go in search of excellence. I have included in the section which follows a few churches from the late Edwardian years, and some from the inter-war period which reflect the gradual change of style. But it is really only after 1950 that church architecture finally threw off its Gothic antecedents and embarked single-mindedly in new directions. Some of the churches which follow are generally accepted as the finest that have been built in the capital in this century; others are relatively little known. But I hope the reader will share my view that some of them at least

are first-class, showing continuing vitality of design in ways which can enrich the worship of today's congregations. In the 1990s, two especially stand out – and both are entirely new replacements for churches destroyed by fire – St Paul's, Harringay, a miniature treasure-house of art; and St Barnabas, Dulwich. In their very different ways, both are full of hope for the third millennium.

St Jude-on-the-Hill, Hampstead Garden Suburb

Hampstead Garden Suburb is one of the most successful and influential exercises in town planning of the early years of this century, drawing on earlier experience in Bedford Park, Port Sunlight, Bournville and Letchworth. At its heart, around Central Square, is a group of buildings – the parish church of St Jude with its vicarage, the Free Church and its manse, and the Institute-designed by Sir Edwin Landseer Lutyens (1869-1944).

Lutyens, the greatest English architect of the first third of the twentieth century, had made his reputation in the domestic field and had been influenced by the Arts and Crafts Movement and by Norman Shaw. A 'strong feeling for architectural geometry is always present in his work' (Watkin) and this may be sensed at St Jude's.

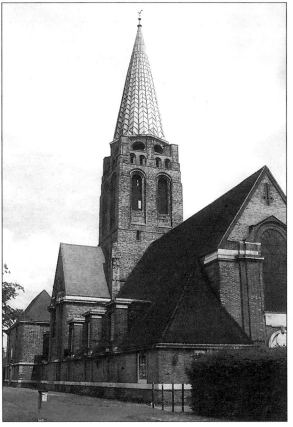

(Fig 384) **St Jude-on-the-Hill, Hampstead Garden Suburb.**

(Fig 385) **St Jude-on-the-Hill, Hampstead Garden Suburb** *The nave, domed crossing and chancel.*

The design of this church broke new ground: at the height of the Edwardian era (1909) the repudiation of Gothic is total; there is not a pointed arch in the building. The only nineteenth-century church at all comparable is perhaps the atypical but seminal Christchurch, Streatham (1842), but there the campanile is separate from the nave. St Jude's, however, is cruciform, the central tower rising above the crossing to be surmounted by a Byzantine spire – majestic, imperious, Elgarian (Fig 384). Across the square, the Free Church has to be content with a low dome – is there a symbolic meaning here? – but there is no denying the effectiveness of the juxtaposition of the whole group.

The interior is quieter but no less impressive. Again the overall style is Byzantine, but it is a modern, western interpretation of Byzantium. Above the nave is a barrel-vaulted roof, with a ceiling painted by Walter Starmer showing New Testament scenes (the wise men and the shepherds, Christ healing the blind and the lepers, and Christ stilling the storm). The dome over the crossing (Fig 385) is painted with the Cruci-fixion, and over the chancel is Christ carrying the Cross. The west window, also designed by Starmer, is a complex composition, with St Jude holding the cross in his right hand and this building in his left; below is his symbol, a ship, and above Christ in glory surrounded by the symbols of the four evangelists. The aisles have open timber roofs (surely not structural?). The floor of the chancel is of brick and marble, and on each side are iron screens dating from the early eight-eenth century. To the north is the Lady Chapel,

the oldest part of the building, and to the south is the chapel of St John.

Access: Nearest Underground station: Golders Green. Walk north along Finchley Road, taking the fourth turning on the right (Hoop Lane). Continue along Meadway, then turn left into Heathgate which leads to Central Square.

St Barnabas, Shacklewell Row, Hackney

Like Eton College at Hackney Wick (p 170), the Merchant Taylors' School founded a mission in Hackney, and the church there was built by Sir Charles Reilly (1874-1948) in 1910. It is completely hidden by the mission building and surrounding structures, and so the exterior is plainly built of yellow stock brick and concrete.

The church is not at all Gothic, the overall style again being Byzantine (cf Holy Redeemer, p 173). And the sparseness of the decoration makes it very much a product of the early twentieth century, even if the full age of modern architecture has not yet arrived. For its day, therefore, it looks forward to a future bleaker than the Victorians imagined – it is almost as if the cataclysm of 1914 had already happened

The nave is covered with a concrete tunnel-

(Fig 386) **St Barnabas, Shacklewell Row** *The nave and chancel.*

vault supported by brick arches. There are passage aisles on each side, with segmental arcades, the aisles extending westwards to the baptistry. Between nave and chancel is a tall wooden rood and screen, added in 1934, with reading-desks or ambones on each side (Fig 386). At the east end is the chancel and apse, and a small south chapel. The cross and candlesticks in the chancel are of hammered pewter, and were designed by the architect (Clarke [b]). I found the church, now nearly 90 years old, very consonant with modern attitudes to worship.

Access: Not an easy church to find, and the church is usually closed. From Liverpool Street Station, by bus 149 to Kingsland High Street, and walk along Shacklewell Lane; Shacklewell Row is on the left.

St Silas the Martyr, Kentish Town

The relatively unknown architect, Ernest Charles Shearman (1859-1939) was articled to Charles Barry junr. and assisted him for nine years. He built six churches in the London area, one of which (St Matthew, Wimbledon) was destroyed in an air-raid in 1944. St Silas was his second church, and one of the best of his works. The earliest building here was a mission church dating from 1884, but the present church was built between 1911 and 1913. In style it is unmistakably modern, although with undoubted Gothic overtones: but it certainly looks forward to the twentieth-century future rather than back to the Gothic Revival past. The architect himself wrote that 'the church is designed on the basilican model with wide nave affording the whole congregation an uninterrupted view of the sanctuary and the pulpit; the altar being the centre of the apse.' I am indebted to Dr John Salmon for many of the

(Fig 388) **St Silas, Kentish Town** *The arcades and chancel.*

details of this church and of St Gabriel's, North Acton.

From the exterior (Fig 387), the eastern apse, the high-pitched roof and the narrow clerestory windows are striking, and all are typical of Shearman. The building is austere, of brick, with hardly any stone dressings. There is a semicircular window to the right of the double porch; above is a gabled transept. There are no windows in the aisles.

The nave (Fig 388) has acutely pointed arcades of six bays, the columns without capitals; there is a narrow aisle on each side. The chancel is divided from the nave by a low brick wall and is dominated by the ciborium above the altar (Fig 389), designed by the architect. The chancel ends in a polygonal apse; behind the sanctuary a nar-

row ambulatory leads to the Lady Chapel. The whole church is bedecked with statues and shrines, enriching the basic simplicity of the building. As Salmon says, Shearman designed this church to be beautified by its people; and so it is.

(Fig 389) **St Silas, Kentish Town** *The high altar with ciborium above.*

(Fig 387) **St Silas, Kentish Town.**

Access: Nearest Underground station: Chalk Farm. Turn left out of the station, and then right into Prince of Wales Road; the church is in St Silas Place, a short distance along on the left.

St Alphage, Burnt Oak

The 1920s were not, on the whole, a vintage time for church-building: perhaps the horrors of the war were too recent, and modern architecture was not really in its stride. But here in Burnt Oak, then a newly developing suburb, was built a church which 70 years later still has the power to evoke admiration and awe. The exterior is of brick, but the stone for use within was quarried in France and worked in England. At the time of St Alphage's consecration, in 1926, the Great War was still fresh in people's minds, and the stonework was said to symbolise Anglo-French amity.

(Fig 390) **St Alphage, Burnt Oak.**

(Fig 391) **St Alphage, Burnt Oak** *The nave from the sanctuary.*

St Alphage's is, I believe, the only Anglican church designed by the architects, Messrs Nicholas and Dixon-Spain. The exterior (Fig 390) is incomplete, for lack of funds prevented the building of the planned south-eastern tower. Perhaps because of this, the south elevation seems rather monotonous, the repeated clerestory and aisle windows perhaps a little too regular. But there is a good west front, with an arcaded loggia forming the main entrance to the church.

Doubts, however, are swept away by the interior: nave and chancel are undivided, so the whole church is a unity, amply lit by the tall clerestory windows Fig 391). The cross-beams under the roof are panelled and decorated, and the suspended rood was painted by Gertrude Halsey. Simple arcades divide the narrow aisles from the nave. Over the pulpit is a sounding-board which would be a credit to the eighteenth century! The altar stands on a marble floor, and behind it a shallow apse, flanked by tall pilasters, helps to focus attention on the sanctuary. St Alphage's, which had a narrow escape from fire a few years ago, is beautifully decorated and maintained, and the interior is a joy to behold. When it was first built, the interior decor was said to be 'a study in ivory and gold', and it is still so today.

Access: Nearest Underground station: Burnt Oak. Turn right out of the station and walk towards the A5; then turn left, and after a short distance St Alphage's will be found near the corner with Montrose Avenue on the left.

St Saviour, Eltham

St Saviour's is one of the most striking and effective churches of the inter-war years; perhaps, indeed, the finest London parish church of the first half of this century. The architect is Nugent Francis Cachemaille-Day (1896-1976), who had worked as a young man for Goodhart-Rendel. He travelled in Germany and used expressionist forms in a dramatic way (Harwood and Saint).

(Fig 392) **St Saviour, Eltham.**

His design for this church won the Medal and Diploma of the Royal Institute of British Archi-

(Fig 394) **St Saviour, Eltham** *The sanctuary.*

(Fig 393) **St Saviour, Eltham** *The interior, looking west.*

tects in 1933.

Built of purple-grey brick, the exterior (Fig 392) is stark and uncompromising, earning the local nickname of 'Colditz'. The east end is higher, the sanctuary being continued upwards in the form of a tower.

The atmosphere inside is much lighter, warmer and more attractive. The dom-

(Fig 395) **St Saviour, Eltham** *Figure of Christ, by Donald Hastings.*

inating impression is of tremendous verticality (Fig 393), conveyed by the tall piers whose angles face the nave and by the very tall leaded windows at the west end and in the chancel (Fig 394), the latter being filled with blue glass. The full height of the sanctuary is emphasised by the black, red and green cross which hangs against the background of the east window, with the reredos below. The most moving feature is the concrete statue of Christ by Donald Hastings behind the altar (Fig 395). To the south of the sanctuary is the Lady Chapel.

The nave windows are of pre-cast concrete units, filled with yellow and white glass. On each side are narrow passage-aisles, and there is a west gallery. Beneath the gallery is the font, made of cast concrete. The pulpit is of brick, with jagged projections, jutting out in a prickly manner.

Access: By train from London Bridge to Mottingham Station, then by bus 124. The church is in Middle Park Avenue.

St Thomas the Apostle, Hanwell

St Thomas' church, Hanwell is a rare treasure – a modern suburban building, well-loved and cared for, and nearly always open and welcoming to visitors. It was built in 1933-34, the rather

(Fig 396) **St Thomas, Hanwell** *The east end, with the Calvary by Eric Gill.*

traditional architect being Sir Edward Maufe (1883-1974). He was said to be strongly influenced by Swedish work in the 1920s (Bingham et al), and his best-known building in England is Guildford Cathedral. But good though

that is, many feel that it is exceeded by this church in Hanwell.

The design is clean, and, like many great buildings, deceptively simple, but furth-

(Fig 397) **St Thomas, Hanwell** *The nave, looking west.*

er study reveals unexpected subtleties. It is built of brick from South Wales, and the first surprise awaiting the visitor is the arresting Calvary by Eric Gill at the east end, facing the main road (Fig 396), the cross of the sculpture forming the tracery of the circular east window.

The interior (Fig 397) is dominated by the reinforced concrete vault with a series of arches which extend laterally to the aisles. As is usual in churches of this period, the aisles themselves are

narrow, and the windows are very tall lancets with a hint of Y-tracery. The sanctuary (Fig 398) is notable for the attractive reredos, designed in 1911

(Fig 398) **St Thomas, Hanwell** *The sanctuary, with the reredos by Cecil Hare.*

by Cecil Hare for the church of St Thomas, Portman Square, and transferred here in 1934. Fittings from the 1930s include the font and statue of St Christopher in the children's chapel by Vernon Hill, and stained glass in the west window by Moira Forsyth.

Access: Nearest Underground station: Boston Manor. Turn left out of the station, and walk along the main road to the church, which is on the left-hand side.

St Gabriel, Noel Road, North Acton

Built in 1934, more than 20 years after St Silas, Kentish Town, externally this is one of Shearman's most impressive suburban churches (Fig 399). It is especially noted for the four-petal rose window on the wall of the south transept, with broad cruciform transom and mullion. Other windows have tracery more or less in the Decorated style.

(Fig 399) **St Gabriel, North Acton.**

The apsidal east end has tall narrow lancets, the north aisle no windows at all. There is no tower.

The interior (Fig 400) has narrow aisles, with arches both transverse and longitudinal, some

exhibiting notched brick. There is a west gallery. The chancel (Fig 401) is raised, and on the south side are two Gothic arches opening into the Lady Chapel. On each side of the entrance to the chancel are terracotta plaques

(Fig 400) **St Gabriel, North Acton** *The nave from the east end.*

(Fig 401) **St Gabriel, North Acton** *The north arcade and apsidal east end.*

by George Tinworth (1843-1913). That on the north shows Moses and the serpent, and on the south Christ being taken down from the Cross. They were commissioned by the Prince of Wales (later Edward VII) for his wife Alexandra and were exhibited in the Paris Exhibition of 1878, and were formerly in Sandringham Church, Norfolk. They were given to St Gabriel's in 1930. The unusual font is probably Victorian. The interior has recently been reordered for worship, with the altar being placed centrally.

Access: Nearest Underground station: North Acton. Turn right out of the station into Victoria Road. Cross Western Avenue and walk along Horn Lane. Noel Road is the second on the right and the church is on the right-hand side.

Holy Cross, Greenford

Central Middlesex, the epitome of inter-war semi-detached suburbia, still retains a series of small medieval village churches near to the Western Avenue, mostly dating from the thirteenth century – Ickenham, Northolt, Greenford (Fig 402) and Perivale – and all are worth visiting. Between the two World Wars, there was a massive growth of population in this area, and the old churches suddenly became quite inadequate. At Greenford, the happy solution was to build a new church alongside the old one, resulting in two churches in one churchyard.

(Fig 403) **Holy Cross, Greenford** *The new church, built in 1939-41.*

(Fig 404) **Holy Cross, Greenford** *The timbered nave and roof.*

(Fig 402) **Holy Cross, Greenford** *The medieval church, typical of the small village churches of Middlesex.*

Sir Albert Richardson (1882-1964), a champion of traditional styles, designed the new church which is notable especially for its open timbered interior. Externally, the church rather dwarfs the old building, but the juxtaposition is not displeasing. At the west end is an oriel window and a small spire (Fig 403) and clerestory windows extend the whole length of the building. Inside, a complex array of timber posts ascend to the roof, with arched braces and tie-beams (Fig 404); the design is said to be derived from contemporary Swedish building (Bingham et al). The altar was originally at the east end, but is now accorded a more central site, in conformity with modern liturgical practice.

Access: Nearest Underground station: Greenford. The church is half a mile to the south along Oldfield Lane, passing beneath Western Avenue by means of a pedestrian underpass.

St James, Clapham

Twenty-four years after the building of St. Saviour's, Eltham, Cachemaille-Day designed this new church of St James, Clapham, to replace an earlier building destroyed in the war. The exterior is certainly less forbidding than Eltham, and even more than at that church, the architect has seized the opportunity to bring colour into the church, especially in the low east window. The following description is abstracted from an article by the

(Fig 406) **St James, Clapham** *The nave, looking east.*

architect in a booklet published to record the opening of the church in 1958.

The exterior has been carried out in a modern but not aggressively functional design, and a fairly lofty tower, also of modern design forms part of the scheme (Fig 405) and is surmounted by a tall cross in wrought iron. The building is based on a reinforced concrete frame, and the architect was able to impart an interesting arched form to the roof of somewhat vault-like character (Fig 406). Instead of the usual large east window, a wrought-iron grille has been fixed on a reinforced concrete beam over the glazed lower window. Compensation for the absence of a large east window may be said to lie in the west window (Fig 407), which is a large one, and represents in scenes the history of the three saints in the New Testament given the name of James. The east end is slightly apsidal, the sanctuary (Fig 408) being chastely and simply furnished. The Holy Table has been given due emphasis as the principal furnishing of the church; the stained glass window behind is full of colour and was executed by Mr Erridge of Messrs Wippell & Co Ltd; it shows the supper at Emmaus. There is ample space along the communion rail for communicants to circulate to and fro without congestion, and it is possible to walk completely round the Holy Table. (Here, Cachemail-

(Fig 405) **St James, Clapham.**

(Fig 407) **St James, Clapham** *The west end of the nave.*

(Fig 408) **St James, Clapham** *The chancel.*

(Fig 410) **All Saints, Hanworth.** *Intersecting concrete arches, with the lantern above and corona of lights below.*

le-Day is showing his emerging debt to the Liturgical Movement.) The Table, choir and clergy stalls, pulpit and lectern are made of African mahogany; all these furnishings were provided by Wippells. At the west end, the font, of veined Italian marble, came from the bombed church of St Saviour, Ealing.

Access: Nearest Underground station: Clapham Common. From the station, cross to Clapham Park Road; walk along this road and then fork right into Park Hill, where the church is on the right.

All Saints, Hanworth

After Clapham, Cachemaille-Day proceeded to Hanworth, where he provided some much-needed architectural distinction for a dull part of suburbia. All Saints church was built in two stages – the west end, consisting of entrance-hall or narthex and two chapels, was constructed in 1951-52, the body of the church following some five years later. The increasing influence of the Liturgical Movement is plain to see at Hanworth, for here the altar is appreciably nearer to the

congregation than in his earlier churches.

From Uxbridge Road, the church appears as a series of horizontal rectangular blocks, topped by a cylindrical lantern (Fig 409) – a rather severe façade, though not so forbidding as at Eltham. But internally, as at Eltham, the prospect is radically different. At Clapham, the series of intersecting arches compose a visually attractive pattern (Fig 406) in the ceiling; at Hanworth, the arches are reduced to two, and the visitor looks up with wonder at these two arches which soar up to the ceiling (Fig 410). These two are complemented by a semicircular arch which demarcates the sanctuary. The nave is lit from above by the central lantern, beneath which is a corona of lights. The plain stone altar is surrounded by gold leaf, and above it is a Cross with the figure of Christ crowned and in priestly vestments (Fig 411). To the right of the altar is the figure of the Virgin Mary with the Christ Child, and to the left Christ the King, holding an orb (symbolising the world) surmounted by a cross. The floor of the sanctuary is laid with mosaic.

Cachemaille-Day's three churches reviewed here offer stimulating comparisons and contrasts

(Fig 409) **All Saints, Hanworth.**

(Fig 411) **All Saints, Hanworth.** *The sanctuary.*

– Eltham (1933), the work of a young man of great promise; Clapham (1953) mellower, the promise has in large part been achieved; Hanworth (1957) mature, almost his final word. Outside London, his major churches include The Epiphany, Gipton, Leeds (1937), St Michael, Wythenshawe, Manchester (1938), St Barnabas, Tuffley, Gloucester (1942) and St Edmund, Northwood Hills, Middlesex (1962).

Access: By train from Waterloo to Feltham station; then by bus

St Paul, Bow Common

This church has often been described as the first significant church to be built in London after the war and is now generally recognised to be a milestone in architectural and liturgical development (Harwood and Saint). Over a century previously, the Ecclesiologists had decreed that the altar, the focus of worship, should be in a deep chancel, on steps elevated above the floor of the nave, and enriched with furnishings full of liturgical symbolism. With St Paul's, Bow Common, the wheel has come full circle: the plain altar has been brought from the chancel into the very centre of the church, and around the Lord's table gather the people of God.

The original St Paul's, consecrated in 1858, was destroyed in the war and the new church was begun exactly a hundred years later. Bow Common has always been a socially deprived area, though of course the character of the population has been transformed since the first church was built. The architects were Robert Maguire (b 1931) and Keith Murray (b 1929), who had been influenced by the ideas of the Liturgical Movement, and the exterior they designed (Fig 412) must have been arrest-

(Fig 412) **St Paul, Bow Common.**

(Fig 413) **St Paul, Bow Common** *The altar brought forward into the body of the church.*

ing when it was first built. The church is square, built of brick and concrete with a glass lantern above.

It is, however, the interior that impresses with its quiet dignity and deceptive simplicity. On entering, every aspect leads to the central altar (Fig 413), plain, and covered with an unadorned canopy, and lit by the lantern above. At the east end is a further altar where the Sacrament is reserved. The central area is demarcated by a peristyle (a square of columns), which provides for an internal processional route when required. Above the columns is mosaic decoration by Charles Lutyens.

Access: Nearest Underground station: Mile End. Turn left out of the station, and walk along Burdett Road. The church is on the left after passing under a railway bridge.

St Mary Magdalene, Peckham

The first church of St Mary Magdalene, Peckham, was built in 1841, when the parish of Peckham was formed out of Camberwell parish. This church was destroyed by a land-mine in 1940, and after the war the parish was united with the parish of St Mark's, which had also been bombed. The new St Mary's was built in 1961-62,

(Fig 414) **St Mary Magdalene, Peckham.**

to the design of Robert Potter (b 1909) and Richard Hare (1924–89).

It is a striking new church (Fig 414), full of light, with the plain communion table at the centre. All that goes on inside can be seen from without, which perhaps takes away some of the mystery from the worship of the church. Yet what is lost from the sense of mystery is more than compensated for by the increase in accessibility and intelligibility – for this is emphatically a church for the people – people of all backgrounds and of all races. The pews are displayed round three sides of the communion table. Above, a geometrical pattern of triangles, rhomboids and quadrilaterals is outlined by the steeply rising roofs, with steeply pitched triangles facing the exterior to the four points of the compass (Fig 415).

Access: By bus from Victoria or Camberwell Green to Queens Road Peckham station; then walk east for a short distance along Queens Road, and turn right into St Mary's Road; the church is on an island site in that road.

(Fig 415) **St Mary Magdalene, Peckham**
The light-filled interior.

St John, Peckham

This church in Meeting House Lane was built in 1965-66, to the design of David Bush (b 1925), replacing four earlier parish churches. The opportunity was taken to design a building suitable for the needs of modern worshippers, and

(Fig 416) **St John, Peckham.**

for this it may be thought to be outstandingly successful. For by the 1960s, the traditional nave-and-chancel church had become quite unsuitable and inflexible for the needs of an inner-city multi-ethnic community such as Peckham.

The main feature of the exterior is the 'tower' – an upward angular prolongation of two-way sloping roofs (Fig 416), giving startling emphasis to the building. The interior of the church proper is dark, even on a sunny day (in contrast to the preceding church); then, as one's eyes become adjusted, a moving scene is revealed. The overall effect is of horizontality, with the windowless east wall appearing triangular in shape (Fig 15, p 15). The altar and the rood above are lit by a cleverly concealed window. The organ pipes high on the left wall act as a foil to the rood. On the right, a stained glass window of seven lights diffuses an array of colours throughout the church; the theme is the Creation, and the design is by Susan Johnson. Notice also the sculpted figure of a mother holding a baby aloft; this was made in fibreglass with a bronzed finish by Ron Hinton.

The stone font was carved from one of the columns of the bombed church of St. Jude.

Access: By bus from Victoria or Camberwell Green to Peckham High Street. Turn into Meeting House Lane, and the church is towards the end of this road on the left.

St Laurence, Catford

The original church of St Laurence, Catford, was built in 1887, the architect being the same H. R. Gough who designed St Cuthbert, Philbeach Gardens. This church fell victim to civic ambition in the 1960s, when the London Borough of Lewisham decided that the site was required for a municipal centre (in the event, only a car park ensued); an alternative site became available 200 years along Bromley Road.

(Fig 417) **St Laurence, Catford.**

The new church was designed by Ralph Covell (1911-88) and was built in 1967-68. It has a 25 foot spire (likened by some to a rocket-launching pad) above the Lady Chapel; and the church itself is a circular building surmounted by a corona (Fig 417). Internally (Fig 418), the pews are displayed around the altar, and modern abstract stained glass set in concrete, designed by T.

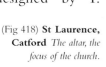

(Fig 418) **St Laurence, Catford** *The altar, the focus of the church.*

Carter Shapland, is prominent in windows all round the building; he also designed the illuminated glass cross above the altar. The glass contributes greatly to the ambience of the church. The Lady Chapel contains a wooden carving in jacaranda wood of the martyrdom of St Laurence by Samuel Wanjau, from Kenya.

Access: Nearest station Catford (trains from Victoria). From the station, walk east along Catford Road to the cross-roads; turn right into Bromley Road, and the church is a short distance along on the left.

St Mary, Barnes

The medieval parish church of Barnes, with its Victorian and Edwardian extensions, was severely damaged by fire on 8 June 1978, and the opportunity thus provided was taken to design a new church retaining as much as possible of the older fabric. The architect was Edward Cullinan (b 1931).

The visitor approaching from the south-east sees the attractive east end of the former south aisle (originally the chancel), with three stepped lancet windows and a small vesica above (Fig 419). Beyond is the south aisle, porch and south-west tower – the latter of brick with facings of stone, dating from the later fifteenth century, adorned with clock and sun-dial. Behind, the new building projects to the north, incorporating a stair-turret at the west end and a vestry at the east.

Before the fire, St Mary's had three parallel independently roofed sections: the medieval nave and chancel had become a south aisle, while to the north had been built a Victorian nave and later a north aisle. The architect evolved an ingenious design, extending the church to the north, providing a new crossing, with projections east and west. The Victorian east window had survived the fire and at the request of the congregation was placed above the altar as a visible

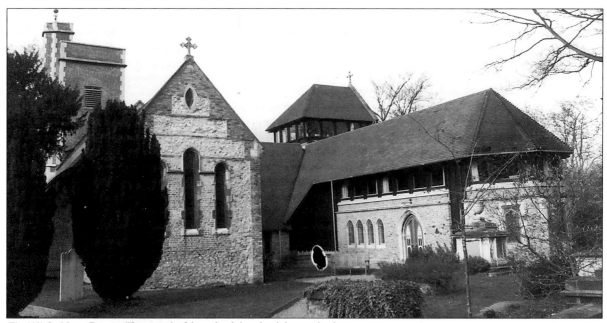

(Fig 419) **St Mary, Barnes** *The east ends of the medieval chancel and the new church.*

(Fig 420) **St Mary, Barnes** *The medieval chancel, now the Langton chapel.*

reminder of the former church.

As one enters through the south porch, an exciting duality of perspective is revealed. To the right is the medieval chancel, now the Langton chapel with its three lancet windows (Fig 420); traces of medieval wall-painting, long hidden by plaster, were revealed here by the 1978 fire. Ahead, through two columns which had previously been inserted in the north wall of the medieval nave, is the new church oriented north-south. The architect describes his work in the church guide: 'Two trusses of multi-coloured steel and wood cross the medieval nave and extend across the top of the columns to become dual ridge trusses for the new nave (Fig 421). Secondary ridge trusses cross the main ridge trusses and run east and west to form transepts. At this crossing and above the altar the high wall containing the old window is raised to a high gable that forms a vertical back to a

(Fig 421) **St Mary, Barnes** *The new nave, looking south from the altar.*

crossing lantern.' The duality is evident in that the medieval nave and chancel can be used for small congregations facing east; or the medieval nave can be read as a narthex or vestibule to a much larger church with a wide nave facing north.

Access: Nearest Underground station: Hammersmith; then by bus.

St Paul, Brentford

This is another church which has been transformed in a similar way, by throwing open the north arcade and building a new nave. Like

Barnes, Brentford is an ancient settlement, and a church has been there since at least the twelfth century. St Paul's church was built in 1867, but by the early 1990s it was in a dilapidated state. An imaginative scheme was devised, retaining the structure of the old church (Fig 422), the chancel

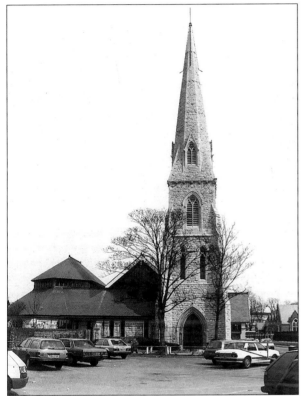

(Fig 422) **St Paul, Brentford** *The Victorian tower and spire, with the new church on the left.*

as at Barnes becoming a chapel, and a new polygonal structure built beyond the former north wall.

The architect of the new St Paul's was Michael Blee (1931-96), and the new interior is a *tour de force*. It is roughly hexagonal in plan, with three projecting triangular oratories from the north wall, each housing modern icons owing something to Byzantine traditions. The former nave, the architect writes, 'has now become a secular narthex defined by the original richly carved columns: it is these which generate the grid or pattern from which all of the remaining

structure derives... It is upon the diamond pattern generated by drawing diagonal lines through these columns that the new worship space on the axis of entry is developed: its height is the product of the Victorian columns, and the oratories owe their intimate geometry to the proportions of the columns and the angles established by the column diagonals. Even the pew supports accord with these angles.'

The visitor enters through a door above which is a sculpture of a man making tents — St Paul was a tentmaker, and

(Fig 423) **St Paul, Brentford** *The marriage of old and new in the chancel.*

the sculptor, Geoffrey Aldred, says that the angular folds in his work reflect the interior of the new building, which itself is a tent-like structure. In the vestibule, the former nave, is a social area, and on the right, the former chancel is now a chapel (Fig 423) where hangs a painting of the Last Supper by John Zoffany (*c.*1733-1810). Through

(Fig 424) **St Paul, Brentford** *The new church.*

the former north arcade, one enters the new church (Fig 424), where a central altar is surrounded by radiating groups of pews. It is a superbly accomplished interior, utilising the best modern workmanship to create an ambience of devotion.

Access: By bus from Northfields Underground station.

This section on twentieth-century churches ends with two superb entirely new churches of the 1990s, each replacing a former church destroyed by fire.

St Paul, Harringay

Not since Cachemaille-Day's church at Eltham has such a riveting new church appeared in London as St Paul's, Harringay by Peter Jenkins (b 1946); if St Saviour's was the outstanding London church of the first half of the century, I would

(Fig 426) **St Paul, Harringay** *The sanctuary from the west gallery.*

venture to say that this is the equivalent of the second half.

St Paul's is not a large church — it seats barely 140 people — yet it stands boldly above the small houses around. As at Eltham, the exterior is a little forbidding, perhaps related to the apparent total absence of windows, which ensures that the congregation is not subjected to the common gaze. The steeply-pitched roof ends in a prominent over-hanging triangular gable; on each side of the inconspicuous entrance, the vertical columns of red brick are divided by horizontal bands of white, with a white plinth at the foot (Fig 425).

The interior (Fig 426) is an intimate study in black and white — black chairs, white walls and ceiling, enriched by the porphyry of the altar, font and simple Stations of the Cross. It is not dark: light comes through the glazed gable-ends, and also through two tall windows in the west end totally hidden from the street by the vertical columns on each side of the entrance. The font, altar and reredos are by Stephen Cox. The reredos, specially made for this church, consists of a series of fragments of travertine marble depicting the crucified Christ, with an empty cross on each side. The fragmentation, exposing the white-washed brickwork behind, gives a new meaning to the familiar words 'This is my body, broken for you'. This powerful image speaks eloquently to today's world.

It is not surprising that St Paul's, Harringay has quickly made its mark, and has become well-known among

(Fig 425) **St Paul, Harringay.**

connoisseurs of modern art. But this is modern art with a difference, expressing to today's generation the age-old Christian message. If there is one modern church that cries out to be visited, this is it.

Access: Nearest Underground station: Manor House.

St Barnabas, Dulwich

Dulwich is a pleasant oasis in south London, and has some notable buildings, including the College and the Art Gallery (by Sir John Soane). The flourishing church of St Barnabas had been built in 1894, and was totally destroyed by fire in December 1992. A new St Barnabas has risen from the ashes, and on 27 October 1996 was dedicated by the Bishop of Southwark.

The loss of the old church was stunning and was complete; in retrospect, perhaps it was a blessing in disguise that the destruction was so total – otherwise there would have been a temptation to preserve as much of the old fabric as possible. It was clear that an entirely new church would have to be built – when I visited St Barnabas in August, 1996, the building was nearing completion, and already it promised to be a distinguished church. I am indebted for much of the following to Keith

(Fig 427) **St Barnabas, Dulwich.**

(Fig 428) **St Barnabas, Dulwich** *The light-filled interior.*

Jackson, vice-chairman of the Parochial Church Council, and to the architect.

The architect is Lawrence Malcic (b 1945) of Hellmuth, Obata and Kassabaum, and Marius Reynolds was the project architect. From the outside, (Fig 427), the most arresting feature is the 107-foot glass spire, constructed on a lattice of stainless steel. 'This element, traditional in form and meaning, but contemporary in materials and technology, witnesses faith in the past and hope for the future. Its transparent nature reinforces ancient use of light as a symbol of divine presence.' (Malcic). Inside, there is light from the structure of the roof, in addition to the large east and west windows.

'The cruciform church is orientated to the cardinal points of the compass, while the entrance is oblique, symbolising the progression from a human world of chaos into a divinely ordered place of calm and repose.' The west end of the church frames the font, salvaged from the former church. The main area for worship, seating 430 persons, is displayed around the central altar. There is just one window at ground level, looking out into the Garden of Remembrance. All the other windows are above eye level, giving views of trees and sky. Four limbs radiate from the altar, the seating being arranged in octagonal form around the central space. The altar stands beneath the spire, and a large corona hangs over it. A chapel for smaller services, together with meeting rooms can be integrated into the main worship space, bringing the total capacity to 650 people. There are no formal aisles, these being inferred only by a change in the height of the ceiling (Fig 428). The stained glass (at the time of writing, not yet installed) has been designed by Caroline Swash, and fabricated by Messrs Goddard and Gibbs; the furniture has been designed and manufactured by Luke Hughes & Co; and the organ was designed by Kenneth Tichell of Northampton.

The new St Barnabas is a lovely church, and there is little doubt that it will be recognised as such by generations to come. But, a recurring theme in this book, there is more to a church than the building: and St Barnabas positively throbs with life. It is this, even more than the exciting architecture, that gives such hope as the church in London moves into the third millennium.

Access: Nearest station North Dulwich (frequent trains from London Bridge). Turn left out of the station, cross Village Way into Dulwich Village; and then take the second turning left into Calton Avenue, where the church is on the right-hand side.

Postscript

The history of London's churches that began in the eleventh century finishes on the eve of the twenty-first century.

What remains is to ensure that these buildings are maintained in all their present wonderful variety for the enjoyment of generations to come. There has been much debate about the future of some of the churches, especially those in the City of London. This is not the place to discuss this issue in detail: but it seems clear to me that in addition to their vital religious and social function (and there is really no division between the two), a major programme of public education is required to ensure two things:

That all the churches in the City of London, and the major ones in Westminster, the West End and East End are open to the public at stated and readily ascertainable times. This plea comes from the heart, for in the course of preparing this book I was often frustrated in gaining entry to some churches, simply because it was not obvious when they would be open. We must not forget that these buildings witness to the faith, even to tourists! Opening the churches will cost money, for they cannot be left unattended.

(2) That no more elements of our architectural heritage are lost. London's medieval and seventeenth- and eighteenth-century churches are now safe from the threat of demolition (though fire remains a major threat, and terrorism an unpredictable hazard; and inappropriate reorganisation of interiors may still wreak havoc). But the threat to Victorian churches remains acute; just as in the last years of the nineteenth century, our forefathers were demolishing Wren's churches with vigour, so in the closing years of this century many Victorian churches have been lost. Steps must be taken urgently to stem this haemorrhage of irreplaceable buildings; and much thought is required to devise alternative uses for those churches for which there is no pastoral need in the foreseeable future. Nowhere is this rescue operation more necessary or urgent than at St Stephen's, Rosslyn Hill, Hampstead.

Bibliography and References

Atterbury, P. and Wainwright, C. (eds.) (1994) *Pugin: A Gothic Passion*. Yale University Press, London.

Baker, B. *A History of the 1724 Chapel known as St Peter's, Vere Street*.

Bingham, N. et al. (1997) *The Twentieth Century Church*. RIBA Exhibition, London.

Brooks, C. and Saint, A. (eds.) (1995) *The Victorian Church*. Manchester University Press.

Bumpus, T.F. *Ancient London Churches*. Laurie, London.

Clark, K. (1962) *The Gothic Revival* (3rd Edition). John Murray, London.

Clarke, B.F.L. (a) (1966) *Parish Churches of London*. Batsford, London.

Clarke, B.F.L. (b) (1969) *Church Builders of the Nineteenth Century*. (2nd Edition). David and Charles, Newton Abbot

Clifton-Taylor, A. (1987) *The Pattern of English Building* (4th Edition). Faber, London.

Cobb, G. (1941) *The Old Churches of London*. Batsford, London.

Cobban, A. D. (1975) *250 Years after Sir Christopher Wren*. Uffington Press, Melksham.

Curl, J.S. (1995) *Victorian Churches*. Batsford/ English Heritage, London.

Downes, K. (a) (1979) *Hawksmoor* (2nd Edition). Zwemmer, London.

Downes, K. (b) (1982) *The Architecture of Wren*. Granada, London.

Eastlake, C.L. (1872) *A History of the Gothic Revival*. With an introduction by J.M.Crook. Leicester University Press (1970).

Esdile, K.A. (1946) *English Church Monuments 1510-1840*. Batsford, London.

Foster, R. (1981) *Discovering English Churches*. BBC, London.

Goodhart-Rendel, H.S. (1949) *Rogue Architects of the Victorian Era*. Journal R.I.B.A. 56. 251.

Hamilton, G. Personal communication.

Harwood, E. and Saint, A. (1991) *Exploring England's Heritage: London*. HMSO, London.

Howell, P and Sutton, I. (eds.) (1989) *The Faber Guide to Victorian Churches*. Faber and Faber, London.

Jeffery, P. (a) (1994) *The Church of St Vedast-alias-Foster, City of London*. The Institute of Ecclesiology, London.

Jeffery, P. (b) (1996) *The City Churches of Sir Christopher Wren*. The Hambledon Press, London.

Jenkins, R. (1995) *Gladstone*. Macmillan, London.

Kaufman, E.N. (1989) in *Howell and Sutton* (op. cit.).

Pevsner, N. (1952) *The Buildings of England: London, Volumes I and II*. Penguin Books, Harmondsworth.

Ruskin, J. (1848) *The Seven Lamps of Architecture*. 1989 edition, Dover Publications, New York.

Ruskin, J. (1851-53) *The Stones of Venice*. Ed. J.G. Links 1960, Da Capo Press, New York.

Saunders, M. (1982) *The Churches of S.S. Teulon*. The Ecclesiological Society, London.

Sekler, E. E, (1956) *Wren and his place in European Architecture*. Faber and Faber, London.

Sitwell, S. (1945) *British Architects and Craftsmen*. Batsford, London.

Stamp, G. and Amery, C. (1980) *Victorian Buildings of London*. The Architectural Press, London.

Summerson, J. (a) (1945) *Georgian London*. Pleaides, London.

Summerson, J. (b) (1953) *Architecture in Britain 1530-1830*. Penguin Books, Harmondsworth.

Summerson J. (c) (1963) *The Classical Language of Architecture*. Thames and Hudson, London and New York.

Summerson, J. (d) (1970) *Victorian Architecture: Four Studies in Evaluation*. Columbia University Press, New York and London.

Symondson, A. (a) (1989) in *Howell and Sutton* (op. cit.).

Symondson, A. (b) (1995) in *Brooks and Saint* (op. cit.).

Taylor, G. (1971) *St Giles-in-the-Fields* (Church guide).

Watkin, D. (1979) *English Architecture: a concise history*. Thames and Hudson, London and New York.

Webb, G. (1937) *Wren*. Duckworth, London.

Whinney, M. (a) (1971) *Wren*. Thames and Hudson, London and New York.

Whinney, M. (b) (1988) *Sculpture in Britain 1530-1830*. Penguin Books, Harmondsworth.

Young, E. and W. (a) (1966) *Old London Churches*. Faber and Faber, London.

Young, E. and W. (b) (1986) *London's Churches*. Grafton Books, London.

Glossary

Abacus: a flat slab above a capital.

Acanthus: a prickly-leafed plant whose leaves are represented in Corinthian capitals.

Advowson: the right of presentation of a priest to a church.

Alabaster: a compact marble-like form of gypsum (calcium sulphate) long favoured for memorial effigies.

Ambulatory: an enclosed walkway.

Apse: the semicircular or rectangular end of the chancel.

Arcade: a range of arches supported by piers or columns.

Arch: a curved supporting structure, made of wedge-shaped sections.

Arched braces: see Roof.

Architrave: the lowest of the parts of the entablature above a column.

Ashlar: blocks of masonry fashioned to even faces and square edges.

Augustinian canons: members of an order whose rule is based on the teachings of St Augustine.

Aumbry: a recess or cupboard to hold the vessels for Mass or Holy Communion.

Baldacchino: a canopy supported on columns.

Baluster: a small pillar or column of artistic outline.

Balustrade: a series of short columns, usually supporting a railing.

Baptistry: part of a church set aside for baptism.

Baroque: a vigorous, exuberant style of architecture prevalent in the seventeenth-century in Europe, and in a modified form from about 1700-1720 in England.

Bay: the space between the columns of an arcade.

Benedictine: a monk or nun of the order founded by St Benedict.

Blind arcade: an arcade of piers or columns attached to a wall.

Boss: a projection at the intersection of the ribs of a vault or roof.

Box-pew: a pew with a tall wooden enclosure.

Broach spire: a spire at the base of which sloping half-pyramids of stone effect the transition from a square tower to an octagonal spire.

Buttress: a mass of masonry projecting from or built against a wall to give extra strength.

Buttress, flying: an arch, or half-arch, transmitting the thrust from the upper part of a wall to an outer support.

Campanile: an isolated bell-tower.

Capital: the top part of a pier or column.

Caryatid: a female figure supporting an entablature.

Ceilure: an embellished part of the roof above the rood.

Chamfer: a bevel or slope made by paring the edge of a right-angled block of stone.

Chancel: the east end of the church containing the altar.

Chancel arch: an arch at the east end of the nave opening into the chancel.

Chantry chapel: a chapel endowed for the saying of Masses for the soul(s) of the founder(s) after death.

Chevron: Norman zigzag moulding on arches or windows.

Choir: the east end of the church where divine service is sung.

Ciborium: a baldacchino.

Clerestory: an upper storey of the walls of the nave pierced by windows.

Coffering: sunken panels decorating a ceiling.

Collar-beam: see Roof.

Colonnade: a row of columns.

Colonnette: a small column.

Composite columns: one of the orders of classical architecture.

Corbel: a block of stone projecting from a wall, often supporting roof beams.

Corinthian columns: one of the orders of classical architecture.

Cornice: the top section of the entablature.

Crenellated: notched or embattled (as in a parapet).

Crocket: decorative projections on the sloping sides of spires, pinnacles, etc.

Crossing: in a cruciform church, the space at the intersection of the nave, chancel and transepts.

Cupola: a domed or polygonal turret crowning a roof.

Curvilinear: see Tracery.

Cushion: in Norman architecture, the rounding-off of the lower angles of the square capital to the cylindrical pier below.

Decorated: historical division of English Gothic architecture, from *c.*1300–1350.

Diaper: a low-relief pattern, often composed of square or lozenge shapes.

Doom: a picture of the Last Judgment.

Doric: one of the orders of classical architecture.

Dormer window: an upright window projecting from a sloping roof.

Early English: historical division of English Gothic architecture from *c.*1200–1300.

Easter sepulchre: a recess in the north wall of the chancel used to house the consecrated Host between Maundy Thursday and Easter Day.

Entablature: all the horizontal members above a column (architrave, frieze and cornice).

Fan vault: see Vault.

Finial: the top of a canopy, gable or pinnacle.

Flamboyant: the last phase of French Gothic architecture, characterised by wavy or undulating window tracery.

Flèche: a slender wooden spire on the centre of a roof.

Fluting: vertical channelling in the shaft of a column.

Frieze: the middle division of the entablature.

Geometrical: see Tracery.

Gothic: the style of architecture characterised by pointed arches, sub-divided into Early English, Decorated and Perpendicular.

Greek cross: a cross with arms of equal length.

Hall church: in which the nave and aisles are of approximately equal height.

Hammer-beam: see Roof.

Hood-mould: projecting moulding over doors or windows to throw off rain-water.

Ionic columns: one of the orders of classical architecture.

Jamb: the straight side of an archway, doorway or window.

King-post: see Roof.

Knights Templar: founded in 1119 for the protection of the Holy Sepulchre in Jerusalem.

Lancet window: the tall narrow pointed window of the Early English period.

Lantern: an open structure over the crossing, with windows all round.

Light: a vertical division of a window.

Lintel: a horizontal stone over a doorway.

Lucarne: a small opening to admit light.

Lunette: a semicircular opening.

Mullions: vertical stone bars dividing a window into lights.

Narthex: a vestibule at the western end of a church.

Neo-classicism: a style of English and French architecture from *c.*1750, characterised by renewed interest in classical forms.

Newel: the central post in a circular or winding staircase.

Norman architecture: the massive Romanesque style of building, from 1066–1200.

Ogee arch: a non-structural arch formed by two S-shaped curves, with the concave parts above coming to a point, typical of the fourteenth century.

Oratory: a small private chapel.

Order: in classical building, a column, with base, shaft, capital and entablature; in Norman building, one of the successively recessed arches of an archway, or at the sides of a doorway, all the parts of a column (base, shaft and capital).

Oriel: an upper-floor bay-window.

Palladian: architecture derived from that of Andrea Palladio, prevalent in England from *c.*1720-60.

Parclose screen: a screen separating a chapel from the rest of the church.

Pedestal: the support of a column.

Pediment: a low-pitched gable placed as a decorative feature above doorways, windows, etc.

   broken pediment: the central portion of the pediment is open.

   segmental pediment: part of the sloping sides is omitted.

Pendentive: a concave triangular spandrel leading from the angle of two walls to the base of a dome.

Peristyle: a range of columns round or within a building.

Perpendicular: a historical division of English Gothic architecture, *c.*1350-1550.

Pier: a column of free-standing masonry supporting arches.

Pilaster: a shallow pier attached to a wall.

Piscina: a basin with drain in the wall to the south of the altar for washing the vessels used during Mass.

Plate tracery: see Tracery.

Plinth: the projecting base of a wall or column.

Polychromy: decoration in many colours.

Porphyry: a very hard rock, purple and white, used in sculpture.

Portico: a roof supported by columns at the entrance to a building.

Portland stone: an oolitic building-stone quarried in the Isle of Portland.

Pre-Raphaelites: a group of painters who, about 1848, sought to return to the style of painters before Raphael (Millais, Burne-Jones, Holman Hunt etc.).

Purbeck marble: an expensive shelly limestone from Purbeck, Dorset, often polished.

Quatrefoil: an ornament divided by cusps into four lobes.

Queen-post: see Roof.

Quoins: dressed stones at the angles of a building.

Ragstone: hard or coarse-textured stone from Kent, rough, brittle and hard to work.

Rebus: a pun, or play on words.

Rendering: plastering of an outer wall.

Reredos: a an ornamental screen or hanging on the wall behind the altar.

Respond: a half-pier carrying one end of an arch and bonded into a wall.

Reticulated tracery: see Tracery.

Retrochoir: an extension of a church to the east of the high altar.

Rococo: the last phase of the baroque style, prevalent on the continent *c.*1720-60.

Romanesque: another name for Norman architecture, defined by round arches and vaults.

Rood: a Cross bearing the body of Jesus, flanked by the Virgin Mary and St John.

Rood-loft: a gallery on top of the rood-screen.

Rood-screen: a screen at the junction of nave and chancel bearing the Rood.

Roof:

   Arched brace: inclined curved timbers, strengthening collar- or hammer-beams.

   Collar-beam: a tie-beam applied higher up the slope of the roof.

   Hammer-beam: a horizontal beam projecting from the wall bearing arched braces.

   King-post: an upright timber connecting a tie- or collar-beam to the ridge-beam.

   Purlins: horizontal timbers parallel with the ridge of the roof.

   Queen-posts: a pair of upright timbers placed symmetrically on a tie- or collar-beam connecting it with the rafters above.

   Tie-beam: a horizontal timber connecting the feet of the rafters.

Rose window: a circular window with tracery radiating from the centre.

Rustication: Large blocks of masonry separated by sunken or chamfered joints.

Sacristy: a room housing sacred vessels, treasures etc.

Sanctuary: the area around the high altar.

Scagliola: an imitation marble, made of cement and colouring matter.

Scallop: decoration on the under surface of a

Norman capital in which a series of truncated cones are elaborated.

Sedilia: recessed seats for priests in the south wall of the chancel.

Spandrel: the space between the curve of an arch and enclosing mouldings.

Stiff-leaf: Early English type of foliage of many-lobed shapes, on capitals etc.

String-course: a projecting line of moulding running horizontally round the walls of the church or tower.

Stucco: plaster-work.

Sword-rest: a wooden or wrought-iron frame for holding a sword, set up when a parishioner became Lord Mayor of London.

Tabernacle: a canopied niche or seat, or vessel containing the Host.

Tester: a canopy or sounding-board over the pulpit.

Three-decker pulpit: a pulpit, with clerk's stall and reading-desk below.

Tie-beam: see Roof.

Tierceron: a secondary rib in a vault, springing from the intersection of two other ribs.

Tower arch: an arch usually at the west end of the nave opening into the ground floor of the tower.

Tracery: rib-work in the upper part of a window.

    Curvilinear: tracery consisting of curved lines.

    Geometrical: consisting of circles or foiled leaf-shaped circles.

    Intersecting: each mullion branches into two curved bars.

    Plate: an early form in which openings are cut through the stone in the head of the window, often producing a Y shape.

    Reticulated: in which circles are drawn at top and bottom into ogee shapes producing a net-like pattern.

Transept: transverse portion of a cross-shaped church.

Transitional: the style of building in which Gothic pointed arches exist alongside Norman archi-tecture, typical of 1160-1200.

Transom: a horizontal bar across the opening of a window.

Tree of Jesse: in which the genealogy of Jesus is traced back to Jesse, father of King David.

Trefoil: an ornament divided by cusps into three lobes.

Triforium: an arcaded wall-passage or blind arcading facing the nave at the height of the roof of the aisle, and below the clerestory.

Triglyphs: blocks with vertical grooves in the Doric frieze.

Triptych: a set of three painted panels, hinged together.

Turret: a small tower, often containing a winding stair.

Tuscan columns: one of the classical orders of architecture.

Undercroft: a vaulted room below a church.

Vault: an arched roof or ceiling.

    Barrel or tunnel vault: of semicircular section.

    Fan-vault: in which all the ribs springing from their origin are of the same length and curvature, and equidistant from each other.

    Groin-vault: two tunnel-vaults intersecting at right-angles.

Venetian window: a window with three openings, the central one arched and wider than the outer ones.

Vesica: an oval, with pointed head and foot.

Volute: a spiral scroll, found on Ionic capitals, and also on Norman capitals.

Voussoir: a wedge-shaped stone used in the construction of an arch.

Wagon roof: the appearance of the inside of a canvas over a wagon, achieved by closely set arched braces, the roof often being panelled or plastered.

Y-tracery: see Tracery, plate.

Zigzag: Norman geometrical decoration found on arches etc.

Index